DATE DUE

MAR 11 '88 RET

1264

Legislative Review of the Budget in California

D. JAY DOUBLEDAY

For Dwight Waldo
Mentor and Friend.

Jay Dubleday

Legislative Review of the
Budget in California

INSTITUTE OF GOVERNMENTAL STUDIES
UNIVERSITY OF CALIFORNIA, BERKELEY
EUGENE C. LEE, *Director*

Legislative Review of the Budget in California

By D. JAY DOUBLEDAY

Graduate School of Public and International Affairs
University of Pittsburgh

OCTOBER, 1967

COPYRIGHT © 1967 BY D. JAY DOUBLEDAY

ALL RIGHTS RESERVED

LIBRARY OF CONGRESS CATALOG CARD NUMBER: 67-64519

PRINTED IN THE UNITED STATES OF AMERICA

BY THE UNIVERSITY OF CALIFORNIA PRINTING DEPARTMENT

HJ
2053
C3
D6

HJ

To 17171

Preface

This study describes and evaluates the methods and organization employed by the California legislature in reviewing the executive budget and enacting appropriations. Both description and evaluation proceed on the assumption that the legislative decisions on the budget should be made in a rational manner and that the legislature should exercise effective control of the use of financial resources. This assumption is consistent with the attitude of California legislators and will, I believe, be widely shared in other circles.

The study analyzes the ways in which legislative machinery and practice tend to enhance or impair rationality, and it suggests changes designed to heighten the rationality of the decision-making process, while maintaining legislative fiscal control. Fundamentally, the evaluative analysis and the reforms proposed stem from the question of how the legislature would structure its organization and procedure if it wished to achieve a high degree of rationality and control. Where normative terms are employed, it should be understood that they refer to these values, unless the context indicates otherwise. Thus, the statement that a particular procedure is an "improvement" means that the procedure tends to increase the rationality of decisions or the effectiveness of control, or both. The relation of the procedure to these values is specified, unless it is obvious or readily inferred from the context.

This is not a study of the politics of the budget, but in proposing reforms I have endeavored to give realistic consideration to the political character of the budget process and of the legislator's role. It must be recognized that on the one hand, organization and procedure have political implications, and on the other, that political factors impose limitations upon the kinds of institutional arrangements that are likely to be considered feasible.

In order to facilitate understanding of the main argument and to provide a relatively full account of organization and procedure for budget review, I have included some historical and descriptive analysis that is only indirectly related to the principal organizing concepts of rational decision and control. Especially full treatment has been accorded to the legislative fiscal analysis staff in the office of the Legislative Analyst and to the Joint Legislative Budget Committee, which supervises the staff. Because of the innovative character of these agencies, their interest for other states, and the key role played by the Analyst in budget review, I have chosen to treat their origins, development, relationships and functions in considerable detail.

Research on the legislative process in California is hampered by the absence of crucial documentation. Debates on the floor and hearings of standing committees are not published or recorded. Only formal actions, such as motions and votes, are published in the journals of the houses. Furthermore, the reports of standing committees on bills referred to them simply recommend passage or list proposed amendments; they do not summarize issues or give reasons for the actions recommended. The investigator must rely upon personal observation and interviews for data about the deliberation that takes place in committee and on the floor of the two houses.

In addition to the documents and other publications cited in the notes, sources for the present study include interviews in 1954 and at various times from 1959 to 1961 with approximately 50 members of the legislature, with almost as many administrative officials, and with the Legislative Analyst, the Auditor General, and with committee and other legislative staff members. In many cases these persons were interviewed more than once. During the process of preparation and review of the 1954–55 budget, I observed a number of executive budget hearings, most of the hearings of the appropriations committees and subcommittees, and almost all of the floor proceedings. In each of the years 1958–61, I observed a portion of the assembly floor proceedings, as well as a few committee hearings. The cut-off date for research was the beginning of 1962, although occasional references are made to later publications and data.

The research was originally undertaken for my doctoral dissertation and was supported in 1953-54 by a Research Training Fellowship of the Social Science Research Council, in 1957–58 by a John Randolph Haynes and Dora Haynes Fellowship in Political Science awarded by the University of California, and in the summer of 1960 by a grant from the California Legislative Internship Program. While absolving them of all responsibility for my findings and interpretations, I am deeply grateful to these institutions and to a host of persons in California government whose generous assistance was indispensable to the study. I am particularly indebted to A. Alan Post, Legislative Analyst, who devoted many hours to answering my questions, read a large part of the manuscript, and helped me in many other ways. Among the many officials of the Department of Finance who gave assistance, I am especially grateful to T. H. Mugford, formerly Chief of the Budget Division, later Director of Finance, and now retired; and to Roy M. Bell, Chief of the Budget Division and later Assistant Director of Finance. Arthur A. Ohnimus, Chief Clerk of the Assembly, shared his extraordinary knowledge of legislative organization and practice with me and facilitated my investigation in other ways. Thanks are also due to William H. Merrifield, Auditor General; Gilbert Lentz, Assistant Legislative Analyst; Larry Margolis, Administrative Assistant to the Speaker; Dan Luévano, consultant to the Assembly Ways and Means Committee and later Chief Deputy Director of Finance; and the many assemblymen and senators who gave freely of their time and knowledge.

Above all, I am deeply indebted to Professor Joseph P. Harris, who suggested that I undertake the study and whose counsel and encouragement were invaluable.

Quito, Ecuador   D. JAY DOUBLEDAY
June, 1966

Contents

TABLES

Chapter I

INTRODUCTION

Early in the year the California legislature begins the annual round of hearings, negotiations, debates and voting from which emerge appropriations necessary to support the programs and services of the state. Headlines announce that the governor's budget calls for record levels of spending, and a few members of the legislature issue statements about trimming the "fat" from the expenditure program. Party spokesmen view with alarm or express cautious satisfaction, while interest groups mobilize their forces in support of the expenditure proposals which concern them. Slowly at first, later more feverishly, the legislative machinery grinds out decisions until, in the closing days or hours of the session, the budget act is passed. The governor usually finds grounds on which to congratulate the legislature for its work, and legislators, although dissatisfied with some of the particulars, concede that the budget is about as good as can be obtained, considering the pressures, compromises, and uncertainties that enter into its review and approval. Once again the skill of the legislature in manipulating the purse strings has been tested.

As the historic basis for the legislature's successful challenge to unbridled executive power, the power of the purse is conventionally viewed as the key to legislative control of public policy, to the effective supervision of the bureaucracy, and to the protection and husbanding of the public treasure. It is a symbol to which all can adhere, whether partisans of legislative supremacy, upholding legislative prerogatives, or apologists for executive and administrative power, insisting that the control of the purse guarantees ultimate and effective legislative control. Yet the extent to which reality corresponds to symbol is a matter for widespread doubt and anxiety. The sheer size of public expenditures, coupled with a steady rise in the level of taxes, debt, and spending, have stimulated widespread public discussion and concern during the postwar period. Growth of the budget is a reflection of more fundamental forces that test the capacity of legislatures to retain effective control of the purse.

1

As the activities of government become more extensive, varied, and complex, the task of controlling policy and overseeing administration is made more difficult. New social problems and changed perceptions of old ones demand attention, while outdated solutions require reappraisal and adjustment. Increasingly the formulation of policy alternatives falls to the executive, aided and influenced by the expert advice of civil servants, while the legislature reviews, approves, modifies, or vetoes. Executive and administrative discretion are broadened, as the legislature perceives the need for flexibility and expertise in the execution of policy, or finds itself unwilling or unable to reconcile conflicting claims. Unable to match the expertise of the bureaucracy, beset by new, shifting, complex forces, pressured by a bewildering variety of interests and organized groups, and overwhelmed by masses of information from every side, the legislature may ponder with reason whether its coordinate constitutional status is secure, its control of affairs effective. In greater or lesser degree, these problems confront the legislature in all its spheres of activity, including review of the budget.

The present study describes, analyzes, and appraises the California legislature's performance of its role in the budget process. With California's expenditures now exceeding $4 billion annually, the problem of budget review inevitably assumes a considerable degree of complexity, and the methods employed cannot be a matter of indifference. With respect to applications outside California, it is true that differences in size, functions, responsibilities and institutional arrangements severely limit the extent to which the analysis of state experience can throw light upon corresponding problems at the national level. However, the states' experience is of considerable interest because their performance has decided impact both upon the citizens and the states' position in the governmental system.

FINANCIAL TRENDS IN CALIFORNIA

It is trite but true that population growth is the key to understanding much of what goes on in California's government, politics, administration, economy, and social relations. From 1940 to 1960, the state's population more than doubled, growing from about seven million to 15.9 million.[1] Table 1 presents data for selected years showing trends in population, expenditures, revenue, and the relationship of taxes to personal income. It will be seen that the trend is upward in all indices, but that in relation to personal income, tax collections have increased at a relatively moderate rate. Population increase, economic growth, and inflation have combined to augment personal income to such an extent that taxpayers as a group pay for the costs of state government with only a little larger share of income than was required in 1938–39 or in 1948–49.

It is of interest to know where the tax money goes. Table 2 gives the general picture for the 1966–67 budget. More than half of the state's total outlay goes to local government, in the form of school apportionments, state contributions for the welfare programs, and shared revenues. Approximately one-third goes for the operating costs of the state government,

TABLE 1

TRENDS IN POPULATION AND STATE FINANCES, SELECTED YEARS, 1938–39 TO 1966–67

Year	Estimated Population July 1st (thousands)	Fiscal Year	Expenditures (millions)	Expenditures Per Capita	Taxes Per $100 of Personal Income
1938...............	6,656	1938–39	$ 286	$ 42.63	$4.64
1943...............	7,570	1943–44	265	33.82	3.11
1948...............	10,064	1948–49	883	86.60	4.17
1953...............	12,101	1953–54	1,381	112.23	4.56
1958...............	14,741	1958–59	1,932	128.65	4.74
1963...............	17,670	1963–64	2,978	168.52[a]	5.49
1966...............	19,324	1966–67	4,049[b]	209.51[a,b]	5.71[b]

Sources: *Budget, 1963–64*, pp. A–19, A–41. *State Support and Local Assistance Budget*, 1965–66, p. A–55; 1966–67, pp. A–17, A–53; *Capital Outlay Budget*, 1965–66, p. xi; *Capital Outlay Budget and Five-Year Construction Program*, 1966–67, p. xvi.
[a] Computed from population and expenditure data.
[b] Estimated.

including debt service. About four-fifths of all state expenditures are allocated to three broad functions: education, highway transportation, and health and welfare.

ANALYTICAL FRAMEWORK

Broadly conceived, the process of controlling the purse embraces a wide range of legislative decisions and activities. Most legislation requires for its implementation the expenditure of funds; the level of total expenditures is determined primarily by the policies and programs embodied in substantive legislation. Revenue and appropriation measures affect budget aggregates and the allocation of resources among programs; the ratio of value received to resources expended is influenced by legislative determinations of administrative structure and procedure, by legislative investigations of administration, and by the postauditing of expenditures by an agency independent of the executive branch. Legislative criticism, questions, and more or less formal stipulations may also affect the spending programs.

TABLE 2

BUDGETED EXPENDITURES, 1966–67

Expenditures Included in Budget Totals	(Millions)	Percent
Support...	$1,352.4	33.4
Local Assistance.................................	2,325.1	57.4
Capital Outlay....................................	371.1	9.2
Total...	$4,048.6	100.0
Expenditures from Bond Funds Not Included in Budget Totals.....................	569.4	....
Grand Total......................................	$4,617.9ᵃ	....
Salary Costs for 166,533.3 Personnel Man-Years......	$1,317.1	....
Functional Distribution of Expenditures for Support and Local Assistance		
Education...	$1,653.1	45.0
Health and Welfare...............................	795.5	21.6
Transportation...................................	470.0	12.8
Resource Development.............................	136.2	3.7
Corrections......................................	120.7	3.3
Fiscal Affairs...................................	65.5	1.8
Business and Commerce............................	40.4	1.1
Public Safety....................................	31.1	0.8
Shared Revenue...................................	203.9	5.5
Other..	161.0	4.4
Total...	$3,677.4	100.0ᵃ
Functional Distribution of Capital Outlay Including Expenditures from Bond Sources		
Resource Development.............................	$419.1	45.1
Highways...	321.1	34.5
Education..	134.4	14.5
Corrections......................................	29.1	3.1
Health and Welfare...............................	17.1	1.8
Other..	8.6	0.9
Total...	$929.4	100.0ᵃ

Sources: *Support and Local Assistance Budget* and *Capital Outlay Budget and Five-Year Construction Program*, 1966–67.
    ᵃ Components do not add to total, due to rounding.

The present study is concerned with one major aspect of control of the purse: the process of examining and modifying the annual expenditure program formulated by the executive. Although attention is given to determining the relationship between aggregate income and outgo, the process of reviewing and enacting revenue measures is excluded in order to keep the study within manageable proportions.

The scope of the study is further limited by the point of view adopted for purposes of description and analysis. The process of budget review is examined in terms of the organization, procedures, and practices employed by the legislature to make decisions, to ensure a degree of rationality in the decision-making process, and to exercise control over spending. Stated negatively, the study does not attempt to analyze the politics of the budget, although the appraisal of machinery cannot ignore the political context. Neither does it make a systematic examination of budget review as an instrument for holding the bureaucracy accountable. Both the politics of the budget and the problem of accountability are, however, legitimate spheres of inquiry and an adequate theory of the legislative role in the budget process must include them both.

Assumptions

The present study assumes that legislative review of the budget as it operates in most American legislatures has as one basic purpose the making of decisions about policies, programs, and allocation of resources. It also assumes that legislatures aim to make these decisions in a more or less rational manner and that rationality is a desirable goal. It assumes further that a third basic objective is the control of spending, interpreted in several senses as indicated below. Finally, it assumes that procedures, practices, and organizational machinery play an important role in determining the rationality of decision-making and the effectiveness of control of spending.

The last assumption finds justification in the long-standing preoccupation of political science with the consequences of institutional arrangements. Truman points out that procedural and structural elements impose limits on the stream of politics, noting specifically that in the legislative process they are rarely neutral in their effects on access to key points of decision.[2] Bailey finds that the relationship of formal structure and procedure to legislative behavior has not received the attention it deserves,[3] and Eulau notes that the behavioral approach to the study of politics includes an interest in the "institutional parameters" that influence and are influenced by political behavior.[4] The assumption that structure and procedure influence the output of institutions is, of course, no more than a starting point for analysis, since the nature and extent of this influence is a matter for empirical determination. The examination of the consequences of structure and procedure is a fundamental objective of the present study.

Decision-Making

The California legislature makes hundreds of decisions about appropriations each year. It has developed an elaborate system of committees, procedures, and staff assistance, designed to facilitate orderly decision-making upon the basis of substantial deliberation. Although this system serves purposes other than decision-making, such as legislative oversight and communication, members of the legislature tend to emphasize its decision-making functions. There is, in short, ample justification for analysis of the budget process in terms of decision-making. The use of a decisional framework does not postulate a goal for the legislature which it does not share, nor impose upon the phenomena of budget review an alien analytical scheme.

Rationality

The concept of rationality is a familiar one in the literature of budgeting. Stated in economic terms, an expenditure decision is rational if it equates the marginal cost of governmental service with marginal benefit. This principle may be applied to the allocation of resources as between governmental activities: the allocation should be such that the last dollar spent for higher education produces benefits equal to the last dollar spent for corrections or highways. It may also be applied to the allocation of resources between the public and private sectors: resources should be transferred to the public sector until the benefits received from the expenditure of the last dollar collected in taxes are equal to the satisfactions lost by the taxpayer who gives up that dollar.[5]

From a theoretical standpoint, this criterion presents a serious difficulty, for the community is not a single entity with a single schedule of utility preferences, but an aggregation of individuals having varying patterns of preferences. Because interpersonal comparisons of utility cannot validly be made, according to economic theorists,[6] there is no way to sum satisfactions and dissatisfactions in order to strike a balance at the margin. Although the problem of interpersonal comparisons also exists with respect to the private sector, market values may be presumed to reflect satisfactions in important degree. Most government goods and services, by contrast, are not sold, and hence there is no way of assigning values to them on the basis of the prices they bring in the market. In the absence of prices, it is impossible to compare objectively the values to be derived from alternative allocations among functions in the public sector or as between the public and private sectors. At best, decision-makers make judgments regarding the marginal social benefits of particular expenditures, but whether these approximate the allocation that would emerge from the dollar voting of "sovereign" consumers in a market is impossible to determine.[7]

The principle of equating benefits and costs at the margin does not provide the decision-maker with a determinate solution to allocation problems. Nevertheless, a budget necessarily entails a determinate allocation between higher education and highways, as well as between public and private uses. We may assume that the allocations will be more nearly rational if they are based on more rather than less search for alternatives and for information about their consequences, more rather than less deliberation on alternatives and their consequences, more rather than less consideration of the preferences of significant "publics."[8] At some point, of course, the costs of information-gathering and deliberation will exceed the increased satisfactions to be derived from a better allocation of resources. Decision-makers, as well as those who evaluate their procedures, must make rough judgments regarding the point at which costs outweigh possible benefits.

The classic concept of rational choice assumes that the decision-maker examines all of the alternatives before him, considers all of the consequences of each alternative, and selects one alternative upon the basis of an evaluation of all of the sets of consequences. His consideration of consequences includes an appraisal of the likelihood that they will in fact occur. This model has been criticized for assuming that all alternatives are "given," that all consequences are known, and that the decision-maker has at hand complete knowledge of his preference ranking for all possible consequences.[9] In fact, many alternatives are never considered because they do not occur to the decision-maker. Knowledge of consequences is always incomplete, and evaluation of consequences is imperfect because they must be imagined while they still lie in the future.[10] Analysis must then begin with recognition that rationality is limited in important ways.

The classic model assumes that the rational decision-maker optimizes— selects the alternative that promises the greatest satisfaction given his estimate of consequences and his preferences. March, Simon, and Guetzkow have suggested an assumption more in keeping with the actual behavior of decision-makers: they "satisfice," selecting a satisfactory or "good enough" alternative. They illustrate this conception by distinguishing the procedure of trying to find the sharpest needle in the haystack from that of searching the haystack for one sufficiently sharp for sewing.[11]

Lindblom's Incremental Method

Agreeing with Simon that the behavior of decision-makers is a far cry from that suggested by the classic model of rationality with optimization, Lindblom finds reason to be optimistic about the degree of rationality permitted by what he terms the method of "successive limited comparisons" or the "incremental method,"[12] explained in his article on the "science of muddling through." This method differs from the classic model in several ways. The latter assumes that values and goals are clarified, alternatives are then analyzed, and optimal means are selected for achieving the goals and realizing the values in view. All alternatives, all consequences, and all values are considered, and there is heavy use of theory in analyzing the problem of choice. By contrast, in the incremental method the clarification of goals is not a separate step from the analysis of alternatives; they proceed together in close relationship, with consequent limited use of ends-means analysis. The decision is taken not on the basis of the optimal alternative, but rather on the basis of agreement among interested parties that the decision is "good"—though they may disagree about what it is good for. There is no attempt to analyze comprehensively all of the alternatives, consequences, and values affected, and there is very limited use of theory. Generally, the method involves successive comparison of the status quo with a limited number of possible "small" changes. This method has three principal advantages: (1) the decision-maker's task is greatly simplified because the alternatives considered are limited to those involving small changes from the status quo; (2) agreement among interested parties, as the test of a good decision, tends to ensure that relevant values will not be neglected; and (3) because consequences of small changes can be judged on the basis of experience and reasonable prediction, it is unnecessary to resort to intervening theory, which may offer little guidance.

We may now indicate the manner in which the concept of rationality will be employed in the analysis of legislative budget review. It is recognized at the outset that rationality will at best be limited and imperfect, and it is assumed that within limits the degree of rationality may vary. We are interested in discovering ways in which rationality is enhanced or diminished by procedural and structural factors. To judge whether particular budget decisions are irrational, in the sense of failing to equate marginal costs with marginal social benefits, would be an impossible task. Rather, the rationality of the decision-making process will be assessed by analyzing the extent to which the process requires or encourages the consideration of alternatives, their consequences, and the values associated with consequences.[13] We are interested not only in discovering the factors that limit or enhance rationality, but also in the extent to which these factors are subject to modification.

Wildavsky has justly criticized the literature of budgeting for proposing budget reforms that too often neglect significant political implications.[14] It cannot be assumed that the members of the legislature have only one paramount goal—rational budgetary decision-making. Rather, it must be recognized that they have multiple goals which reflect personal interests, institutional identifications, and the goals of political groups. Prompt rejection is the probable fate of reform proposals that stress the single goal of rational decision-making while neglecting others.

Politics and Rationality

It remains to consider a possible objection to the use of rationality in the analysis and appraisal of budget decision-making, namely, that it denies or discounts the political character of the budget process. Certainly, it would be folly to deny that goals to be achieved, interests to be served, and values to be realized through the budget are determined by political processes. But neither is it satisfactory to conceive of the budget process as simply the mobilization of forces, persuasion, and mutual influence, with contests settled by voting. For, at bottom, the budget is an attempt to determine on more or less objective criteria what resources are needed to achieve determined goals. Inevitably, budget decisions are based upon an element of rational calculation, of instrumental consideration. Given an objective, the decision-maker is interested in knowing the cheapest way and the shortest path, for resources are scarce and goals are many. Given multiple objectives, he is also interested in achieving balance in the distribution of resources among them. In specific cases, of course, individuals or groups will prefer that some alternatives remain unexplored, that some consequences be ignored, or that some values be neglected. But over the longer run, and especially in the numerous routine budget decisions, the vast majority of legislators will benefit from more, rather than less, consideration of alternatives, consequences, and values. They will benefit in terms of their own electoral aspirations, in terms of their conception of their roles in the budget process, and in terms of maintaining the position of the legislative institution in the political system.

It must be recognized, of course, that goals are often determined through decisions concerning resources. The amount and quality of medical care to be provided in mental hospitals is not determined by substantive legislation or by a prior decision to provide a specified level of service; rather it is determined by the amount and kind of staffing, equipment, supplies, and buildings provided through the annual budget. Nevertheless, an element of rational calculation generally enters into the latter determination, for the decision-maker is interested in knowing what will be the results, in terms of patients cured or improved, of varying combinations and levels of resources. And he will be interested in the basis upon which results are predicted, as well as the accuracy of prior forecasts.

Most budgetary issues, even those that are highly "political," exhibit instrumental aspects, for they are usually means of realizing more abstract values or higher goals. A salary increase for state employees, for example, often entails intense political conflict. In part this issue may be viewed as instrumental. Higher salaries may be seen as means of achieving a greater degree of equity, higher morale, higher standards of performance in public administration, or improved ability to compete in the employment market.

Within limits, processes of rational calculation can be employed in deciding issues. Although there is much room for debate about the objectives themselves and about the effect of a salary increase upon them, and although information about consequences may be used to rationalize decisions taken on strictly political (i.e., vote-getting) grounds, it is nevertheless possible that a review of alternatives and consequences will clarify the ends-means relationship and play its part, along with political forces and motivations, in determining decisions.

Control of Spending

Legislative control of expenditure may have a variety of meanings, ranging from the formal authority to appropriate funds, through application of funds in accordance with "legislative intent" and maintenance of a balanced budget, to the avoidance of a level of expenditure that is "too high." The present study does not undertake to analyze the problem of control of spending in all of its ramifications; rather it emphasizes the manner in which control enters into budget review, the significance of the legislative fiscal analysis staff in exercising control, and control limitations resulting from continuing appropriations and a large number of segregated funds.

In some of its meanings, legislative control of expenditures is closely related to rational decision-making, and indeed one analyst has defined control in terms of knowledge of the consequences of spending decisions.[15] It seems preferable, however, to maintain a conceptual separation, for it is possible to conceive of a system in which knowledge of the consequences of decisions is superb, but in which administrative compliance is poor, deficit spending is rampant, and constitutional or self-imposed limitations restrict the area of legislative decision-making. Also conceivable is a situation in which rationality is low, because there is little search for alternatives and limited information about consequences, but in which the decisions that are taken are carried out faithfully, budgets are balanced, limitations on the sphere of decision-making are few, and administrative operations are efficient. In short, it seems useful for purposes of analysis to separate the quality of decision-making from the scope of decision-making, as well as from the system which ensures compliance with legislative decisions.

ORGANIZATION OF THE STUDY

Study of the legislature's review of the budget from the standpoint of rational decision-making requires a careful analysis of the role of the relatively large legislative fiscal staff in the office of the Legislative Analyst. This staff is charged with the responsibility of providing the legislature with financial and other information and with making recommendations regarding the amounts that should be appropriated for the state's departments and programs. The origins and development of the Analyst's staff and of the committee which supervises it are reviewed in Chapter III, and its role and functions, including the preparation of a detailed analysis of the budget, are examined in Chapters IV through VI. Chapters VII and VIII deal with budget review by the appropriations committees and with house deliberation. Chapter IX explores the problems of determining aggregate income and outgo and of ascertaining their relationship in an organization that disperses decision-making authority. Some problems of legislative control of spending are examined in Chapter X. The final chapter suggests changes in the legislature's approach to budget review and offers some generalizations regarding legislative budget staffing, based upon California's experience. To provide a basis for the chapters to follow, the budget system as a whole is outlined in Chapter II.

[1] *State of California Budget ... July 1, 1963 to June 30, 1964*, p. A-19. Cited hereafter as *Budget.*

[2] David B. Truman, *The Governmental Process* (New York: Alfred A. Knopf, 1951), pp. 322, 328.

[3] Stephen K. Bailey, "New Research Frontiers of Interest to Legislators and Administrators," in *Research Frontiers in Politics and Government* (Washington: The Brookings Institution, 1955), p. 15.

[4] Heinz Eulau, *Recent Developments in the Behavioral Study of Politics* (Stanford, California, 1961), p. 8.

[5] A. C. Pigou, *A Study in Public Finance*, 3rd ed. (London: Macmillan & Co., Ltd., 1947), p. 31.

[6] R. A. Musgrave, "The Public Interest: Efficiency in the Creation and Maintenance of Material Welfare," in Carl J. Friedrich, ed., *The Public Interest* (New York: Atherton Press, 1962), p. 110.

[7] Jesse Burkhead, *Government Budgeting* (New York: John Wiley and Sons, Inc., 1956), pp. 42–4.

[8] Cf. Edward C. Banfield, "Congress and the Budget; A Planner's Criticism," *American Political Science Review*, XLIII (December, 1949), 1224.

[9] James G. March, Herbert A. Simon and Harold Guetzkow, *Organizations* (New York: Wiley, 1958), pp. 138–9.

[10] Herbert A. Simon, *Administrative Behavior*, 2nd ed. (New York: Macmillan, 1957), pp. 81–4.

[11] March, Simon and Guetzkow, *op. cit.*, pp. 140–1.

[12] Charles E. Lindblom, "The Science of 'Muddling Through,' " *Public Administration Review*, XIX (Spring, 1959), 79–88.

[13] Cf. V. O. Key, "The Lack of a Budgetary Theory," *American Political Science Review*, XXXIV (December, 1940), 1142.

[14] Aaron Wildavsky, "Political Implications of Budgetary Reform," *Public Administration Review*, XXI (Autumn, 1961), 183–90.

[15] Robert Ash Wallace, *Congressional Control of Federal Spending* (Detroit: Wayne State University Press, 1960), p. 5.

Chapter II

THE BUDGET SYSTEM

The legislative phase of the budget process is one of a number of inter-related elements which together constitute the budget system. The legislature's role must be analyzed in terms of its relationship to the rest of the system. Specifically, it is necessary to examine how and by whom the budget is formulated and executed and what provision is made for auditing financial transactions. The present chapter surveys the budget system as a whole, giving particular attention to the formulation of the budget.

ELEMENTS OF THE BUDGET SYSTEM

The basic pattern for budgeting was established by a state constitutional amendment adopted in 1922. The system was modified by the creation of an agency for legislative fiscal analysis in 1941, the adoption of the annual budget in 1946, and the establishment of an independent legislative audit in 1955.

During the administration of Governor Hiram Johnson (1911–17) an "informal" budget procedure was developed. There was a semi-official budget board which included the governor, the Board of Control (three members serving at the governor's pleasure) and the State Controller, a constitutionally independent, elected officer. The board held hearings on departmental requests, made definite recommendations to the legislature, and defended their recommendations before the appropriations committees. While this procedure was a decided improvement over earlier practice,[1] it was not created or regulated by law, and the governor was therefore not obliged to continue its use. No single official held responsibility for formulating the budget; the governor was not required to recommend sources for financing the expenditure program. Recognition of the need for a legal basis for budget procedures led to the constitutional amendment of 1922,[2] which established the governor's responsibility for submitting comprehensive and detailed expenditure plans, and when necessary, recommending sources of revenue.

Governor's Responsibility for Budget Formulation

As amended in 1922 (and in 1946 to provide for annual budgeting), the constitution makes it the duty of the governor to submit to the legislature a "complete plan and itemized statement of all proposed expenditures of the State provided by existing law or recommended by him . . . and of all estimated revenues," together with an explanatory message. The budget must be submitted within the first 30 days of the general session (held in odd-numbered years) and within the first three days of the budget session (held in even-numbered years).[3] Actual and estimated expenditures and revenues for the budget year, the current year, and the prior year must be shown for "each item," and, if proposed expenditures exceed estimated revenues, the governor is required to recommend "the sources from which the additional revenue shall be provided." The governor, and also the governor-elect, may require any state official to furnish any information deemed necessary "in connection with the budget or to assist him in its preparation." The governor is required to submit "an appropriation bill covering the proposed expenditures, to be known as the Budget Bill," which is to be introduced in each house by the chairman of the appropriations committee.

Practice has permitted exception to the requirement that the governor submit a complete plan that includes all expenditures "recommended by him." Although governors have usually included some of the expenditures that would result from adoption of legislation proposed by them, they have often failed to include all such expenditures.[4]

The governor is assisted by the Budget Division, which revises the expenditure estimates of the agencies, estimates revenue, and prepares the budget document. The division is located within the Department of Finance whose director acts on behalf of the governor, gives policy direction to the Budget Division, and takes an active part in formulating the budget.

The Process of Authorizing the Expenditure Program

Both the legislature and the governor participate in authorizing the expenditure program. Annual appropriations are carried by the omnibus appropriation bill (budget bill) and special appropriation bills, with the budget bill enjoying constitutional priority. Until the budget bill is enacted, the constitution prohibits final passage of special appropriation bills in either house, with only two exceptions: those bills which provide funds for the expenses of the legislature, and those recommended by the governor as emergency measures. No appropriation bill, except the budget bill, may contain more than one item of appropriation, which must be for "one single and certain purpose" expressed in the bill. For many years, approximately two-thirds of the expenditure program has been authorized by continuing appropriations, provided in statutes or in the constitution. Consequently, the legislature exercises annual control on only about one-third of the expenditure program.

Article IV of the constitution provides that any item of appropriation in the budget bill, unless "for the usual current expenses of the State," is subject to the petition referendum. Thus, it recognizes that a referendum on the normal operating expenses of the state would be intolerable, resulting in inconvenience or even paralyzing delay. No referendum has ever been held on a budget bill item.[5]

An intensive review of the expenditure program is conducted by the appropriations committees of the two houses (styled the Committee on Ways and Means in the assembly, the Committee on Finance in the senate). Making extensive use of subcommittees, the appropriations committees conduct public hearings at which private persons and departmental spokesmen testify on the budget bill and special appropriation bills. The Legislative Analyst submits to the appropriations committees a lengthy, detailed analysis of the budget bill. In this document and in oral testimony he recommends specific reductions in appropriation items. The appropriations committees propose many changes in the budget bill, most of which are adopted by the houses. In the assembly, further amendments offered on the floor are often adopted; prevailing sentiment in the senate discourages floor amendments, few being proposed and even fewer adopted. For a number of years one or more conference committees have been required to settle inter-house differences on the budget bill.

The final step in the authorization process is the approval of the governor, who has the power to reduce or eliminate items of appropriation in any appropriation bill, including the budget bill, while approving other portions of the bill.[6] Although the governor seldom eliminates or reduces budget bill appropriations, he frequently vetoes or reduces appropriations in other bills.

Budget Execution

Execution of the budget is almost entirely the responsibility of the executive branch. Departments make many of the decisions that implement the budget, but the Department of Finance, acting under the governor's general direction, exercises important controls over their actions. After the legislature has authorized the expenditure program, the departments must submit their operating budgets, reflecting legislative action, to the

Department of Finance for its approval. Finance may revise these budgets before approving them; it may also require further changes in them during the course of the fiscal year.[7] It may modify and must approve requests for funds and budgets to be submitted to the national government, with the exception of those for highways.[8] The Finance Department may authorize special fund departments to spend in excess of appropriations (with the specific consent of the governor if the amount exceeds $25,000).[9]

Budget act provisions permit the Director of Finance to authorize transfers between the two object categories used in the budget act ("salaries and wages" and "operating expenses and equipment") and between construction projects within any single appropriation.[10] Transfers between institutions within a department (for example, hospitals for the mentally ill within the Department of Mental Hygiene) may be authorized by the Board of Control, with the approval of the Director of Finance.[11] The budget act also regularly requires that the Department of Finance approve the establishment of new positions, the reclassification of existing positions, or the filling of positions vacant for a specified period of time.[12]

Exceptions to Finance Department Control

The large budgets of the Division of Highways and the University of California are relatively free from such controls by the Department of Finance. The university has independent status under the constitution;[13] the governor and the legislature do not scrutinize its requests for appropriations in the same detail as they do other budgets, and the execution of its budget is not controlled by the Department of Finance. Future support of the university, which relies heavily on appropriations from the state, might be jeopardized if it departed radically from the expenditure plan presented to the legislature.

The budget of the Division of Highways is required by law to be submitted to the legislature without change by the Department of Finance or the governor. The Highway Commission has authority to execute the highway budget, except that certain transfers require approval by the Department of Finance.[14] Highway expenditures are financed by continuing appropriation of certain proceeds from taxes paid by users of motor vehicles. The disposition of the funds is governed by statutory formulas. The legislature exercises some control over highway expenditures by adjusting rates of taxes, by establishing the termini for the state highway system, by a statutory allocation of 45 percent of construction funds to the northern part of the state and 55 percent to the southern part, and by other statutory provisions. But the Highway Commission determines the routes between termini, establishes freeways, and allocates construction funds. The seven-member commission is relatively independent of the governor. Six of its members are appointed for staggered four-year terms by the governor with the advice and consent of the senate. The seventh, the Director of Public Works, is a member ex officio and the chairman of the commission. He serves at the pleasure of the governor.

During 1966–67, estimated expenditures of the Division of Highways were $736 million, including $339 million from federal funds. The University of California was budgeted to spend $829 million from all sources.[15] In view of the size of these expenditures, limitations upon executive and legislative budgetary control are of great significance.

The State Controller

Participating in the execution of the budget is the State Controller, whose office is established by the constitution and filled by statewide election. The controller conducts a preaudit of claims against the state, checking for legality, correctness, and sufficient provisions of law for payment. Although budget execution is primarily an executive responsibility, the legislature participates to a limited extent, in a manner which will be discussed subsequently.

Independent Postaudit

Until 1955, there was no agency independent of the executive branch that made a systematic examination of financial records in order to verify and report upon the facts of financial operation. The only postaudit was conducted by the Division of Audits of the Department of Finance, with the result that the executive branch was in effect auditing itself. In 1955 the legislature established the Joint Legislative Audit Committee, consisting of three members from each house, and authorized it to appoint an Auditor General, determine the policies to be followed by him, and review his audit reports.[16] With the aid of a staff of 28 auditors,[17] the Auditor General examines and reports annually upon the financial statements prepared by the executive branch.

Annual Budget

The constitution was amended in 1946 to provide for annual legislative sessions.[18] Sessions held in even-numbered years are designated "budget sessions," at which the legislature may consider only the budget bill, revenue measures, bills providing for the expense of the session, and approval or rejection of local government charters and charter amendments. The budget session may not exceed 30 calendar days in length, but a legislative recess of up to 30 days may be taken in order to permit adequate time for the appropriations committees to review the budget.[19] Prior to 1956 there was no provision for a recess at the budget session. An informal procedure was developed whereby the appropriations committees began their review of the state operations section of the budget (but not capital outlay or local assistance) three or four weeks prior to the convening of the session. Although this procedure was reasonably satisfactory, its continuance depended upon the cooperation of the governor, and the appropriations committees were compelled to make their initial review without knowing the budget totals nor the detailed plans for capital outlay.[20]

The general session held in odd-numbered years was limited to 120 calendar days until 1958, when the constitution was amended to exclude Saturdays and Sundays in the computation of the 120 days and to provide for an optional rather than a mandatory 30-day recess during the general session.

Reasons advanced for changing from a biennial to an annual budget were that annual budgeting would (1) increase the accuracy of estimates of revenues and expenditures, facilitating a "continually-balanced" budget; (2) permit better legislative and executive control of expenditure; (3) prevent the accumulation of surpluses leading to legislative extravagance; and (4) make legislators more knowledgeable regarding the budget because they would review it twice as often. Opponents contended that an annual budget would increase state expenditures by providing more opportunities for agencies, legislators and interest groups to press for new or expanded programs.[21]

There is little likelihood that the state will return to biennial legislative sessions and a biennial budget; instead, numerous constitutional amendments have been proposed in the legislature to provide for general sessions each year.[22] The Joint Committee on Legislative Procedure concluded in 1956 that the budget session should be retained, pointing out that annual budgeting "has kept the members of the Legislature in closer touch with the financial condition of the State and with the needs of State Government."[23]

Two considerations argue strongly for retention of the annual budget. First, changes in economic, social, and fiscal conditions occur with a rapidity which warrants annual review and adjustment of both revenue and expenditure programs. Second, because the revenue system of the state is highly sensitive to economic fluctuation, annual review and adjustment of financial plans is necessary; even annual revenue estimates frequently turn out to be substantially in error. Table 3 shows that in the decade of the 1950's actual receipts of the general fund differed from original estimates by as much as 18 percent and by at least 5 percent in every year except three. It is impossible to determine whether the annual budget has increased expenditures. A study committee of the Commonwealth Club of California stated in 1955 that "the state has had a slight but steady increase in cost (discounting economic changes and population increase) over a period which includes both biennial and annual sessions."[24]

It is significant that by 1966, 20 states used annual sessions, 10 of them providing for alternate-year budget sessions, whereas at the beginning of World War II, only four state legislatures met annually.[25]

BUDGET PREPARATION

Organization

The Director of Finance is the most important officer in the administrative organization of the state. In addition to his duties as administrator of the department and chief fiscal advisor to the governor (at whose pleasure

TABLE 3

GENERAL FUND REVENUE ESTIMATES, 1950–59

(millions of dollars)

Fiscal Year	Original Estimate[a]	Actual Receipts	Difference	Difference as Percent of Estimate
1950–51	$ 569	$ 672	$103	18.2%
1951–52	639	734	95	14.9
1952–53	742	774	32	4.3
1953–54	804	798	− 6	− 0.7
1954–55	822	879	57	6.9
1955–56	857	1,005	148	17.3
1956–57	1,014	1,079	65	6.4
1957–58	1,171	1,111	− 60	− 5.2
1958–59	1,239	1,210	− 29	− 2.4
1959–60	1,405	1,491	86	6.1

Source: *State of California Budget*. Data for 1951–55 from *Budget*, 1957–58, p. III.
[a] Adjusted for major changes in revenue legislation not foreseen in original estimates.

he serves), the director's responsibilities include service on numerous boards and commissions. The preparation of the budget is necessarily one of his primary concerns, and he makes major policy decisions, often after consultation with the governor. The extent of the director's participation in decisions of lesser importance varies with the interests and energy of the incumbent, but it is inevitable that many decisions are made by the Budget Division. The director presided at some of the executive budget hearings until such hearings were abandoned. He seldom appears before the appropriations committees, except to make an introductory statement when they begin their deliberations on the budget.

With a staff of more than 80 technical positions, the Budget Division was budgeted to spend $729,000 in 1966–67.[26] The division was reorganized in 1962 to provide for three units: (1) the economic and demographic research unit, with responsibility for making revenue and population estimates; (2) the budget procedures and methods unit, which was given responsibility for continuing studies of budget procedures; and (3) the budget operations unit, which reviews expenditure estimates and exercises control over budget execution. The latter, largest of the three, was divided into five sections: a fiscal control section and four operating sections, each responsible for a group of related agencies or functions.[27]

Central Review of Expenditure Estimates

The preparation and review of departmental budget requests is governed by a timetable provided by the Department of Finance. The formal call for expenditure estimates usually goes to the agencies in June or July, in the form of a letter from the Director of Finance, advising them of policies and assumptions on which budgets should be based. The letter also provides information on population and economic trends, the fiscal outlook, and price levels.

Until 1960, the review process included formal hearings at which agencies defended their budget requests before the Director of Finance or the chief of the Budget Division. The hearings were open to the public and the press. Representatives of the office of the Legislative Analyst, who were always present, occasionally asked questions.

The public character of the hearings discouraged frank discussion. They were useful as a method of transmitting information, but they did not provide an effective instrument for deliberation, and decisions were usually taken at a later time. A survey by the Organization and Cost Control Division found in 1957 that Budget Division and agency personnel were expressing "confusion and doubt" as to the purpose of the hearings, and in some instances believed that there was no need for them.[28] This viewpoint became official policy in 1960. Hearings were abandoned in favor of more informal, less public procedures for consultation within the executive branch.

In reviewing agency requests, the Budget Division tries to determine the needs of the agencies, and it makes revisions considered necessary or desirable in view of specific justifications and the overall fiscal situation. Requests are scrutinized in great detail, down to the last individual position or piece of equipment.

A key question in the review is whether a proposed expenditure is required to process anticipated workload, or whether it will provide new or expanded services. The agencies naturally try to justify as much of their budgets as possible on the basis of workload requirements, and they often disagree with the Budget Division analysts regarding the appropriate classification of particular expenditures.

In order that decisions may be based on more or less objective criteria, formulas and standards have been developed by which the need for personnel can be determined automatically, once the number of units of work has been established. For example, there is a formula for state college teaching staff based on such factors as teaching hours, type of course, enrollment, and non-teaching assignments. A formula for state college library personnel takes into account technical processing of new volumes, mending, inventorying and discarding, sorting and shelving, and manning public service desks and checkout points.[29] The development and use of standards results in a constant demand from the budget staff (and also from the Legislative Analyst) for more and better workload data.

The Budget Division has exhibited a strong "control" orientation with respect to its role in the preparation and execution of the budget, although it has moved cautiously in the past few years in the direction of greater decentralization of decision-making to the departments. The division has sought to guard against wasteful, unjustified, or irregular expenditures, rather than to "liberate" the departments for the achievement of their program objectives. This orientation has been reinforced by the attitude of the legislature and of the office of the Legislative Analyst, which have generally encouraged or accepted strong control by the Department of Finance.

Criticisms and Suggestions for Reform

A 1957 survey by the Division of Organization and Cost Control criticized the Budget Division for "a disproportionate emphasis on mechanics and detail" and insufficient attention to agency programs and their results. It found that there had been no coordinated effort leading to a performance approach to the budget, and that progress in this direction required changes in the attitude of the budget staff (as well as the departments and the legislature). It urged the division to support "strong management groups in the various state agencies," to establish standards within which agencies should operate, and to rely upon a postaudit by the executive branch to ensure compliance with standards. It admonished the division to make clear that it "recognizes the ability and integrity of agency personnel" and to embark on a "deliberate program of relying upon the agencies for budget preparation and budget administration to the greatest extent practical." The division was urged to place its emphasis (for those agencies demonstrating a capacity for effective management) upon "budgetary decentralization, information documents (rather than control documents), and post-review (rather than pre-review)."[30]

Decentralization and emphasis upon program and performance were the key themes in the 1959 proposals for reorganization of the budget process, as presented by the Governor's Committee on Organization of State Government. The committee proposed an overall scheme of reorganization providing for consolidation of departments and other agencies into eight "Agencies" headed by "Administrators." Within the governor's office there would be established an Executive Department, a staff agency having budgetary, management analysis, and planning functions. High level personnel of the present Department of Finance would move into the Executive Department, but other budget staff would be transferred to the agencies, "in order to provide the Administrators with strong management teams," permitting "a high degree of decentralization of management responsibility to the agency level." Basic budget policy would be decided by the governor, in consultation with the cabinet and with the assistance of the Budget Unit in the Executive Department. The Budget Unit would then issue budget policy instructions to the agencies.

The administrator would prepare "the program budget for his agency, not a detailed budget but one based on a broad definition of functions and activities." The Budget Unit would conduct hearings on these proposals, the governor would decide major questions, overall dollar limits would be established for each agency budget, and the administrator would prepare the detailed budget in accordance with these decisions and limits. The detailed budget would focus attention "on the purposes for which money is appropriated, the results being obtained by the various programs, and the results which are expected if requested funds are appropriated." The detailed budgets would be reviewed in the Executive Department to see that they conformed to previous understandings and would then be collated in the governor's budget. Each agency would be responsible for explaining its program to the appropriations committees.

After authorization of the expenditure program by the legislature, administration of the budget would be "a basic responsibility of the Administrator; however, major modifications [would] require approval of the Budget Unit."[81]

Changes in Budget Procedure

In the preparation of the 1961–62 budget, a step was taken in the direction favored by the Committee on Organization of State Government. A tentative dollar ceiling for each agency was established by the Department of Finance, which requested that the agency prepare a detailed expenditure plan within the limit set by the ceiling. Although the Department of Finance reviewed and revised the detailed plans, it showed greater willingness to accept the judgment of the agencies than it had in the past. The

Director of Finance also intimated that the agencies would have more discretion in the execution of their budgets. The tentative ceilings were established without any formal presentation of budget proposals by the departments and agencies. Capital outlay requirements and expenditures from continuing appropriations were estimated and deducted from anticipated revenues. The remaining funds were allocated to departments, the amounts being approximately the same as for the prior year, adjusted for population and enrollment increases at state institutions. No formal hearings were held on the budgets submitted by the departments, and consequently there was no opportunity for the Legislative Analyst to obtain information through that procedure. In many cases ceilings were adjusted upward as the result of conferences between the Department of Finance and the agencies.

The principal objective of the change in procedure was not to decentralize decision-making, but to provide for realistic budget planning by early consideration of available revenues. Formerly the departments had no specific guidance as to the amount of money that might be budgeted for them (although rough indications were communicated informally), and consequently their requests often greatly exceeded available resources. Much time and energy had gone into the preparation and central review of requests which had little or no chance of being accepted.

Inevitably, as it developed, the new procedure tended to decentralize decision-making because the ceilings forced the departments to establish their own priorities, rather than to shift the responsibility to the central review agency. But by its careful review of agency plans, the Budget Division made clear that it would not proceed rapidly with extensive decentralization.[82]

The new procedure did not materially affect legislative review. The Legislative Analyst thought that the new procedure weakened executive review, and that the legislature should compensate by scrutinizing expenditure plans more carefully than ever. He expressed certain reservations about the new method: that it encouraged agencies to defer necessary expenditures (e.g., by asking for new positions while holding others unfilled until funds might be available, when they could be filled without the legislative review required for new positions); that it encouraged departments to expand supervisory personnel to a degree which the Department of Finance would not have permitted in the past; that it permitted the initiation of small new programs which could be expected to expand rapidly; and that it led to "over- and under-budgeting" (e.g., equipment requests budgeted at the level of the previous year without "apparent consideration" of one-time needs).

He also noted that the procedure had limited the information available to his office, which in many cases had been requested not to contact the agencies. Requests by the Analyst for information might have tipped off the agencies to the final decisions of the Department of Finance, which wanted to keep the agencies in the dark. The Analyst conceded, however, that the new procedure had, under current conditions, stimulated the agencies to re-examine their priorities.[33]

The Process of Estimating Revenue

The economic and demographic research unit of the Budget Division bases its revenue estimates upon analyses of economic and population trends, both national and state, and upon a detailed study of the factors which affect the productivity of each tax. To provide a basis for estimating receipts from the corporate income tax and the gross insurance premiums tax, the unit sends questionnaires to a carefully selected sample of corporations and insurance companies. Estimates of 1961–62 receipts from the new (1959) cigarette tax were based upon a correlation involving cigarette consumption, income, population and degree of urbanization in 29 other states, checked by an analysis of trends in receipts from the tax in California.[34] To obtain a consensus of opinion concerning the general economic outlook, a conference is held each year with outstanding economists from government, private industry, and universities. Representatives of the unit also attend the annual national conference of budget estimators.

The basis for the revenue estimates for each tax is explained in detail in the budget document. Re-estimates are made during the legislative session in order to provide up-to-date information as a basis for legislative decisions.

Although the estimating process is highly professional, thorough, and detailed, actual revenues frequently vary by significant amounts and percentages from the estimates because of inability to predict economic developments with sufficient accuracy. The Legislative Analyst has raised serious questions regarding the estimates on only one occasion, a number of years ago.[35] Nevertheless, the process is sufficiently inexact to permit legislators to question the estimates. Usually, the legislature gives no serious review to the revenue estimates, but when additional taxes are proposed, the suggestion is frequently made that the estimates are unduly pessimistic. It is a difficult task for a governor to secure legislative approval of additional taxes; his problems are magnified when legislators question the revenue estimates, whether from political motivation or from honest difference of opinion.[36]

Capital Outlay Process

From 1945–46 through 1961–62 the state spent in excess of $4.5 billion for capital outlay, including about $350 million from the sale of general obligation bonds for construction.[37] A major portion of this amount was for highways. In order to catch up with construction and repair of state institutions and buildings deferred during the depression and World War II, the legislature authorized a $154 million construction program in 1946, which was supplemented by subsequent appropriations. In 1955 the Department of Finance prepared a five-year state building construction program, which has been revised and extended annually, and which was the basis for a series of bond issues authorized by the electorate in subsequent years.[38]

While the legislature gave its general approval to the construction program by submitting the bond measures to the voters, annual control was preserved; the legislature authorizes all projects by means of the budget act or other appropriation acts. Through appropriation decisions, the legislature can alter priorities, control the pace of implementation of the program, and eliminate or add specific projects.

Since World War II, much progress has been made in the development of detailed procedures for reviewing and authorizing capital outlay expenditures for the State Building Construction Program. It includes mainly construction of office buildings, prisons, mental hospitals, state college and University of California facilities, but not highway construction, development of beaches and parks, water development and flood control. In order to gain a more precise understanding of the scope and cost of construction projects before authorizing them, the legislature began in 1951 to appropriate money for preliminary plans, on the basis of which working drawings and construction could be authorized at a subsequent session. Although this procedure resulted in better planning and more reliable estimates of cost,[39] departments frequently proposed changes in the original plans after the projects had been authorized, with resulting changes in cost estimates and delays. Fifteen to 18 months sometimes elapsed between legislative authorization and the letting of contracts.

Present practice incorporates further changes made in 1956 in order to speed up the process. An appropriation is made for preliminary plans, but before they are drawn, extensive discussion takes place among the interested agencies (including the Department of Finance and the Legislative Analyst) to reach agreement on the scope of the project, its related program, type of structure, and space needs and utilization. If the project is approved, preliminary plans are drawn by the Division of Architecture, reviewed by the Department of Finance, the agency concerned, and the

Legislative Analyst. When necessary, plans are modified. If it has sufficient priority, the project is included in the governor's budget. If the project is approved by the legislature, working drawings can be authorized (by the Public Works Board) as soon as the legislature adjourns, usually about one year after the original submission of the proposal to the Department of Finance. Because preliminary plans are now prepared in greater detail than they were formerly, and because agreement on scope is reached before the project is presented to the legislature, few changes are required after the appropriation is made. Although considerable time and money have been invested in a project by the time it is presented to the legislature for funding, this investment is rarely lost; if the project is not authorized the first time presented, it is usually approved in a subsequent year.[40]

Although the new procedure has expedited budgeting and initiation of capital improvements, it has been criticized by the Legislative Analyst on the ground that information about projects is not received early enough or is incomplete. As a result, he is unable to make firm recommendations to the legislative committees regarding the projects. The Analyst proposed in 1961 that agencies be required to submit major construction proposals by January 15 (instead of April 1) in order that detailed plans could be prepared by October 1. This schedule would permit thorough review by the Department of Finance prior to inclusion of a project in the budget, and review by the Analyst prior to submitting recommendations to the legislature.[41]

Large gains have been made in the development of standards for construction and space utilization. The Legislative Analyst reported in 1959 that in the Department of Mental Hygiene, for example, "a considerable amount of standardization has taken place even to the extent of a standard ward building with a minimum number of standard variations for different types of patients, such as standard patients, infirm and bedridden patients, geriatrics, etc." Standards exist for bed space, day room and occupational therapy space, dining area space, toilet and bathing facilities, and office space. Design and construction materials for hospitals have also been "fairly well standardized."[42] Varying degrees of standardization have also been achieved for the construction of state office buildings, state college facilities, and correctional institutions.[43]

THE BUDGET DOCUMENT

"Our State Government," said Governor Warren in his 1950 budget message, "serves every phase of our social and economic life; to present its activities and fiscal requirements in a comprehensive manner requires quite a large book."[44] The 1966–67 budget document contained more than 2,000 pages and was divided into four separate publications dealing respectively with (1) current operations and local assistance, (2) capital outlay, (3) budgets for local agricultural fairs, and (4) details of existing positions. The first of these included the governor's budget message.

The budget message highlights the principal elements of the governor's financial plan for the year. It discusses the relationship between income and outgo, sources of additional revenue or other means of financing the expenditure program, expenditures for major functions, proposed new expenditure programs, and capital outlay. It explains the reasons for the governor's recommendations and underlines basic factors affecting the budget, such as population growth and the magnitude of continuing appropriations.

The document contains extensive summary statements, including narrative discussion of revenues and expenditures and numerous schedules, tables and charts. In the summaries, as in the detailed budgets, estimates for the budget year and the current year, and actual amounts for the prior year, are provided. Data are presented on the condition of funds, bonded debt, federal aid expenditures, and the appropriation sources for estimated expenditures (budget act, prior year appropriations, or continuing appropriations). The general fund surplus and current and past year expenditures are reconciled with previous estimates. Expenditures are presented by character, function, organization unit, and type of fund source.

Within each of the sections dealing with state operations, capital outlay, and local assistance, the estimates are organized by function and organization unit. Thus, under the heading "Fiscal Affairs" are grouped the Department of Finance, the Treasurer, the Controller, the Franchise Tax Board, and the Board of Equalization. Within a department, estimates for state operations are broken down by organization unit, object categories ("personal services," "operating expenses," and "equipment"), and, in some cases, by subfunctions or activities. The number of positions in each class for each organization unit is shown in the *Budget Supplement;* information about positions appears in somewhat less detail in the main document. Equipment does not appear in detail, and operating expense is broken down into such categories as "communications," "traveling—in-state," "traveling—out-of-state," "printing," "rent," and the like. The estimates for departments and other organization units are accompanied by narrative explanations of objectives and programs, including changes proposed in the budget year, and by statistical indices of workload, unit costs, workload standards, and staffing formulas.

THE BUDGET BILL

The budget bill contains more than 350 items of appropriation, providing for proposed expenditures not authorized by prior year or continuing appropriations. The appropriations are in lump sums, and a single appropriation may provide all of a department's current operation funds. Most appropriations carry a schedule of two items: (1) personal services, and (2) operating expense and equipment. These are not appropriations but are upper limits upon expenditures for the object categories. Similarly, appropriations for capital outlay are lump sums, with a schedule of amounts for individual projects.

CONCLUSIONS

The most important conclusion to be noted from the preceding outline of the California budget system is that responsibility for the preparation and execution of the budget is placed upon the governor. Extensive and complex organization and procedures have been developed for formulating, authorizing, and executing the budget, and a basic deficiency in the system was removed when provision was made in 1955 for an independent post-audit by an agency responsible to the legislature. In the processes of budget preparation and execution, progress has been made in establishing standards of performance and in planning and budgeting for capital improvements. At the same time, the desirability of decentralizing greater budgetary authority to the operating departments has recently been emphasized by the state's central management analysis unit and by a distinguished Committee on Organization of State Government. Cautious steps in this direction have been undertaken by the Department of Finance. The values of the annual budget, adopted in 1946, are recognized, and there is no serious thought of returning to the biennial budget.

An important part of the budget system is the staff agency that assists the legislature in fulfilling its responsibilities for budget review and authorization. It is essential to understand the role and functions of that agency in order to describe and appraise the legislature's performance of the review of the budget. The following chapter treats the origins and development of the Joint Legislative Budget Committee, and the office of the Legislative Analyst, for whose supervision the committee is responsible.

[1] In 1926 Governor-elect C. C. Young described earlier practice as follows:
When I first entered the legislature in 1909, there was little short of chaos as far as any orderly provisions for state expenditures were concerned. There had been no audit of the state finances for over 20 years. The finance committees of the two houses were scenes of a blind scramble on the part of the various institutions and departments of the state in an effort to secure as large a portion as possible of whatever money might happen to be in the treasury. Heads of institutions encamped night after night in the committee rooms, each alert for his own interest regardless of the interests of other institutions. "Log rolling" and trading of votes on appropriations bills was the common practice among members of the legislature.
"State Finances and the Executive Budget," Commonwealth Club of California *Transactions*, XXI (December 14, 1926), p. 442. For the background of the 1922 amendment, see also E. A. Wolcott, "The Executive Budget Wins in California," *National Municipal Review*, XIII (March 1924), 134–5.

[2] *Cal. Const.*, Art. IV, sec. 34 (Amend. 1922).

[3] N.B. Beginning in 1967, annual general legislative sessions were provided for by the constitutional revision of 1966. The sessions were not limited as to duration or subject.

[4] The Legislative Analyst stated in 1945 that only three budgets since 1922 had conformed to the constitutional requirements, and noted a number of recommendations made by Governor Warren for which no provision had been made in the 1945-47 budget. *Report of the Legislative Auditor to the Joint Legislative Budget Committee* (1945), pp. 4–7.

[5] Winston W. Crouch, *Initiative and Referendum in California* (Los Angeles: The Haynes Foundation, 1950), pp. 48–9. The phrase "usual current expenses" also appears in Article I, sec. 1 (Amend. 1911), which provides that, with certain exceptions including appropriations "for the usual current expenses of the State," no act shall go into effect until 90 days after adjournment of the legislature. The purpose of this provision is to permit the filing of referendum petitions. In 1953 the Legislative Counsel expressed "serious doubt" that certain capital outlay provisions of the 1953 budget bill would go into effect immediately, despite the usual language in the bill that "inasmuch as it provides for an appropriation for the usual current expenses of the State [this act] shall ... take effect immediately." The Legislative Counsel's opinion cited *McClure v. Nye* (1913), 22 Cal. App. 248, which held that appropriations for the construction of temporary buildings at a state college, building and furnishing cottages at a correctional school, and completing a dam and reservoir at a state mental hospital were not usual current expenses, and consequently could not take immediate effect under Article IV, sec. 1. The Legislative Counsel contended, however, that the budget act unquestionably would have immediate effect, if an urgency clause were adopted and the bill passed by a two-thirds vote of all members elected to each house, as provided by Article IV, sec. 1. "Budget Bill—No. 10043," *Assembly Journal*, May 22, 1953, pp. 4429–31. An urgency clause has regularly been included in subsequent budget acts in order to insure their immediate effect.

[6] *Cal. Const.*, Art IV, sec. 34.

[7] *Cal. Govt. Code*, secs. 13320–22.

[8] *Ibid.*, sec. 13326.

[9] *Ibid.*, sec. 11006.

[10] E.g., Budget Act of 1965, sec. 27.

[11] *Cal. Govt. Code*, sec. 16304.6.

[12] See Budget Act of 1965, secs. 20, 31.

[13] Art. IX, sec. 9 (Amend. 1918).

[14] *California Streets and Highways Code*, sec. 143.1. Legislative control of the highway budget is discussed in *Reports on Legislative Review of State Highway Funds* ..., Assembly Interim Committee on Ways and Means (Assembly Interim Committee Reports, 1963–5, vol. 21, no. 9, 1965), pp. (9)–25.

[15] *Capital Outlay Budget and Five-Year Construction Program*, 1966–67, pp. 60, 226, 228; *Support and Local Assistance Budget*, 1966–67, p. 311.

[16] *Cal. Stats.* (1955), chap. 1699.

[17] "Biennial Report of the Joint Legislative Audit Committee," (1964), p. 4 (process).

[18] *Cal. Const.*, Art. IV, sec. 2 (a).

[19] See note 3, above.

[20] "Argument in Favor of Senate Constitutional Amendment No. 4," *Proposed Amendments to Constitution, Propositions, and Proposed Laws ... to be Submitted to the Electors ... November 6, 1956*, Secretary of State (1956), p. 13.

[21] "Argument in Favor of ... and Against Senate Constitutional Amendment No. 25," *Proposed Amendments to Constitution, Propositions and Proposed Laws ... November 7, 1944*, pp. 5, 6; "Argument in Favor of Assembly Constitutional Amendment No. 10," *Proposed Amendments ... November 5, 1946*, p. 7.

[22] See note 3, above.

[23] "Report of the Joint Committee on Legislative Procedure," 1956, p. 15 (process). The Citizens Legislative Advisory Commission recommended, however, that consideration be given to returning to biennial sessions. "Report ...," *Assembly Journal*, May 14, 1957, p. 4549.

[24] Commonwealth Club of California, "Indirect Factors in Government Cost," *Transactions*, L (December 12, 1955), p. 10.

[25] *The Book of the States, 1966–67*, p. 41.

[26] *Budget Supplement: Detail of Authorized Salaries and Wages Contained in the 1966–1967 Budget*, pp. 343–4; *Support and Local Assistance Budget*, 1966–67, p. 576.

[27] *Analysis of the Budget Bill of the State of California for the Fiscal Year July 1, 1963 to June 30, 1964*, Report of the Legislative Analyst to the Joint Legislative Budget Committee (1963), p. 348. Cited hereafter as *Analysis*.

[28] *General Management Survey of the Department of Finance*, Survey 852 by the Organization and Cost Control Division of the Department of Finance (1957), p. 175.

[29] *Budget*, 1961–62, p. 232.

[30] *General Management Survey of the Department of Finance*, pp. 157–8. Many other criticisms and recommendations were made by the report, pp. 155–84.

[31] *The Agency Plan for California*, report by Governor's Committee on Organization of State Government (Sacramento: 1959), pp. 11–15. Four agencies were created by statute in 1961 and a Department of General Services was established in 1963.

[32] The foregoing is based on interviews with Department of Finance officials; *Budget*, 1961–62, pp. vi–vii; John E. Carr, "Budgeting for the State of California," *The Tax Digest*, 38, (November, 1960), 247–8.

[33] *Analysis*, 1961–62, pp. VII–VIII. The *Analysis* made no further comments on the ceiling procedure in 1962 and 1963.

[34] *Budget*, 1961–62, pp. A-15–A-16.

[35] Statement by Legislative Analyst A. Alan Post at the Panel on Fiscal Analysis of the Legislative Service Conference, held at New Orleans, September 29, 1953. (Discussion

recorded by the Council of State Governments.) The Analyst's budget analysis has not taken serious exception to the estimates since the 1953 statement.

[86] Governors Knight and Brown both had occasion to defend the revenue estimating process after they had sought taxes on the basis of revenue estimates which turned out to be too low. *Budget*, 1957–58, p. III and 1961–62, p. vii. From 1959 to 1961 Brown found himself in a running battle with Republican opponents, who charged that the taxes he pushed through in 1959 were unnecessary and urged that taxes be reduced in 1960 and 1961.

[87] Computed from data in *Budget*, 1961–62, p. A-34, and "Preliminary Summary: Legislative Action on Budget Bill and Major Revenue and Appropriations Bills, 1961 General Session," prepared by Office of Legislative Analyst (June 21, 1961), p. 6 (process).

[88] *State Building Construction Program*, report of the Department of Finance to the Joint Legislative Budget Committee (Senate, 1955). In 1966 the five-year construction program was presented as part of the capital outlay section of the budget document.

[89] *Analysis*, 1955–56, p. 760.

[40] The foregoing is based on interviews with Lew Clingan, Supervising Construction Analyst, Budget Division, December 12, 1957 and December 2, 1959; "Capital Outlay Program Procedures," Department of Finance [1958] (mim); and "Procedures For State Capital Outlay Program," prepared by Legislative Analyst (December 12, 1958) (mim). Capital outlay procedure is summarized in *Analysis*, 1965–66, pp. 954–7.

[41] *Analysis*, 1961–62, pp. 789–92.

[42] *Analysis*, 1959–60, p. 862.

[43] *Ibid.*, pp. 752–4, 759–61, 791–3, 838–9.

[44] *Budget*, 1950–51, pp. III–IV.

Chapter III

THE JOINT LEGISLATIVE BUDGET COMMITTEE AND THE LEGISLATIVE ANALYST

To provide a basis for analyzing the process of budget review, some relevant characteristics of the California legislature are examined briefly in the following section. The remainder of this chapter gives an account of the origins and development of the Joint Legislative Budget Committee and the Legislative Analyst.

CHARACTERISTICS OF THE LEGISLATURE

Californians do not enjoy a reputation for being a modest folk, and the members of the legislature are proud of themselves, their facilities, and their ways of doing things. Their pride is not without justification, for each member enjoys a commodious office, secretarial assistance, and the services of several staff agencies—the Legislative Counsel, the Legislative Analyst, the Auditor General, and, in the lower house, the Legislative Reference Service. Committee chairmen have the services of an administrative assistant (usually termed "consultant"). Committees meet once or twice weekly in well-appointed rooms to hear witnesses and take action on bills. Members receive $6,000 per year plus per diem allowances during sessions and when traveling on committee business between sessions. Relative to the time devoted to the job of being a legislator, compensation is modest indeed.[1]

Although the tradition of the part-time legislator dies hard, growing demands upon the time of members are forcing its abandonment. When the legislature is in session, the members' days are crowded with house sessions, committee meetings, and conferences with lobbyists, administrators, constituents, other legislators and staff, and in the period between legislative sessions much time is devoted to interim committee investigations. A survey published in 1958 found that about four-fifths of the responding legislators were spending one-half or more of their time on legislative duties, and 30 percent stated that they were spending full time on legislative work during general session years.[2] In the 1965 general session members introduced 5,021 bills, of which 2,070 became law, somewhat less than the record output of 1957. The folkway which requires that every bill be granted a hearing in committee, if the author requests it, adds to the workload.

The size of the houses is small enough to permit a degree of informality in procedure and to encourage a high level of interaction among members. With a membership of 80, the assembly is smaller than the lower houses of most states. Compared with other upper houses, the 40-member senate is of average size.

Organization

Key elements in the formal legislative organization are the speaker of the assembly, the president pro tempore of the senate, the Senate Rules Committee, and the standing committees of both houses. In addition, interim investigating committees perform important functions in highlighting issues and fact-finding, with the chairmanship of such a committee being one important means of advancement to legislative leadership. The speaker of the assembly and the president pro tempore of the senate are elected by the respective houses. The speaker appoints committees (except the Rules Committee) and committee chairmen, refers bills to committee, and, as presiding officer, controls debate and decides points of order. Although the chairman of the Rules Committee is appointed by the speaker, the other six members are named by the party caucuses, three by each party. The president pro tempore is the leader of the senate, but he acts as presiding officer only when the lieutenant governor steps down. The selection of committee members and chairmen and the reference of bills are functions of the five-member Rules Committee, of which the president pro tempore is chairman. The discretion of the Rules Committee in committee appointments is considerably limited by the practice of naming both chairmen and members of standing committees on the basis of seniority.

Almost all bills that win committee approval are passed by the house, some with floor amendments. Many die in committee, however, either because the author chooses not to press for them, or because they fail to find favor. The house has the power to force withdrawal of bills from committee, but this power is rarely invoked, and almost never with success. Normally, bills are heard if and when the author desires, although committee chairmen very occasionally "lose" bills or delay hearings on the ground that the schedule is crowded. Virtually all hearings and votes on bills take place in public session, when the committees listen to lobbyists, legislators, citizens, or administrators who wish to testify.[3] Committees meet according to a fixed schedule. Members serve on several committees, but attention is given to the schedule in making appointments, and few members receive assignments to two committees that meet at the same time.

Both houses use a calendar that is virtually automatic; bills are placed on the calendar in the order in which they are reported from committee and are taken up in order unless the author requests postponement.

Partisanship

Since the days of Hiram Johnson, partisanship has played a varying but limited role in the legislature.[4] The speaker of the assembly and the president pro tempore of the senate have almost always been members of the party in control of the house, but the speaker has normally received the support of some part of the minority. Official election of the president pro tempore is always unanimous, the real choice having taken place beforehand in a caucus of all senators behind closed doors. Committee chairmen always include some members of the minority party. Until the late 1950's at least, it often appeared that rural-urban, North-South and liberal-conservative cleavages were more important than party differences. In the senate, especially, party counted for little.

As late as 1957, 58 percent of the members of the legislature considered that parties had little or no impact in the legislature, but only one-fourth of a 50 percent sample held this opinion in 1960.[5] Buchanan has reported that in 1959, a majority of one party in the assembly opposed a majority of the other on 49 percent of the contested roll call votes, in contrast to 31 percent in 1949, 36 percent in 1951, and 34 percent in 1957. Even so, party cohesion remained low relative to other states.[6]

Interest Groups

From the rise of lobbyist Artie Samish in the 1930's until the 1950's, interest groups played a much more influential role in the legislature than did parties. The "revolution" of 1951 marked the beginning of a decline in the power of lobbies in the assembly. The house leadership, which was subservient to certain interest groups, met defeat on the issue of the speaker's power to appoint the Rules Committee. In the following session the insurgents took control of the house. Although the senate never experienced such a revolution, lobby influence waned as a result of Samish's conviction on charges of federal income tax evasion, changes in the personnel of the senate, sensational revelations concerning the Board of Equalization's administration of liquor control, and prosecutions in which a former speaker and an assemblyman were convicted.

Despite distasteful experiences with certain lobbies, the members of the California legislature recognize the valuable functions that lobbyists perform. The latter converge on Sacramento by the hundreds during each session, quite openly and often helpfully explaining the views of their clients on legislation. It would be wrong to suggest that interest groups do not continue to have enormous power, but increased legislative salaries, the strengthening of parties, a change in climate, and new blood have reduced noticeably the extraordinary influence of certain lobbies, and have partially redressed the balance among contending groups.

Summarizing some of the salient characteristics of the California legislature, we may note (1) moderate and growing partisanship, (2) growing and onerous workload, (3) a highly developed committee system playing a crucial role in determining the legislative output, (4) extensive and high-quality staff services and excellent physical facilities, and (5) numerous and diversified interest groups, accepted as legitimate participants in the legislative process.

ESTABLISHMENT OF THE BUDGET COMMITTEE AND THE NEED FOR STAFF

In 1941 the legislature created the Joint Legislative Budget Committee and the office of the Legislative Analyst,* agencies that were destined to form basic elements in the California budget process and models for other states to copy. Before analyzing the present functions, organization, and procedures of these agencies, it is well to consider two questions: Why did the legislature establish such machinery in 1941? How have these agencies evolved over the course of more than two decades?

A concurrent resolution adopted in the closing days of the 1941 regular session made it the duty of the Budget Committee

to ascertain facts and make recommendations to the legislature ... concerning the State Budget, the revenues and expenditures of the State, and of the organization and functions of the State, its departments, subdivisions and agencies, with a view of reducing the cost of the State Government, and securing efficiency and economy.[7]

The committee was to represent the leadership of the two houses, for it consisted of the assembly speaker, the president pro tempore of the senate, four assemblymen appointed by the speaker, and four senators each selected by one of four important senate committees: Finance, Revenue and

---

* Until 1957 the title of the Legislative Analyst was Legislative Auditor. The change of names was made in order to avoid confusion with the Auditor General, a post created in 1955. In the present work, Legislative Analyst is used throughout.

Taxation, Governmental Efficiency, and Judiciary. The new committee received authority to select its own chairman, to make its own rules, to create subcommittees, to subpoena witnesses and records, to meet during or between sessions, to appoint a Legislative Analyst and other staff and to prescribe the Analyst's duties.

The resolution made clear that the Budget Committee was not just another run-of-the-mill interim investigating committee, of which the legislature created 32 at the 1941 session.[8] Normally, such committees went out of existence at the convening of the next regular session after their establishment, but the Budget Committee was to continue in existence during "any succeeding session" until appointment of a new committee. Furthermore, the resolution provided for a new joint rule concerning the membership, organization, and powers of the committee. This was a departure from custom, for the legislature did not normally place in the joint rules provisions regarding particular interim committees. The exceptional treatment of the Budget Committee underlined the legislature's expectation that the committee would be a permanent agency.

The Budget Committee was different in yet another respect. It received an appropriation of $40,000, nearly one-fourth of the total appropriated for interim committees by the 1941 session and substantially more than any other committee received.[9] It is also significant that the authors of the resolution were the president pro tempore and the other four members of the Senate Rules Committee.

The creation of the Budget Committee in 1941 is to be understood in terms of financial and political circumstances of the depression years. Since the early thirties, the state general fund had shown a deficit at the end of each biennium, although a small surplus was expected by the end of the 1941–43 biennium.[10] The state had been obliged to pay bills with registered warrants, and much-needed improvements in the state's physical plant had been deferred. During the 1941 session there was serious discussion of a possible reduction in taxes, or alternatively, the authorization of a construction program.[11] The recurrent financial difficulties of the depression decade led the legislature to consider improvements in its organization and procedure for making budgetary decisions.

The development of sharp antagonisms between a major part of the legislature and Governor Culbert Olson provided political motives for the establishment of the Budget Committee. One of the key battles during the Olson administration was the struggle over the budget in 1939.[12] The Budget Committee was potentially useful as a weapon in the legislature's conflict with the executive branch.

The legislature sought two objectives: first, to secure more objective, more accurate, and more complete information on state finances, and second, to tighten legislative control over expenditures. An assembly subcommittee had charged in 1940 that there had been "many instances" in which "misleading or incorrect" information had been given to the legislature by the executive branch:

The principal offender has been the Department of Finance, where the staff includes a number of budget troopers who know all the tricks of the trade and who have no compunction about deceiving the Legislature and then laughing heartily when adjournment day comes.[13]

The subcommittee had recommended the establishment of a budget officer in the Legislative Counsel's office to study the budget during preparation, and to report his findings to the legislature.[14]

In 1941 the senate adopted a resolution outlining its policy regarding taxes, the budget bill, and special appropriation bills, and emphasizing the need for a legislative staff agency to assist in fiscal matters:

We state first that the adoption of the resolution providing for a Legislative Budget Advisor should be one of the most urgent matters before the present State Legislature. This . . . will provide us with the necessary information and advice. . . . [The budget advisor] must begin his work soon, to the end that every unnecessary item of expense, big or little, may be eliminated. . . .[15]

In its first report the Budget Committee stated that the need for better information was a basic reason for its creation:

Succeeding Legislatures for years have felt that they were handicapped because of lack of information, particularly so in considering State appropriations and the Governor's budget. This arose from the fact that the Legislature did not have reliable information and facts free from bias and prejudice and political considerations upon which it could base its decisions and its legislation.[16]

Whereas the governor had a trained budget staff at his disposal, the legislature had relied on legislative committees, which were ineffective because of time limitations, lack of continuity, and lack of competent staff.[17] The legislature "needed some instrumentality whereby it could secure its own information, free from the control and influence of the adminstration."[18]

The second objective—tighter legislative control over expenditures— was intimately related to the aim of securing more and better information:

The repeated instances of expanding the State pay roll and the making of jobs through establishing a large number of administrative assistants, coordinators, public relations men, and other political jobs, which in some instances were contrary to the expressed will of the Legislature, indicated the desirability of the Legislature's keeping informed as respects the administration and particularly the reorganization of the various departments of the State. The expansion of old services of government and the establishment of absolutely new services . . . during legislative interims without any approval of the Legislature and in some instances without the Legislature's making any specific appropriations for such new service, gave a further reason for having a representative of the Legislature continuously on the job to observe these matters.[19]

The Assembly Subcommittee on Budgetary Control had also placed heavy stress on the need for tighter control of expenditures. For example, it found abuses in the use of the emergency fund during the administrations of both Governors Merriam and Olson, including the construction of an Indian Museum at Sutter's Fort and the remodeling and refurnishing of the governor's office. A major part of $5 million appropriated to the emergency fund for flood relief had been diverted to other purposes. The Department of Finance had created 110 new jobs despite the legislative cut in its budget that had been intended to eliminate almost all of the 108 proposed new positions. Cuts in special fund budgets "so carefully made" by the legislature in 1939 had been rendered meaningless because the Department of Finance, acting under its authority to approve deficiency expenditures by special fund agencies, had restored the amounts deleted. The subcommittee recommended that the legislature "specify in detail just what the money appropriated is to be used for," prohibit "juggling funds," require approval of the State Controller before the emergency fund could be used, clearly define "emergency," take from the Department of Finance the power to authorize deficiency spending by special fund agencies, and transfer the auditing function from the Department of Finance to the Controller.[20]

During 1939–41, legislative concern about fiscal information and control was also expressed in a number of measures, several of which provided for some kind of legislative agency for fiscal analysis.[21] In 1941 the legislature passed, but the governor vetoed, a bill which would have created an independent postauditing agency.[22]

Three developments in the early history of the committee were favorable to its survival and growth in influence. The first was the selection of an able and aggressive Legislative Analyst to serve as its chief of staff. The second was the committee's demonstration of its usefulness during a special legislative session called shortly after the United States entered World War II. The third was the marked improvement in legislative-executive relationships after Governor Warren took office in 1943; the committee's capacity for effective performance was substantially increased by the cooperation extended to it by the new governor.

The First Legislative Analyst

In October, 1941 the Budget Committee appointed as Legislative Analyst, Rolland A Vandegrift, who was to hold the office until his death in

1949. Vandegrift had been Director of Finance from 1931 to 1934, and before that had served as director of research of the California Taxpayer's Association, which he had helped to organize.[23] He displayed extraordinary ability to collect and retain factual information, and he brought to his position extensive knowledge of California government. His arguments for proposed budget reductions were often shrewd and persuasive, although not always capable of standing up under careful analysis. He threw himself energetically into the work of the Budget Committee, zealously pursuing the objectives of economizing, ferreting out waste and inefficiency, and uncovering misbehavior. He identified strongly with the legislative branch, and was prepared to go to great lengths to secure legislative control of expenditures. In 1947 he recommended that the legislature "incorporate the Budget Document itself" into the budget act, a step that would have entailed itemization of appropriations in minute detail.[24] He was aggressive, outspoken, and, at times, contentious. Thus, he criticized members of the legislature for wasteful use of the services of the Legislative Counsel:

...a considerable amount of time of the Legislative Counsel Bureau is wasted through improper consideration and indiscriminate requests. For example, the *carte blanche* authorization given by some members of the Legislature to citizens interested in legislation to have any bills drawn which they wish is frequently an extravagant waste of time of the Legislative Counsel Bureau....Frequently the requests of legislators themselves are so indefinite as to place an undue burden on the imagination as well as the technical skill of the Legislative Counsel Bureau.[25]

Vandegrift's rigorous standard of frugality and his willingness to enter the lists against the exalted as well as the lowly, are illustrated by his comments on budget requests of the Supreme Court in 1948. He scolded the Supreme Court for requesting an automobile for each justice and the sum of $1,000 to replace their worn and patched robes; he preferred existing policy under which they were reimbursed for official use of their private cars and purchased their own robes.

This request for robes at state expense, and that for an automobile for each justice, we believe is beneath the dignity of the Supreme Court, which should be looked upon with honor and esteem not because of the trappings of the office but because of its high regard, which is exerted through the excellence of the minds and characters of the justices of the Supreme Court and the translation of their intellectual attributes to a logical and just interpretation of the law.

In a remarkable display of logic, he argued that if robes and automobiles were to be provided for the Supreme Court, the state should furnish work clothes and an automobile for each state employee.[26] Nor did the governor escape criticism. When Warren proposed in 1945 to increase medical services in mental hositals, Vandegrift commented:

Why, in the middle of a war, when the services of trained nurses and doctors are at a premium, should this expenditure be proposed? Wounds of soldiers continue after the fighting ends and long after the glory dims.[27]

In the same year, his report to the Budget Committee devoted 46 pages to dissecting the governor's six-page budget message.[28] He took issue with the governor's statement that in preparing the budget he had attempted to adhere to a policy of "strict economy"; criticized the governor for recommending new programs for which no financial provision was made in the budget; and questioned the governor's assertion that highways, hospitals, and institutions of higher learning had been neglected in the prewar period.[29] On the ground that unit costs were increasing, Vandegrift disagreed with the governor's view that the budget provided for a continuation of service in accordance with the standards that the legislature had established, and quarreled with the governor's explanation for the increases that had taken place during the 20th century in the cost of state government.[30]

Vandegrift deserves a substantial measure of the credit for the establishment of the Budget Committee as an important institution in the California budget system, and for shaping the role of the committee and its staff. Eschewing the role of the self-effacing staff assistant with a "passion for anonymity," he seized the opportunity to make the office of Legislative Analyst a positive force in the process of making financial decisions. That he did so with the express approval of the Budget Committee does not detract from the importance of his own boldness and energy in pursuit of that goal. When invited to make recommendations to the legislature regarding spending proposals, he accepted the responsibility with enthusiasm, nor did he permit caution, much less timidity, to restrain him from vigorous objection to expenditures or practices that he considered unwise or unnecessary. The early reports of the Budget Committee, unmistakably reflecting Vandegrift's style and tone, recounted the achievements of the committee and its staff in glowing terms. His boldness, his "penny-pinching" tendencies, his contentiousness, and his need to be in the center of the stage stimulated negative reactions from some legislators as well as from adminstrative personnel, but on balance, his qualities contributed greatly to the shaping of influential roles for the Budget Committee and especially for the Legislative Analyst himself.

Special Session of 1941

About two months after the Budget Committee held its first meeting, Pearl Harbor was attacked, and in the extraordinary legislative session convened shortly thereafter to consider measures to cope with the emergency, the committee played an important role. The governor recommended enlargement of the State Guard and substantial appropriations for the emergency fund.[31] For the duration of the special session the legislature enlarged the committee to a membership of 22 and directed it to study and report on all matters included in the governor's proclamation.[32] After extensive hearings the committee, and ultimately the legislature, accepted nearly all of the recommendations of the Legislative Analyst regarding appropriations, reducing the governor's request from $28 million to $16 million. Included in the governor's request was $9,250,000 for the emergency fund which would have been subject to allocation by the governor. The legislature appropriated most of this sum to departments, thereby partially removing it from the governor's control.[33]

The Budget Committee's own assessment of its role in the 1941 special session appeared in its 1943 report to the legislature:

... the appropriations were not made ... in the way of a blank check by having all appropriations made to the emergency fund and allowing the Governor to distribute them as he saw fit. ...

Through relying on the recommendations of the enlarged Legislative Budget Committee and its staff, the legislature was not stampeded into turning over the treasury to the governor because of the Pearl Harbor incident. ...

The only reason that satisfactory results were secured in this emergency in relation to appropriations followed from the fact that the Legislative Budget Committee was already organized and the Legislative Auditor [Analyst] was already intimately familiar with the entire operation of the State Government, and also that he already had in hand available for the committee basic information which could be used at a moment's notice.[34]

Even if allowance is made for exaggeration in this estimate, it seems clear that the leading role played by the Budget Committee and the Legislative Analyst in the special session did much to place the committee in a position of prominence and to demonstrate its potential usefulness to the legislature.

Cooperation with the Governor

The bitter animosity which had characterized legislative-executive relationships during the Olson adminstration gave way to an era of good feeling after Warren was elected in 1942. Even before he took office, he approached the chairman of the Budget Committee and requested assistance in preparing an "economy budget." He invited the Legislative Analyst to attend the executive budget hearings, private and public, and to "participate in the final consideration of the budget items with the Governor-elect before these were finally determined." As a result of the Analyst's participation, appropriation requests were "materially" affected.[35] Warren's 1943 budget message stated that "in all of our Budget hearings we have exchanged views with your Legislative [Analyst] and feel indebted to him for many valuable suggestions."[36] Two years later the Analyst took part in the public budget hearings "as if he were a member of the budget staff," participating in many decisions reached at these hearings, but not in those taken privately by the Department of Finance or the governor.[37]

Another important area of cooperation between the governor and the legislature was in the planning of the postwar building program. The Legislative Analyst

worked with the Director of Finance and the several departments concerned on the Postwar Building Program, helping to schedule priorities, estimate needs accurately, hold down costs by better planning and ... distribute available funds on an equitable basis and assisted in the procedure of setting up the appropriations for reserves for those purposes.[38]

Finally, the Warren administration was careful to follow legislative intent regarding appropriations, consulting the Budget Committee when, in the execution of the budget, questions of intent arose.

By soliciting its assistance and counsel, Governor Warren lent prestige to the Budget Committee and magnified its role in the budgetary process. Furthermore, without his cooperation, the committee's task of obtaining information would have been difficult. Although Warren became more aloof in later years, his early attitude toward the Budget Committee helped it to become firmly established.

DEVELOPMENT OF THE BUDGET COMMITTEE AND THE STAFF

The resolution that created the Budget Committee was silent as to the Legislative Analyst's precise functions. It was soon made clear that he was not to perform an audit function in the sense of an examination of records to ascertain and verify the facts of financial operation. A function which did emerge, as early as the 1941 special session, was that of making recommendations to the legislature and its committees regarding proposed appropriations. At the next general session in 1943, he presented an overall analysis of the governor's budget, analyzed the appropriations proposed in the budget bill, and recommended a specific amount to be appropriated for each item.[39] The basic pattern established in 1943 has been followed ever since, and making recommendations regarding proposed appropriations has always been the most important function of the agency.

Precedent was also established at an early stage for the Legislative Analyst to make recommendations regarding matters of policy, as distinguished from questions of cost estimates or resources needed to carry on programs and activities. In 1943 he recommended the consolidation of several revenue agencies into a department of taxation and revenue,[40] and his analysis of the 1945–47 budget contained a number of policy recommendations.[41] Subsequent reports by the agency have included many policy recommendations, including some requiring changes in existing statutes.

The Committee and the Analyst's Recommendations

As might be expected, the establishment of a high degree of freedom for the Legislative Analyst to make recommendations was accompanied by a tendency for the Budget Committee to take less and less responsibility for the specific proposals of its staff. At first, the committee gave rather specific instructions to the Analyst to guide him in making his budget analysis. In 1945, for example, the Analyst listed 20 points on which he had received specific instructions from the committee, such as that no dormitories should be provided at the university or state colleges and that there should be no provisions for commodity price increases in the appropriation to the emergency fund.[42] Such instructions were soon abandoned. The committee normally limits its guidance to certain procedural matters and the general injunction that the staff show the legislature how to balance the budget without new or additional taxes.

In 1943 the Analyst's recommendations regarding appropriations were published as reports of the committee, although the committee members reserved the right to disagree with them because some had not read the reports.[43] The Analyst's recommendations on the 1947 budget bill were adopted by the committee, but in 1948 Chairman Rich thought that to do so was the "wrong policy,"[44] a viewpoint to which the committee has adhered ever since. Nor does the committee normally adopt the recommendations in other reports by the staff regarding administrative organization and procedure, administrative programs, and financial policy.[45]

Not only has the Budget Committee ceased to adopt the recommendations of the staff, but it has also virtually discontinued the practice of making recommendations of its own, of sponsoring legislation, and even of making regular reports to the legislature. The committee has not made a formal report to the legislature on its activities since 1947, and it has rarely sponsored legislation since 1949, although individual members have introduced bills arising from the work of the committee.[46] The many reports made by the staff constitute a partial record of the committee's activities and are in that limited sense a report.

The Legislative Analyst summarized the role of the Budget Committee very well in 1953:

It manages the staff in behalf of the legislature. . . . The committee does not take

positions on policy questions. . . . They leave the question of a position on a particular report or a particular recommendation of the staff to be transmitted
through them to the legislature and to be considered by them acting not as members of the Budget Committee, but as members of the legislature acting in a standing committee . . . and that serves the purpose of not committing the Budget Committee to any particular position that might be taken by the Legislative [Analyst].
It's a staff recommendation and they can take it or leave it, as members of standing
committees. It gives greater freedom to us as members of the staff; it gives greater
freedom to them, they feel, as members of the legislature.[47]

Senator George Miller, Jr., who became chairman of the Budget Committee in 1959, believed that the committee should play a more decisive
role in guiding the staff and should take more responsibility for its recommendations. The committee minutes make this clear:

The Chairman suggested that the committee hold a briefing session prior to the
printing of the *Analysis of the Budget Bill* in order to bring the committee members up to date on what is being recommended in regard to general policy items
in the *Analysis*. It was suggested that these policy items be summarized and an advance report be submitted by the Legislative Analyst to all members of the committee at that time. In this way the committee can determine the broad policy
matters which it will support.[48]

At the following meeting of the committee a member objected to this suggestion on the ground that the Budget Committee was not a policy-making
committee, but only a fact-finding committee.[49] Chairman Miller replied
that ". . . this is a policy-making committee in respect to the facts that it
submits to the legislature." Although the committee would not take decisions on specific proposals contained in the reports of the Analyst, "the
manner and what is presented to the legislature should not be left to the
staff." The committee would not say that it was "either for or against this,
but this should be submitted, this should not be submitted; this is of value,
this is not of value."

This "fine line," as the chairman called it, was accepted by the committee, but the question would not down, for at the same meeting an issue
arose regarding the disposition of a report by the Analyst on the newly-
established and controversial Fair Employment Practice Commission. The
report criticized the staffing and expenditure requests that the commission
had submitted to the Department of Finance and took issue with the commission's interpretation of its authority under the law.[50] It was moved that
"we accept this report and at the budget hearings we can take up [sic]
whatever action we choose. . . ." The chairman said that the question was
whether "to accept this report and have it incorporated in the full report
[i.e., the Analyst's *Analysis of the Budget Bill* for the 1960–61 budget] and
recommended to the legislature." The question was not whether the com-

mittee would adopt the report as its own, but only whether it would permit the *Analyst's* recommendations to be submitted to the legislature.

That an extended discussion was necessary to decide on the disposition of the report is evidence of the committee's recognition that a decision to permit (or not to permit) submission of the report to the legislature would imply approval of the recommendations, even though the committee did not formally adopt them. The motion was amended to say that the committee would "receive," rather than "accept" the report. But Chairman Miller's interpretation of the significance of the amended motion raised further doubt. He considered that if the report were "received," the committee would signify thereby that it wanted to take a "real good look" at the Fair Employment Practice Commission and would put the commission on notice that the committee members would give the Analyst's recommendations serious consideration. "Receiving" the report would not be rejecting nor accepting it, but it would be a recommendation that the legislature "take a good look at it." On the other hand, failure of the committee to "receive" the report would, according to Miller, prevent the inclusion of its substance in the *Analysis of the Budget Bill*.

Assemblyman Jesse Unruh, chairman of the Ways and Means Committee, expressed strong reservations about the direction in which Chairman Miller appeared to be moving:

... I certainly am not inclined to be in the position of having signed this report—I, parenthetically, disagree with it. ... If we are going to attempt to do what I think the chair has had in mind all this year—that is, to give the weight of the Legislative Analyst's recommendations more than simply the recommendations of A. Alan Post—put some of the prestige of the committee behind it, then I think we have to work out some sort of definition [of terms] whereby we can take a middle ground on this. I don't want to keep this entirely out of the report [i.e., the *Analysis of the Budget Bill*]. On the other hand, if it's going to be in there as a recommendation of this committee and we're moving this committee in the direction of giving more support to the Legislative Analyst himself, then I'm going to have to vote against this. ... If we can say that this is the report of the Analyst himself and does not bear the recommendation of the committee, then I'm willing to let it in, but not if it's going to be the recommendation of the committee.

At this point the committee recessed to have lunch and to resolve the issue privately. After lunch there was no further discussion. Without dissent, the committee passed a motion that the report "be received." It is clear that the committee was not yet prepared to take responsibility for the specific recommendations and findings of the Legislative Analyst, nor even to offer unambiguous signs of support for them. The duty assigned to the committee in 1941 "to ascertain facts and make recommendations to the Legislature" would continue to be delegated almost completely to the staff.

Until 1951, the continuation of the Budget Committee depended on the inclusion of an authorizing provision in the joint rules at each legislative session. In that year the legislature enacted a statute[51] giving permanent status to the committee, the purpose being to strengthen its position against any opposition that its activities or those of the staff might arouse.[52]

SUBSTANTIVE INTERESTS OF THE BUDGET COMMITTEE

The problems with which the Budget Committee has concerned itself are fundamentally those which gave rise to its creation: (1) securing information to aid in fiscal decision-making, and (2) strengthening legislative control of expenditure. In the case of the former, the committee's primary role has been that of providing and broadly supervising a fiscal staff that transmits information both to the committee itself and to other committees and individual members. This function is considered below in chapters dealing with the Legislative Analyst and the review of the budget by the appropriations committees.

With respect to the second problem, the Budget Committee has endeavored to strengthen legislative control of expenditures in two ways. It has worked to secure economy and efficiency, and it has tried to ensure that the legislature plays its rightful role in making fiscal determinations. The committee staff has been important in these efforts.

In its search for economy and efficiency, the committee looked into such areas of possible extravagance as administrative and legislative printing, public information personnel, unnecessary or unauthorized use of state automobiles, travel costs, and sick leave with pay. It sponsored a variety of bills dealing with such areas and sought to secure economies in small matters as well as large. The committee's first report stated that it had purchased almost all of the equipment for its own office from the surplus stock of the liquidated State Relief Administration, and that "costly letterheads and other expensive printing have been eliminated, and other office costs strictly controlled."[53] As a further economy measure, some 50 bills sponsored by the committee in 1943 were introduced in only one house in order to avoid the costs of companion bills.[54]

Especially during its earlier years, the committee was much concerned with ways and means of exercising effective control over fiscal determinations. The committee criticized failure to follow legislative intent. At an early meeting, for example, an assemblyman "inquired why Miss Flannigan had been kept on by Mrs. Clark, in a position by a different title, after her old position was abolished by the Legislature."[55] The committee sponsored a few proposals to eliminate certain special funds and continuing appropriations, and was instrumental in the establishment of the Joint Legislative Audit Committee and the Auditor General in 1955. Several efforts were made to reduce executive discretion in the execution of the budget; the most far-reaching was a measure introduced in 1943[56] to create a Board of Budget Appeals consisting of the Controller (an elected constitutional officer independent of the governor), the Director of Finance, and a third member to be elected by concurrent resolution of the legislature.

In effect, the bill would have enacted into law the detailed budget contained in the budget document (as modified by the legislative action on the budget bill). Any departures from the detailed expenditure plan would have required the approval of the Board of Budget Appeals. Since only one member of the board would have been appointed by the governor, the measure would have vastly reduced the governor's power over budget execution. The approval of the board and the governor, instead of the governor alone, would have been required to authorize deficiency spending from special funds. Existing authority of the Department of Finance to control budget execution would have been curtailed in other ways. The bill was passed by the senate but died in the assembly. Nevertheless, it brought about a conference between the governor and the Ways and Means Committee "out of which came the agreement and assurance of the Governor that he would see that budgetary control was exercised and the legislative intent in relation to appropriations followed." The governor and the Director of Finance consulted the Ways and Means Committee minutes and the Legislative Analyst when they were in doubt as to legislative intent. The Budget Committee averred in its 1945 report that the result of this agreement was a saving of "many millions of dollars."[57]

The agreement to abide by legislative intent was reaffirmed subsequently, and the Department of Finance continues to adhere closely to this policy. In 1948 the Director of Finance assured the Budget Committee that

It is the policy of the Department of Finance when the Legislature has eliminated a position from the budget recommended by the Governor not to permit this position to be filled except in an emergency situation which this department believes justifies such employment.[58]

Occasionally, the Department of Finance has appealed to the Budget Committee itself for clarification of legislative intent.[59] It has requested committee approval for filling positions deleted by the legislature, transfers, use of the emergency fund, or incurring of deficiencies. Although the committee has sometimes been unwilling to pass on such questions, its reluctance has usually been based on the circumstances of the particular case rather than any general principle.

Most of the bills sponsored by the Budget Committee failed to pass, or, in a few cases, were vetoed. Many of them were of minor importance, although the establishment of the Auditor General was a major reform. The committee's successful effort to secure closer adherence by the administration to legislative intent was also an achievement of considerable importance.

The Budget Committee has taken little interest in the revenue side of the budget, with the exception of total revenues. Although its traditional policy has been in opposition to additional or increased taxes, the committee has not entered the field of tax policy with recommendations regarding the structure or rates of taxation.

THE BUDGET COMMITTEE'S CURRENT PROCEDURE

The committee has usually met four or five times during the course of a year,[60] the principal function of the meetings being to hear reports from the Legislative Analyst. Meetings have always been held in Sacramento; in the past the committee received requests to "leave Sacramento and investigate various things,"[61] but it declined to do so. The meetings of the committee were public (except those concerned with personnel matters and the like) until 1959, when executive sessions ("work sessions") were instituted in order to encourage uninhibited discussion of the committee's work. It had been found that some members, fearing political repercussions, were reluctant to decide in public that certain studies and investigations should be made.

At the public hearings held prior to 1959, the Analyst gave oral presentations based on written reports distributed to the committee. Representatives of the Department of Finance were always present and had the opportunity to comment on the Analyst's reports. Usually upon invitation, but sometimes at their own request, other state officials occasionally appeared before the committee to reply to criticism or questions from the Legislative Analyst. Representatives of private organizations or local government agencies rarely testified at the committee's hearings.

Thus, the Budget Committee has operated in a fashion quite different from that of most interim committees. It has not held hearings in various parts of the state to secure the views of private organizations and of state and local officials, and, as we have noted, it does not make reports and recommendations to the legislature. The primary purpose of its meetings is to receive information from its own staff.

Reports presented to the Budget Committee treat administrative organization and procedures, programs, and fiscal trends and problems. The responsibility for deciding which subjects should be studied is largely left to the Analyst, although the Budget Committee approves the program that he develops and makes some suggestions of its own. Before reports are presented to the committee, the Analyst makes some effort to secure the views of the administrative units concerned, unless the report deals with "policy."

Such consultation has the advantage of helping to ensure that the reports are factually accurate; moreover, the Analyst prefers to be able to report to the committee that the agency has agreed with his recommendations or, better still, has begun to implement them.

Implementing the Analyst's Reports

There is no single procedure by which recommendations contained in reports of the Analyst are implemented. As noted earlier, the Budget Committee normally does not adopt the reports. Frequently, it refers them to the departments concerned for consideration and sometimes for reply. In some cases the reports stimulate members of the committee to introduce legislation. The most likely mode of implementation is through action on the budget bill at a subsequent legislative session. Frequently, deficiencies in administrative organization and procedure reported to the Budget Committee are noted in the *Analysis of the Budget Bill* presented to the appropriations committees at a subsequent session. Such deficiencies may be the basis for recommendations by the Analyst that specific reductions be made in the budget of the department concerned. The appropriations committees may, by criticism, direction, or formal resolution urge or insist that the deficiencies be corrected. In some cases the Department of Finance or the department concerned takes action on its own initiative to implement the Analyst's recommendations.

Although these various modes of implementation provide flexibility and are by no means ineffective, it appears likely that a more systematic approach would be beneficial. When specific recommendations or criticisms are made by the Analyst, the committee should request that the department concerned, and where appropriate, the Department of Finance, make a written report to the committee indicating the extent to which they agree with the Analyst, reasons for disagreement, and steps (if any) proposed to be taken to implement the recommendations. If such a procedure were adopted, it would be necessary to make clear that the departments would not be obliged to accept the Analyst's recommendations. The requirement of a written reply would give the committee the benefit of facts or considerations missing from the Analyst's report, and would force the department to consider criticisms and recommendations seriously and to give a reasoned justification of its position. If the reply were deemed unsatisfactory, further action on the matter might take the form of a hearing by the Budget Committee, legislation, or modification of the department's budget.

BUDGET COMMITTEE MEMBERSHIP

The Budget Committee elects its own chairman, and it has always chosen a senator. From 1945 through 1955 the chairman of the committee was also

TABLE 4
Percentage of Republican Seats in Houses and on Budget Committees, 1941-65*

Year	Assembly	Budget Committee (Assembly Members)	Number of Seats By Which Minority Under-represented	Senate	Budget Committee (Senate Members)	Number of Seats By Which Minority Under-represented
1941	48%	60%	...	60%	100%	2
1943	55	80	1	58	100	2
1945	53	80	1	68	100	1
1947	60	80	1	65	100	1
1949	56	60	...	65	100	1
1951	58	80	1	70	100	1
1953	68	60	...	70	100	1
1955	59	60	...	60	100	2
1957	53	57	...	50	71	1
1959	41	29	1	33	43	...
1961	41	14	2	25	29	...
1963	35	29	...	33	14	1
1965	39	29	...	37	14	1

Source: *Final Calendar of Legislative Business.*
* One vacancy in assembly, 1951, 1955, 1957; in senate, 1943 and 1947. Two senate vacancies in 1965. One independent, 1945. One senator changed registration from Republican to Democratic at the end of the 1959 session; he is counted as Republican in 1959.

the chairman of the Senate Finance Committee. The membership of the Budget Committee has included strong representation from the leadership of the two houses. The joint rule creating the committee required that the speaker of the assembly and the principal leader of the senate, the president pro tempore, be members of the committee. Although this requirement was removed in 1955, the president pro tempore has continued to serve on the committee. Until 1947 the joint rules provided that each of four important senate committees select one of its members to serve on the Budget Committee. All senate members of the committee are now appointed by the Rules Committee, which is elected by the senate. From the beginning, assembly members have been appointed by the speaker.

Once appointed, committee members continue to serve until they resign from the committee or fail to be re-elected to the legislature. Seniority, the principal consideration in the appointment of senate standing committees, is much less important in the appointment of standing committees of the assembly and of interim committees of both houses, including the Budget Committee. Nevertheless, many members of the Budget Committee have had considerable seniority when appointed; few receive appointment before they have acquired at least three years of legislative experience.

Legislative leaders serving on the Budget Committee have included, in addition to the speaker and president pro tempore, the chairmen of the appropriations committees, usually one to three members of the powerful Senate Rules Committee, which appoints committees and refers bills in the upper house, and occasionally the chairmen of the committees on revenue and taxation. The chairman of the appropriations committee of the assembly (Ways and Means) has been a member since the beginning; the chairman of the senate committee (Finance), since 1945. It is important to note that, in effect, the governor names the chairman of the Ways and Means Committee, whose service on the Budget Committee tends to strengthen the governor's access to the committee. Service by legislative leaders on the Budget Committee is evidence of the importance assigned to the committee by the legislature and creates a presumption that on the whole the activities of the committee and its staff have reflected predominant opinion in the two houses.

Throughout the history of the Budget Committee, there has been extensive overlapping between its membership and that of the appropriations committees. The senate rules have required since 1945 that four senate members of the Budget Committee be appointed to the Finance Committee.[62] In 1962, nine of the 14 members of the Budget Committee were members of appropriations committees. In addition, Budget Committee membership has also overlapped significantly with those of the committees on revenue and taxation. Such memberships greatly facilitate communication among the several financial committees.

Partly because the Budget Committee has been representative of the leadership of both houses, it has had considerable prestige, and competition for appointments has been keen. In order to make more places available, the committee was enlarged from 10 to 14 members in 1957.[63]

It is reasonable to believe that the effectiveness of a committee is increased if its chairman and members serve long enough to gain familiarity with the committee's work. From 1941 through 1961, 34 assemblymen and 21 senators served on the Budget Committee, the mean lengths of service being 3.4 years and 5.5 years respectively. The first chairman, Senator William P. Rich, served 10 years; his successor, Senator Ben Hulse, served six. The chairman has supplied leadership and taken special responsibility for supervision of the staff; consequently, the long tenure of the first two chairmen provided important continuity in the shaping of the committee's functions and procedure.

The State of Washington requires by law that the two political parties be given equal representation on their Legislative Budget Committee.[64] No such requirement exists in California, and Table 4 shows that the majority party has often been overrepresented on the Budget Committee. Until 1959 no Democratic senator served on the committee, although the Democrats would always have been entitled to one or two seats if party representation on the committee had been proportional to strength in the senate. The assembly Republicans were overrepresented about half of the time from 1941 until 1959, when the Democrats took control of the house and, in turn, gave themselves disproportionate representation.

STAFF OF THE BUDGET COMMITTEE

The Budget Committee began operations in 1941 with a staff of three: the Legislative Analyst, his assistant, and a secretary.[65] By 1948, the staff (excluding clerical positions) had grown to 10.[66] In the decade 1956–65, the number of technical staff fluctuated between 29 and 33.[67] By comparison, a 1961 study showed that similar agencies in other states—that is, legislative agencies primarily concerned with budget review and fiscal analysis—had fewer than 10 technical positions in every case, the median being two.[68] California's executive budget staff is nearly three times the size of the Legislative Analyst's staff. Nonetheless, relative to the executive staff, the legislative staff is sufficiently large to permit the legislature to enjoy a position of strength vis-à-vis the executive in the budgetary field.

The significance of comparative staff sizes is limited by the fact that the functions of the legislature's Budget Committee and the executive's Budget Division differ in important respects. Both perform budget analysis and review functions, but the Budget Division has much more extensive responsibility for budget execution. An important part of the Analyst's resources is devoted to management studies, whereas the Budget Division relies largely on another agency for this activity. The Analyst also renders legislative reference services.

The Budget Committee has delegated to the Legislative Analyst the authority to appoint and discharge members of the staff. The staff, including the Analyst, serves at the pleasure of the committee and does not have civil service protection. Although individual legislators occasionally influenced appointments to the staff in the early years of its existence, sometimes with unfortunate results, the merit principle is now well established.[69] The State Personnel Board assists in the classification of positions, compensation is commensurate with that for comparable civil service positions, and fringe benefits, such as participation in the state retirement plan, are similar to those enjoyed in the civil service.

After he became Legislative Analyst in 1950, A. Alan Post made a definite effort to build a professional staff of persons having university training in business and public administration, political science, economics, and other social science or professional fields. Although the senior positions are held by mature and experienced persons, some of whom were originally recruited by Vandegrift, many staff members appointed during Post's administration have been young men recruited directly from colleges and universities.

The work of the office of the Legislative Analyst is divided among staff members on the basis of function and the organization of the executive branch. One unit, for example, is responsible for budgets and legislation relating to education, including the University of California, the state colleges, the Department of Education, and the public school system. Each unit performs all work relating to the functions and agencies assigned to it, including the analysis of the agencies' budgets, the preparation of studies of their organization, procedures, and programs, the analysis of related appropriation and cost bills, and the compilation of information for members and committees of the legislature.[70]

There is one important departure from the principle of organization by function: capital outlay requests of all agencies are analyzed by a single unit. The technical nature of construction and the magnitude of the state capital improvement program make this a reasonable exception. The functional basis of organization of other activities has the obvious advantage of permitting staff members to become well informed over a period of time about the programs and organization of the agencies for which they are responsible. Also, continuing relationships with the personnel of a limited number of agencies may facilitate the collection of information and may increase agency cooperation with the Analyst's office.

Criticisms of the Analyst—1949

The legislature, the Budget Committee and the Legislative Analyst have adopted policies and practices designed to ensure that the staff will render satisfactory service to the legislature and will avoid activities that might make the Analyst's office vulnerable to attack. Some of these policies were adopted as the result of criticisms directed at Legislative Analyst Vandegrift in 1949. The Budget Committee met in January of that year to consider whether the committee should be continued as a joint committee or whether each house should have its own committee. Three powerful assemblymen[71] complained that Vandegrift had become a "publicity agent," had violated confidences, had not complied promptly with legislators' requests for information, and had embarrassed members by opposing their bills and issuing public statements that contradicted those of legislators. Randal F. Dickey, Chairman of the Rules Committee, said that "about forty different legislators" had approached him with criticisms of Vandegrift. He suggested that the latter considered himself "a separate department of the State of California" and had "gone entirely too far in releasing publicity." Assemblyman Ernest R. Geddes thought that there had been "some interference" with the legislative process. He objected to Vandegrift's statement that state-supported child care centers had been created for "bridge-playing mothers" and cited a specific instance in which Vandegrift had in effect recommended that a member drop his bill. The chairman of the Budget Committee conceded that the committee had heard complaints on other occasions, and another member had heard that Vandegrift " 'spouted off' too much." The members of the Budget Committee pointed out that they had instructed Vandegrift to report to the committee and had asked for his recommendations.[72]

Vandegrift said that he had never issued a "written release," although he had answered questions from the press, that delay in supplying requested information to legislators was in some cases the result of the complexity of the fact-finding task, that two or more legislators sometimes requested the same information, and one of them might conclude that Vandegrift had violated a confidence by releasing the information when in fact a fellow legislator had made the release, and that he had "in no sense" suggested that a legislator drop his bill.[73]

Geddes was the principal author of the bill in question (AJR 3). It asked Congress to make the Kellogg Horse Farm available to the state as an addition to the San Dimas branch of California State Polytechnic College. Vandegrift had written to the Budget Committee chairman advising that this would be a costly venture, and also recommending that San Dimas be closed because a divided campus is unsound. The chairman had circulated the letter to the other members of the committee and to the Senate Rules Committee.

Duties of the Analyst Clarified

As a result of these complaints, the joint rules were amended in 1949 to clarify the duties of the Legislative Analyst.[74] For the first time the rules explicitly required the Analyst to "make recommendations to the Budget Committee and under their direction to the committees of the Legislature" concerning revenues, expenditures, functions and organization; and to assist the appropriations committees in consideration of the budget bill, all bills carrying express or implied appropriations, and all legislation "affecting state departments and their efficiency." These provisions gave explicit sanction to existing practice and strengthened the position of the Legislative Analyst by specifically authorizing him to make recommendations to legislative committees.

Other changes imposed certain restrictions. The amended rules provided that, when any legislator or committee requests documents or information under the control of the Legislative Analyst, the latter must "at once" secure the permission of the Budget Committee to make the information available, inform the author of the request when the information will be supplied, and in the event of delay in procuring the information, communicate this fact to him. The rules already prohibited the staff from revealing the content or author of such a request, except to the Budget Committee. A new provision prohibited disclosure even to members of that committee.

These formal limitations upon the staff have been supplemented by committee policy especially designed to control public statements and release of information and reports. In 1951 the committee directed that no report of the Analyst to the Budget Committee be released to the press until the committee or its chairman had approved the release. All members of the committee were to be supplied with copies prior to release of a report under authorization of the chairman.[75] Great care is taken to comply with this policy. The Legislative Analyst does not issue press releases or give statements to the press. Although he was formerly permitted and even encouraged to address citizen groups such as the California Taxpayers' Association, recent committee policy discourages public statements, except those made before committees of the legislature. The sensitivity of legislators on the question of public statements is indicated by a resolution introduced in 1955 which requested the Budget Committee to prohibit the Analyst from divulging recommendations or findings except before legislative committees or as directed by the Budget Committee or the appropriations committees. The author, Senator Luther E. Gibson, objected to certain public statements made by the Analyst, including a recommendation that the Maritime Academy (located in Gibson's district) be closed because its costs were too high.[76]

Although the legislature has authorized the Analyst to make recommendations regarding proposed legislative measures, the Analyst recognizes that other kinds of participation by him and his staff in legislative campaigns would be inappropriate and imprudent. When the Analyst appears before a committee to object to a bill on grounds of cost, lack of administrative feasibility, inconsistency with existing policy, and the like, he risks the displeasure of the author and other supporters of the bill. If he makes no objection, opponents of the measure may be disappointed. The Analyst cannot avoid incurring the displeasure of some members some of the time, although cases in which members react with intense hostility are rare. In order to protect the office against criticism, the Analyst and his staff strictly limit their activities to testifying before committees and submitting formal reports; they do not "buttonhole" legislators or attempt to influence legislation by other means. Moreover, the Analyst follows certain procedures that facilitate harmonious relationships with legislators. The author of a bill receives a copy of the analysis and recommendations at least 24 hours before they are to be presented to the committee considering the bill. This procedure apprises the author of the Analyst's position and of the basis for his cost estimates and recommendations. In some cases authors have persuaded the Analyst that his estimates are erroneous and have secured their revision. Somewhat similar objectives are served by the practice of sending to the author a copy of estimates of a bill's cost prepared by the Analyst at the request of another member.[77]

BUDGET COMMITTEE EXPENDITURES

From its establishment in 1941 until the end of 1960, the Budget Committee spent in excess of $3 million. In the first seven years of its operation it spent about $162,000, less than one-third of its present annual rate of expenditure. Table 5 shows that the committee's expenditures have steadily increased during recent years, exceeding $500,000 in 1964–65. Nearly 90 percent of the committee's costs are for the salaries and wages of the staff. Other components include staff travel, printing, equipment and supplies, and travel and per diem expense of the committee members.[78]

The committee's funds, like those of other committees, are appropriated from the contingent funds of the two houses. The appropriation is made on the basis of estimates prepared by the Legislative Analyst and presented to the rules committees.

SUMMARY

Seeking more objective and accurate fiscal information as well as tighter control of expenditures, the legislature in 1941 created the Joint Legislative Budget Committee and a fiscal analysis staff. During the following decade the committee and its staff emerged as important institutions in the California budget system. The committee now spends more than $500,000

TABLE 5

EXPENDITURES OF THE JOINT LEGISLATIVE BUDGET COMMITTEE, 1956–65

Calendar Year	Total Expenditures Exclusive of Those Reimbursed Under Contract	Reimbursements For Services Under Contract
1956	$307,712	$19,346
1957	353,014	20,919
1958	367,787	33,357
1959	389,709	8,493
1960	390,153	8,226
1961	417,840	5,862
1962	432,206	11,914
1963	464,586	2,096
Fiscal Year		
1963–64	491,576	5,024
1964–65	544,450	9,820

Source: "Annual Report of the Legislative Analyst to the Joint Legislative Budget Committee," 1956–65 (mim).

annually, largely to retain a professional staff of about 30 technicians, who are recruited and paid on the basis of merit. Legislators' complaints regarding the activities of the Legislative Analyst in the 1940's resulted in action by the legislature and the committee to safeguard the confidential relationship between the staff and its legislative clients and to restrict public statements by the staff, other than those made before legislative committees.

In its early history, the Budget Committee took positions on substantive policy, but now confines itself to general supervision of the staff, procedural instructions, and review of staff reports. The Legislative Analyst has wide discretion in making recommendations to the legislature and its committees. Any implementation of his recommendations results from the actions of the appropriations and other standing committees or from voluntary acceptance by administrative agencies; the Budget Committee does little to bring about their acceptance. However, overlapping membership between the Budget Committee and the standing fiscal committees provides a link by which findings and recommendations reported to the Budget Committee may be communicated to and supported in the standing committees.

[1] N.B. The constitutional revision of 1966 provided that legislators' salaries and expenses were to be set by statute (requiring a two-thirds vote in each house for passage) instead of being spelled out in the constitution. The statute that went into effect concurrently with the revision, set salaries at $16,000 per year after January 3, 1967, placed a limit on rates of future adjustments and dealt with the computation of retirement allowances.

[2] The Mangore Corporation, "The California Legislator," a report presented to the Citizens Legislative Advisory Commission (Los Angeles: 1958), p. 14 (process).

[3] On the organization and operation of committees, see Jay Doubleday, *Standing and Interim Committees of the California Legislature*, report prepared for the California Citizens Legislative Advisory Commission (Assembly Rules Committee, 1959).

[4] The following paragraphs on parties and interest groups draw liberally upon William Buchanan's study, *Legislative Partisanship: The Deviant Case of California*, University of California Publications in Political Science, Vol. XIII (Berkeley and Los Angeles: University of California Press, 1963).

[5] *Ibid.*, p. 128.

[6] *Ibid*, p. 127.

[7] *Cal. Stats.* (1941), res. chap. 117.

[8] C. C. Young, *The Legislature of California* (San Francisco: Commonwealth Club of California, 1943), p. 283.

[9] The second largest appropriation was $25,000, and two other committees received $15,000. *Ibid.*, pp. 283–5.

[10] *Budget*, 1941–43, p. A2.

[11] See Senate Resolution 106, *Senate Journal*, 1941, p. 1694, and the report of the Subcommittee of the Senate Finance Committee on a State Building Program, *Senate Journal*, June 6, 1941, p. 2407.

[12] For the executive-legislative conflicts during the Olson Administration, see Robert E. Burke, *Olson's New Deal for California* (Berkeley and Los Angeles: University of California Press, 1953).

[13] "Report on Budgetary Control," Subcommittee on Budgetary Control of the Assembly Revenue and Taxation Fact-Finding Committee, *Assembly Journal*, May 21, 1940 (1st Ex. Sess.), p. 561. See also pp. 559–60.

[14] *Ibid.*, p. 562.

[15] Senate Resolution 106. Apparently the "resolution" referred to is SCR 22, creating the Budget Committee.

[16] *First Partial Report*, Joint Legislative Budget Committee, 1943, p. 8.

[17] *Ibid.*, p. 16.

[18] *Ibid.*, p. 5. The need for information is discussed at length, pp. 5–6, 8–10.

[19] *Ibid.*, p. 6.

[20] "Report on Budgetary Control," cited above, pp. 559–61. The Assembly Revenue and Taxation Fact-Finding Committee commended the recommendations of its Subcommittee on Budgetary Control to the assembly, noting, however, that "the evils in connection with budgetary control, or the lack of it, did not first arise with the present administra-

tion; this administration merely continued the practices with even greater objections." "Report of Assembly Revenue and Taxation Fact-Finding Committee," *Assembly Journal,* May 21, 1940 (1st Ex. Sess.), p. 557.

[21] 1939: SB 1258; 1940 (1st Ex. Sess.): ACR 27; 1941: AB 939, AB 2176, AB 2177, AB 2215, SB 340. In the First Extraordinary Session of 1940, a resolution was adopted requesting the Legislative Counsel to prepare a measure to establish a "legislative budget bureau or like agency." *Cal. Stats.* (1940, 1st Ex. Sess.), res. chap. 50, p. 257. The Legislative Counsel drafted alternative proposals (AB 2176 and AB 2177 [1941]) and submitted a report, "A Legislative Budget Bureau for California."

[22] AB 1129. In 1939 Governor Olson had urged the creation of an auditor general *(Senate Journal,* May 17, 1939, pp. 2122–4). One of his objections to the 1941 measure was that it would have taken from the Department of Finance auditing functions necessary in the study of budget requests and would have limited its ability to supervise fiscal operations. A 1954 report by Price Waterhouse and Company concluded that there were "strong grounds for entertaining such fears in view of the wording of the bill." "Accounting and Auditing for the State of California—Section One: Recommendations and Report," a survey for the Joint Legislative Budget Committee (1954), p. A-44 (process).

[23] "A Mean Man With Your Money," *Fortnight,* March 4, 1949, p. 8.

[24] *Analysis,* 1947–48, pp. 19, 47–8.

[25] *Report of the Legislative Auditor to the Joint Legislative Budget Committee* (1945), p. 127.

[26] *Analysis,* 1948–49, p. 21.

[27] *Report of the Legislative Auditor* . . . (1945), *op. cit.,* p. 59.

[28] *Ibid.,* pp. 31–76.

[29] The governor's view was consistent with that of the senate in 1941, which adopted a resolution stating: "The urgent need of remodeling the institutions and of making certain improvements and additions is a matter of common knowledge. . . ." SR 106 (1941), *Senate Journal,* May 14, 1941, p. 1695. Governor Olson's budget message in 1941 said that the state was "badly in need of additional buildings." *Budget,* 1941–43, p. VII. In 1937, Governor Merriam referred to the failure of the voters in 1935 to approve a bond issue for capital improvements, "despite the imperative need for new buildings and betterments, and in the face of extremely deplorable conditions in many of our institutions. . . ." *Budget,* 1937–39, p. VI.

[30] The governor mentioned population growth, demands of the people for service, continuous increase in the cost of living, and assumption by the state of obligations formerly considered the financial responsibility of local government. Vandegrift argued that population growth could not be given as "the major cause" for the increases, but this was a straw man, for the governor had only said that it was *one* of "four major reasons." Vandegrift agreed that there had been a demand "of the people" for additional services, but lamented that these demands frequently "have been promoted by interested groups and seldom by a concerted demand by a majority of the people. Too often the average taxpayer has no voice in the matter of government costs but only the organized groups are articulate." Vandegrift noted that the cost of living had had ups and downs during the century. Finally, he suggested that some would disagree that the functions supported by state subventions were local functions. With respect to education, for example, he said: "There are those who will argue that public education, since it is provided for in the Constitution, is a State responsibility and not a local." *Report of the Legislative Auditor to the Joint Legislative Budget Committee* (1945), pp. 36–42.

[31] *First Partial Report,* Joint Legislative Budget Committee, p. 10.

[32] *Cal. Stats.* (1941, 1st Ex. Sess.), res. chap. 30.

[33] *First Partial Report*, pp. 11–14. According to that report the legislature reduced the governor's requests by $30 million; the amounts mentioned in the text indicate a reduction of $12 million and are derived from the Budget Committee's report and the governor's message to the special session. *Senate Journal*, December 19, 1941 (1st Ex. Sess.), pp. 8–11.

[34] *First Partial Report*, pp. 12, 14.

[35] *Ibid.*, p. 17.

[36] *Budget*, 1943–45, p. iii.

[37] *Report of the Joint Legislative Budget Committee* (1945), pp. 44–6.

[38] Letter from Legislative Analyst Vandegrift to Budget Committee Chairman Rich, dated January 24, 1949, attached to Budget Committee "Minutes," January 25–26, 1949. The minutes of the committee are typewritten or mimeographed, and are on file in the office of the Legislative Analyst. They are referred to hereafter as "Minutes."

[39] "Second Partial Report of the Joint Legislative Budget Committee to the Legislature," *Senate Journal*, March 20, 1943, pp. 662–710; "Third Partial Report. . . ." *ibid.*, May 5, 1943, pp. 3039–73.

[40] "Second Partial Report. . . ." *Senate Journal,* March 20, 1943, p. 703.

[41] *Report of the Legislative Auditor to the Joint Legislative Budget Committee* (1945). Among the recommendations were: that the legislature refuse to appropriate anything for school subventions over and above the amounts required by the constitution (p. 47); that the legislature accept the governor's proposal to establish a reserve of $40 million for postwar highway construction (p. 48); that the establishment of outpatient mental hygiene clinics be deferred until after the war (p. 284); and that a general reserve of $50 million be established (p. 72).

[42] *Ibid.*, p. 19.

[43] *Senate Journal*, March 20, 1943, p. 662 and May 5, 1943, p. 309.

[44] "Minutes," February 27–29, 1948, p. 1.

[45] In 1952 the chairman of the Budget Committee said that "at no time" were the recommendations of the Legislative Analyst "to be considered as binding upon the members of the Committee, since they do not represent Committee action, being only the advice offered by the Legislative Auditor [Analyst] to the Committee for consideration." "Minutes," October 17, 1952, p. 3.

[46] Even in the earlier period, sponsorship was a somewhat ambiguous matter. Senator Breed, a member of the Budget Committee, was surprised to find that he was a co-author of some Budget Committee bills, but Chairman Rich urged him not to be concerned—they could fight about them after they were introduced. (Interview, Senator Arthur H. Breed, Jr., November 27, 1957.) An exception to the general practice was SB 299 (1957), introduced at the request of the Budget Committee.

[47] Statement by Legislative Analyst A. Alan Post at the workshop on "Legislative Fiscal Analysis" of the Legislative Service Conference, held in New Orleans, September 28–October 1, 1953. (Recording by the Council of State Governments).

[48] "Minutes," September 10, 1959, pp. 1–2.

[49] The following discussion is based chiefly on a tape recording of the Budget Committee meeting of December 19, 1959, in the possession of the committee. Quotations are the author's transcription from the recording.

[50] "Fair Employment Practice Commission Budget Request for 1960-61," (December 11, 1959) (mim).

[51] *Cal. Stats.* (1951), chap. 1667. Voting for the bill in the assembly were 34 Republicans and 17 Democrats; nine Republicans and 14 Democrats opposed. There was no opposition in the senate. Opposition to the bill in the assembly stemmed in part from a belief that committees are more effectively controlled if they are established by rule, the customary

method of creating committees. (Letters to the author from Assemblymen Stanley T. Tomlinson, February 23, 1955, and Ralph M. Brown, March 3, 1955.) Perhaps it also reflected the belief during the early years of the committee's existence that it was a "senate committee," i.e., dominated by senate members.

[52] Interview, Senator Ben Hulse, then chairman of the Budget Committee, February 17, 1954.

[53] *First Partial Report* (1943) p. 7.

[54] "Minutes," March 5, 1943, pp. 1–2.

[55] "Minutes," January 6, 1942, p. 4.

[56] SB 824 (1943). Other measures were SB 805, SB 806 (1943), SB 1060, SB 1065 (1945), SB 1332 (1947).

[57] *Report of the Joint Legislative Budget Committee* (1945), pp. 35, 38.

[58] Letter of July 8, 1948, from Director of Finance James Dean to the Joint Legislative Budget Committee, attached to "Minutes," July 9–10, 1948. The policy was reaffirmed in 1951, "Minutes," September 29, 1951, p. 5.

[59] "Minutes," July 9–10, 1948, pp. 8–9; July 14, 1950, pp. 19–22, 24–5, 26–9, 30–1; October 26, 1951, pp. 1–2, 4–10; November 30, 1951, pp. 1–2; September 10, 1954, p. 5.

[60] It met only twice in 1961.

[61] "Minutes," January 26, 1949, p. 3.

[62] Senate Rule 11.

[63] *Cal. Stats.* (1957), res. chap. 340, pp. 4805–8.

[64] "1959–61 Biennial Report of the Legislative Budget Committee to the Legislature," (Olympia, Washington: n.d.), p. 30 (process).

[65] "A Mean Man With Your Money," *Fortnight,* March 4, 1949, p. 7.

[66] *Analysis,* 1948–49 p. [2].

[67] Year-end data from "Summary of Activities. . . ," in Annual Reports of the Legislative Analyst to the Joint Legislative Budget Committee, 1956–65 (mim).

[68] *Fiscal Services for State Legislatures,* The Council of State Governments, RM–352 (Chicago: 1961), pp. 12, 14–19. Excluded from consideration here are (1) general legislative services agencies that perform fiscal functions, and (2) fiscal agencies that perform both post auditing and budget review and fiscal analysis functions.

[69] A committee of the Citizens Legislative Advisory Commission recommended in 1961 that the employees of the Legislative Analyst's office continue to be exempt from civil service in order to preserve flexibility in recruitment procedure and to avoid civil service delays. It found that the "nonpartisan character of the employment insures that job security is not threatened by political changes within the Legislature." "Report of the Committee on Legislative Aids to the Citizens Legislative Advisory Commission," (March 1, 1961), p. 5 (process).

[70] A. Alan Post, "The Functions of the Legislative Analyst," in *Legislators' Orientation Conference, 1961,* Joint Committee on Legislative Organization (1961) p. 78.

[71] Randal F. Dickey, Chairman of the Rules Committee, Ernest R. Geddes, Chairman of the Committee on Finance and Insurance, and Jonathan J. Hollibaugh, Chairman of the Committee on Revenue and Taxation.

[72] "Minutes," January 25–26, 1949, pp. 7–11. Vandegrift had been criticized in 1945 for publicity activities. "Minutes," January 26, 1945, p. 6.

[73] "Minutes," January 25–26, 1949, pp. 12–14.

[74] *Cal. Stats.* (1949), res. chap. 75. See especially pp. 3076–8.

[75] "Minutes," September 29, 1951, p. 34.

[76] Senate Resolution 172, 1955 Regular Session; Interview, Senator Gibson, March 10, 1958.

[77] Vandegrift made recommendations to the governor as to whether particular bills should be signed or vetoed. His successor discontinued this practice because he thought that a legislative staff agency should not make recommendations regarding bills approved by the legislature. However, the original analyses and recommendations prepared by the Analyst for committees are available to the governor.

[78] "Summary of Activities . . ." in Annual Report of the Legislative Analyst to the Joint Legislative Budget Committee, 1956–65 (mim).

Chapter IV

FUNCTIONS OF THE LEGISLATIVE ANALYST

This and the following two chapters analyze the office of the Legislative Analyst and examine its utility for rational budget decision-making and control of spending. For the sake of simplicity we will often employ "Legislative Analyst" or "Analyst" to refer collectively to the fiscal analysis staff, and will distinguish between the head of the office and the rest of the staff only when necessary for clarity.

Except for the function of general legislative research and reference services, all of the principal activities of the Legislative Analyst are concerned with expenditure control and fiscal decision-making.[1] These activities may be summarized as follows:

1. preparation of a lengthy analysis of the governor's budget and the budget bill, including recommendations on each item of appropriation in the budget bill,

2. preparation of analyses of hundreds of special appropriation bills, implied cost bills, and revenue measures,

3. preparation of reports on fiscal trends and developments,

4. preparation of reports on financial aspects of programs,

5. studies of administrative organization and procedure,

6. general legislative research and reference for individual legislators and for committees, and

7. participation in budget preparation and execution.

For present purposes the most important of these functions is item 1, the analysis of the budget and the budget bill, which is reserved for detailed discussion in the latter part of this chapter. Item 7, the Analyst's participation in budget preparation and execution, is examined in Chapter VI.

FISCAL BILL ANALYSIS

The Legislative Analyst prepares reports on revenue measures, special appropriation bills, and bills that entail costs even though they do not appropriate funds. These last are often called "implied appropriation bills," "implied cost bills," or simply "cost bills." The Analyst deals with all appropriation bills and cost bills that are referred to the appropriations committees. He also prepares cost analyses for other committees. Until a few years ago, these reports customarily included recommendations as to the amounts, if any, that should be spent for the purposes of the bills. For some years, analyses of all revenue measures have been prepared for the committees on revenue and taxation, but these do not include recommendations except with respect to questions of revenue administration.

Typically, the analysis of a bill states concisely (in a paragraph or a page) the purposes and effects of the bill and how much it would cost or change revenue collections. In some cases dollar estimates are not included because there is no satisfactory basis for them. The Analyst requests a cost estimate with substantiating material from the agency concerned. This information is included in the analysis, although the Analyst reserves the right to disagree. In the case of cost bills and appropriation bills, attention is given not only to the costs in the first fiscal year, but also to those expected in future years. Initial year costs may be misleading because (1) the measure does not take effect until sometime during the coming fiscal year, (2) the program will not be in full swing throughout the fiscal year, or (3) the program can be expected to expand in the future.

REPORTING FISCAL TRENDS AND DEVELOPMENTS

The Analyst usually reports to the Budget Committee in the autumn regarding the general fund outlook for the next two fiscal years, basing his analysis on current and projected rates of expenditure and revenue collection. From time to time he prepares reports showing trends in state finance. For example, a 1959 report presented the annual expenditures from general fund sources for capital improvements in the past decade, estimated the costs of servicing the debt incurred for capital outlay, projected future construction requirements, and recommended a policy for future financing.[2] Trend data are often included in reports on the financial aspects of particular programs. In general, however, the Analyst does not make comprehensive projections of the components of future expenditures and revenue totals. Projections of totals are normally limited to a two-year period.

Soon after the conclusion of each session of the legislature, the Analyst prepares a summary of legislative and executive action on the budget, reporting the changes in budget totals, the resulting effect on the condition of the general fund, and the major program augmentations and other fiscal decisions taken during the session. The explanation included in the Analyst's summary makes it a valuable supplement to the *Summary of Financial Legislation* issued annually by the Department of Finance. The latter contains more complete summary tables and lists of enactments, but includes no explanatory narrative.

FINANCIAL ASPECTS OF PROGRAM

Many of the Analyst's reports treat financial aspects of state policies and programs, both existing and proposed. Some are purely informational, but many include recommendations for changes in legislation or administrative policy and practice. Some focus primarily upon ways and means of financing programs; others survey the objectives, accomplishments, and problems of programs, as well as the factors that affect their cost. Studies of the financial aspects of programs have included surveys of broad functional areas such as education, public welfare, care of the mentally ill, and corrections. Others have dealt with more limited subjects such as the performance of the Recreation Commission, research and programs concerned with alcoholism, the all-year school, use of aircraft in wildland fire control, local community mental health programs, prison education, public medical care, and many others.

STUDIES OF ADMINISTRATIVE ORGANIZATION AND PROCEDURE

The Analyst's management studies range from very detailed analyses of procedure to surveys of broad functions and large agencies. The study that led to the mechanization of motor vehicle registration was extremely detailed (". . . studied out completely and to the closest detail by our staff even to the floor location of equipment").[3]

In 1958 the Analyst made detailed recommendations regarding procedures in the Credential Unit of the Department of Education. They included the following:

. . . .

2. Attach IBM receipt card to permanent folder while being processed, thus eliminating the necessity for filing and later pulling IBM card from file.

3. Prepare standardized procedure for recording evaluations.

4. Reduce the amount of clerical jobs performed by the technical staff.

5. Consolidate the numerous form letters.

6. Make reference list of all form letters.

7. Make more use of form letters, thus reducing the need for dictated letters.

8. Performance rating line and time counts for transcribing typists should be taken only once yearly, except in rare cases, when new electric typewriters are installed.

9. Discontinue sending each district superintendent a carbon copy of the list of persons in his district who receive or renew a provisional credential.[4]

Most of the Analyst's management studies are of a less detailed character, although some deal with rather narrow questions, such as the desirable number of members and basis for membership of the Poultry Improvement Commission.[5] Examples of other management problems include automobile replacement policy, state purchasing practices, real property operations, space utilization and cost, and capital outlay procedures. In addition, the Analyst makes surveys of the organization and operation of departments and other units.

GENERAL LEGISLATIVE REFERENCE AND RESEARCH

The responsibilities of the office of the Legislative Analyst have required its staff to become familiar with, and accumulate data concerning substantive programs of the state, administrative management, and finances. It is not surprising, therefore, that legislators and legislative committees have turned to the office for general reference and research services. Reliance upon the Analyst was made all the more necessary by the fact that neither a legislative council nor a legislative reference service existed until the assembly established a one-house reference service in 1961. Seven hundred and thirty-four reports and research assignments were undertaken in 1965, compared with 295 completed in 1955.[6]

The Analyst's office frequently contributes a major part of the staff work required by interim committees, providing research services and consultation, and in some cases assigning staff members to committees. Interim committees sometimes contract with the Budget Committee for staff services. In the peak year of 1958, reimbursements under such contracts were $33,357.08.[7]

Mary Ellen Leary, political writer and editor, noted in 1956 a strong assumption in some quarters that the Legislative Analyst would become *the* general research agency of the legislature. This view, however, was not universally shared:

There are legislators, members of the public, and informed lobbyists who insist that an office primarily conditioned to approach all government issues from an economy angle is fundamentally unable to accomplish enlightened legislative research. These people feel that no bold solutions, no approach based upon new spending, no original thinking could issue from the Legislative [Analyst's] Office. However, many who have used his services do not hold this opinion.[8]

For a time the Analyst emphasized the advantages of relying on his office for general research activities, pointing out that there is "inherent overlap" between fiscal research and general research, and "the creation of an independent staff for the latter function would appear to create duplication and unnecessary cost."[9] In 1961 the Citizens Legislative Advisory Commission and a joint legislative committee issued a report outlining a proposal for a separate legislative reference service.[10] A bill to implement this recommendation passed the assembly, but failed in the senate, whereupon the assembly created its own, one-house legislative reference service.[11] It may be expected that the general research activity of the Analyst will continue to be extensive in the foreseeable future, inasmuch as the new reference service is confined to one house and will require some time to become fully established and accepted.

ANALYSIS OF THE BUDGET BILL

The *Analysis of the Budget Bill*[12] is a weighty document of more than 1,000 pages. Legislators do not read it from cover to cover, of course; the members of subcommittees of the appropriations committees refer to the sections that treat particular appropriations assigned to them for review. Often, important passages in those sections are read to the subcommittees by the Analyst or his representative during hearings.

Despite its formidable size, the *Analysis* is not a comprehensive treatment of the entire expenditure program of the state. Almost all of it is devoted to an examination of the expenditures authorized by the budget act, which normally account for about one-third of the total spending program. The remaining two-thirds, authorized by continuing appropriations, normally receive only brief treatment.

BUDGET COMMITTEE INSTRUCTIONS

Although the Budget Committee has specifically directed the Analyst to include certain types of information in the *Analysis,* the committee has provided only the most general guidance regarding the basis on which the Analyst should make recommendations. Typically, the Analyst is instructed to make recommendations that will permit the budget to be balanced without the imposition of additional taxes.[13] Neither the policy of avoiding tax increases nor the committee's general exhortations in favor of economy give any guidance regarding the programs which should be recommended for reduction.

The Budget Committee has laid down certain procedures to be followed in preparing the *Analysis*. The Analyst has been directed to:

1. Make specific recommendations for or against each proposed appropriation.

2. Report any instance in which the administration has failed to carry out the expressed intent of the legislature.

3. Call attention to each proposed new service provided by the budget.

4. Point out each item in the budget that has been denied by the legislature in the past.

5. Propose research and special studies on problems of program, operation, or finance.

6. Propose statutory changes to improve administration and bring about economies in operation and program.[14]

In addition, the committee has sometimes instructed the Analyst to include information on specified subjects, notably, the availability of reserves or other funds that might be used to balance the general fund budget.[15]

FORM OF THE *ANALYSIS*

The *Analysis* consists of a few pages of general discussion of the budget as a whole followed by an item-by-item examination of the budget bill appropriations. Occasionally, a separate section is devoted to a special subject (e.g., proposed bond issues and state bonded debt, in 1962). The general discussion of the budget varies in content, but usually reviews the revenue and expenditure totals, the basis and accuracy of revenue estimates, the condition of the general fund, and the governor's proposals for financing general fund expenditures. Other matters that have been discussed in this section include: trends in revenue and expenditure, new programs proposed in the budget, the condition of various reserve funds, bonded debt and policy with respect to debt financing of capital improvements, and changes, improvements, or defects in the budget document, the budget bill, and budgeting procedure. In earlier years, suggestions were made for general economies relating to such matters as long-distance telephone calls, postage, automobile operation, clerical and equipment pools, food costs in institutions, and control of equipment purchases. In 1945 and 1947 a lengthy discussion of aspects of the budget system included constitutional requirements for budget preparation and the extent to which the governor had complied with them; the extent to which the budget document controls the execution of the budget; the power of the legislature to modify the form of the budget bill and place limitations on expenditures; and legislative authority to modify continuing appropriations.

Item-by-Item Analysis of Appropriations

The item-by-item analysis of the appropriations in the budget bill follows the pattern of the bill and the budget document; separate sections treat (a) state operations, (b) capital outlay, and (c) local assistance. Each numbered item of appropriation in the bill is the subject of a comment and a recommendation (unless, in the case of capital outlay projects, no recommendation is made because insufficient information is available at the time of writing the *Analysis*). Recommendations are almost always specific as to the amount that should be appropriated and, if reductions are proposed, the positions, equipment, operating expense, projects, or programs that should be deleted or reduced.

The treatment of each item of appropriation for current operations begins with a tabular presentation of the total amount requested, estimated expenditures in the current year, percentage increase, and total reductions recommended by the Legislative Analyst. Immediately following is a summary of the recommended reductions, showing the positions and other items proposed for deletion, the amounts, and the page and line in the budget document where each item appears. These tabular presentations are followed by a narrative analysis, the organization and content of which varies. Usually, it recites the basic function of the agency, outlines major changes in program contemplated in the budget year, explains the reasons for increases in appropriations, and justifies the Analyst's recommendations for reductions. Increasingly, this analysis has included discussion of the accomplishments of the agency and selected problems of its operation. Tables are frequently employed to show trends in expenditures, enrollments, institutional population, caseloads, per capita costs of institutional care, characteristics of institutional population, and the like.

General Analyses

Each institution in the large departments—state colleges in the Department of Education, hospitals in the Department of Mental Hygiene, and correctional facilities in the Departments of Corrections and Youth Authority—receives a separate appropriation. In recent years, a general analysis has been offered regarding problems and programs common to all of the mental hospitals, and many requests are treated on a department-wide basis rather than an institution-by-institution basis. A general analysis of higher education has preceded the more specific discussion of the budgets of the state colleges and the University of California.

Nature of Recommendations

The hundreds of recommendations in the *Analysis* include not only proposed reductions in appropriations, but also recommendations regarding the financing of expenditures, administrative organization and procedure, and problems deserving special study. Normally, the *Analysis* recommends either that the appropriation proposed by the governor be approved or that it be reduced, but on rare occasions it has recommended that an appropriation be increased by a small amount. For example, the *Analysis* proposed in 1957 that the budget be augmented to establish a research program to evaluate the rehabilitative results of correctional programs.[16] In general, however, the Legislative Analyst believes that the departments, the governor, legislators, and interest groups will discern and urge the need for expenditures, and that his role should be limited to that of recommending ways to reduce the expenditure program.

Reducing Appropriations

Recommendations for reductions fall into two classes: (1) program recommendations and (2) resource recommendations. The former are based on the contention that an activity should not be performed on the scale contemplated by the budget, or should not be performed at all; the latter on the contention that an activity can be performed on the scale contemplated with fewer resources—personnel, equipment, supplies, and services—than the budget provides. Resource recommendations are often based upon indicators of workload, such as institutional population, caseload, licenses issued, applications processed, tax returns audited, and the like. Where such indicators are not available, they are based upon an assessment of the "need" for the resources as indicated in the justification prepared by the agency. The considerations that enter into assessment of need are as varied as the activities of the administrative agencies. Much of the *Analysis* is devoted to discussion of resources—the need of a unit for a stenographer, of an institution for a machine to make meat patties, of an agency for printing, of an executive for an administrative assistant, or of a prison for additional guards.

Program recommendations include proposals to eliminate or curtail existing programs and to reject new programs or expand old ones. New programs and program expansions have been the most frequent targets of the Analyst's recommendations, which often involve substantial sums. Each year during the period 1955 through 1963, the Analyst recommended reductions in budgeted amounts for treatment and other programs of the Department of Mental Hygiene. On the average, these proposed cuts were well over $1 million per year—not a large sum in relation to the budget of the department ($159 million in 1963–64, excluding capital outlay), but significant in relation to the particular programs affected. For the most part, proposed new programs or program expansion were the targets of these recommendations which included the deferral, restriction or termination of programs relating to: training in psychiatry for physicians,[17] after-care facilities,[18] convalescent leave,[19] day care treatment centers,[20] and outpatient mental hygiene clinics.[21] Other recommendations sought to restrict increased allotments per patient for drugs and medical supplies,[22] or to cut back the research program of the Department of Mental Hygiene.[23]

With relatively few exceptions, recommended reductions are specific as to the amounts and items proposed for deletion from the budget. Unallocated reductions are rarely proposed. Occasionally, recommendations are made for percentage or "round-figure" reductions that are more or less arbitrary. For example, in 1961 the *Analysis* recommended approval of only one-half of the 583 positions requested for strengthening of treatment services in the Department of Mental Hygiene.[24]

Financing Expenditures

Some of the more important policy recommendations made by the Legislative Analyst deal with the sources of financing: the extent to which those who derive special benefits from a program should bear the cost, the division of the financial burden for certain programs between state and local government, the extent to which the state should resort to debt financing for capital improvements, and the manner in which certain reserve funds, special funds, and revenues should be used. A few important recommendations of this type may be cited: (1) In 1959 the *Analysis* recommended abandonment of the traditional policy whereby students attending the University of California and the state colleges pay no tuition fees; it recommended that tuition fees be set at a level that would permit a reduction of about $11.5 million in the appropriations for the university and the state colleges.[25] (2) In 1955, when the governor proposed a $200 million bond issue to help finance a five-year program of capital improvements, the Analyst recommended that taxes be increased and expenditures curtailed in order to avoid the debt financing.[26] (3) In the same year the Analyst recommended, as an alternative to increased taxes, that the $75 million "Rainy Day Fund" be used to balance the budget.[27] This fund had been established by the legislature to provide a source for financing general fund expenditures in any year in which actual general fund revenues might fall below budgeted estimates.

Changes in Administrative Organization and Procedure

The *Analysis* has recommended numerous changes in adminstrative organization and procedure. In some cases specific reductions in appropriations are proposed on the basis that recommended modifications will reduce costs. In others, such changes are justified on the ground that they will reduce costs in the future or will improve the effectiveness of operations. Recommendations for changes in basic organization (e.g., that revenue functions be consolidated in a single department of revenue) have been relatively few, but less far-reaching proposals for reorganization or procedural change are numerous. Such recommendations range from simplifying the Controller's claim auditing process[28] to the elimination of handwritten duplicate records of the Public Utilities Commission,[29] or merging two divisions of the Department of Industrial Relations having similar functions, but differing clienteles.[30]

Recommendations for Studies

The *Analysis* has included many recommendations that studies be made of administrative organization, methods, and programs. Such recommendations often specify the agency that should make the study (legislative interim committee, department concerned, Department of Finance, Legislative Analyst, Auditor General, consulting firm, or some combination of these). The objectives of such recommendations, in addition to the obvious one of securing more or better information relevant to budget questions, are (1) to secure a definite legislative mandate that a problem be explored, and hence to encourage the administrative agency to take the matter seriously; (2) to initiate a campaign for acceptance of recommendations that are controversial, hence unlikely to be adopted immediately; and (3) to lay the groundwork for future evaluation of program accomplishments.

SUMMARY

The numerous reports issued by the Legislative Analyst are a valuable source of information regarding state finances, programs, and administrative management. Many of them deal with special subjects with which the legislature is currently concerned—highly controversial subjects in some cases. Straightforward and factual, they couch findings and recommendations in moderate, undogmatic terms, avoiding the contentious and the sensational. Typically, they are relatively brief and condensed, designed to be sparing of the time of legislators, who are deluged with printed matter from every side.

Findings and recommendations contained in the reports issued throughout the year frequently find their way into the *Analysis of the Budget Bill.* This document is a detailed critique of approximately one-third of the expenditure program of the state, prepared on the basis of a few procedural guidelines. With the exception of a customary policy against tax increases, the Budget Committee does not provide substantive policy directions. The *Analysis* includes recommendations to reduce appropriations, affecting both program and resources for supporting program, and recommendations regarding financing of expenditures, administrative management, and studies relating to budgetary questions.

To a very considerable extent, the *Analysis* determines the alternatives that are considered by the appropriations committees. It also provides much of the information available to the committees regarding consequences of alternatives. Because the rationality of committee decisions depends in important degree on the *Analysis,* the following chapter is devoted to a detailed evaluation of the *Analysis* itself.

[1] The Legislative Analyst receives the registrations of lobbyists and maintains a file of information that they are required by law to report. This function is purely custodial and is not related to the primary purposes of the office.

[2] "Capital Outlay Expenditures from General Fund Sources for the Period July 1, 1950 to June 30, 1960 with a Proposed Policy for Future Financing," (December 11, 1959) (process).

[3] "Report of the Joint Legislative Budget Committee to the Fifty-Seventh Session of the California Legislature," *Senate Journal,* June 20, 1947, p. 3509.

[4] "Department of Education Credential Unit Procedures," (October 23, 1958), p. 7 (process).

[5] "Report on Number of Members of Poultry Improvement Commission," (1951) (mim).

[6] "Summary of Activities for 1965," Annual Report of the Legislative Analyst to the Joint Legislative Budget Committee (1966), p. [1]; "Summary of Activities for 1957," (1958), p. 3 (mim).

[7] "Summary of Activities for 1958," (1959), p. 3 (mim).

[8] "The Legislature," in *California State Government: Its Tasks and Organization,* Participants' edition of background papers prepared for California Conference on State Government, September 13–16, 1956, pp. 29–30.

[9] A. Alan Post, "California's Joint Legislative Budget Committee and Legislative Auditor," in *Legislators' Orientation Conference, 1956* (Assembly, 1956), pp. 47–53. See also his statement in the same publication for 1959 (pp. 45–6).

[10] *Legislative Reference Services for the California Legislature,* report of the Citizens Legislative Advisory Commission and the Joint Committee on Legislative Reference Library (February, 1961).

[11] HR 350 (1961).

[12] *Analysis of the Budget Bill of the State of California for the Fiscal Year . . . Report of the Legislative Analyst to the Joint Legislative Budget Committee.* Before 1948 the *Analysis* was published under the following titles: "Second Partial Report of the Joint Legislative Budget Committee to the Legislature," and "Third Partial Report . . ." *Senate Journal,* March 20, 1943, pp. 662–710, and May 5, 1943, pp. 3039–73; *Report of the Legislative Auditor to the Joint Legislative Budget Committee* (1945); *Analysis of the Budget and Budget Bill for the Fiscal Year July 1, 1947 to June 30, 1948 . . .* (1947).

[13] *Analysis,* 1949–50, p. VI; 1952–53, p. V; 1953–54, p. IX; 1955–56, p. 1; "Minutes," Joint Legislative Budget Committee, October 10, 1957, p. 1.

[14] A. Alan Post, "The Function of the Legislative Analyst," in *Legislators' Orientation Conference, 1961,* Joint Committee on Legislative Organization, pp. 79–80.

[15] "Minutes," September 16, 1953, p. 5; *Analysis,* 1955–56, p. 1; 1959–60, p. V.

[16] *Analysis,* 1957–58, pp. 56, 167.

[17] *Analysis,* 1958–59, p. 436; 1959–60, pp. 495–8; 1960–61, p. 283.

[18] *Analysis,* 1957–58, p. 480; 1958–59, p. 441; 1960–61, p. 279; 1962–63, pp. 412–13.

[19] *Analysis,* 1960–61, p. 278.

[20] *Ibid.,* pp. 306–7.

[21] *Analysis,* 1959–60, p. 531; 1960–61, pp. 315–16; 1962–63, p. 437; 1963–64, p. 417.

[22] *Analysis,* 1958–59, pp. 451–4; 1959–60, p. 499.

[23] *Analysis*, 1962–63, p. 392.

[24] *Analysis*, 1961–62, p. 445.

[25] *Analysis*, 1959–60, p. 290.

[26] *Analysis*, 1955–56, p. 759.

[27] *Ibid.*, p. 28.

[28] *Analysis*, 1954–55, pp. 219–24.

[29] *Analysis*, 1958–59, p. 638.

[30] *Analysis*, 1963–64, p. 559. This recommendation has been made repeatedly.

Chapter V

EVALUATION OF THE *ANALYSIS*

Utility of the *ANALYSIS* in Rational Decision-Making

In several important ways the *Analysis* strengthens the ability of the legislature to make rational budget decisions and to maintain control of expenditures:

1. It conveys useful information in convenient form.
2. It offers specific and considered alternatives.
3. It appraises the performance of agencies and programs and presses for the establishment of performance standards.
4. It examines critically the justification for proposed expenditures and programs.
5. It strengthens legislative control of expenditures by reporting deviations from legislative intent and practices that might impair control.

Although these functions overlap, each is of sufficient importance to warrant separate consideration.

Presentation of Selected Information

One value of the *Analysis* is that it brings together selected information not available in any other single source. Some of the information is in the budget document: amounts and percentage of increase in particular units or object categories of expenditure, numbers and classes of proposed additional positions, certain workload data, general statements of the functions of departments and sub-units, and other information. The *Analysis*, however, is more convenient and readable than the unwieldy budget document. The latter is primarily a book of figures; its narrative explanations are greatly condensed. The *Analysis* offers more complete interpretation of program changes and issues, and argues the merits of proposed expenditures, whereas the budget document often contents itself with asserting the need for them.

Since much of the information in the *Analysis* comes from the budget document, the departments themselves, and printed reports, the question may be raised whether the legislature should not obtain its information directly from the administration. Legislators interviewed by the author expressed a high degree of confidence in the accuracy of the information supplied by departments. Nevertheless, it is to be assumed that the departments will present information in such form and with such interpretations as will encourage favorable consideration of their budget requests. It is difficult for the legislator to frame the right question and to interpret the response in the light of other relevant facts and considerations. To a degree that is not generally possible for part-time legislators, the staff members of the Analyst's office are able, by reason of experience and full-time attention to the job, to discern what information is needed, to frame suitable inquiries, and to examine critically the significance of information provided. At the same time, it should be recognized that the *Analysis* is in part an attempt to make up for some of the deficiencies of the budget document. Legislative insistence on correction of those deficiencies might have had a greater tendency to improve the formulation and presentation of the budget than does the provision of a supplementary source in the form of the *Analysis*. Improvement of the budget document would not remove the need for the *Analysis,* but would relieve the latter of the need to provide information and explanations that should come from the administration.

Presentation of Alternatives

The *Analysis* presents the legislature with a set of proposals alternative to those in the governor's budget. They include not only recommendations for spending less money than the governor proposes, but also suggestions for spending given sums in alternative ways. For example, in 1957 the *Analysis* raised the question of whether it would not be wiser to use money budgeted for building residence halls at state colleges to construct additional instructional facilities, assuming that the legislature would have to choose between these alternatives because of limited available funds. The *Analysis* noted that a new college with enrollment capacity of approximately four thousand students could be built for the cost of residence halls capable of housing three thousand. Although residence halls would serve the needs of students not living within commuting distance of a college, they would not increase the total number of students accommodated in existing instructional facilities.[1]

The legislature does not lack for alternatives; numerous spending proposals are introduced at every general session, and the members of the legislature are capable of identifying programs that might be abolished, curtailed, or expanded. The special value of the alternatives offered by the *Analysis* is that they are limited in number, they are specific, and they are based upon a certain amount of information and study, not upon hunch or vague notions that an agency or program is inefficient or unnecessary. The *Analysis* presents a set of alternatives superior to anything that the appropriations committees would develop for themselves or could glean from other sources. Committee members do not have the time or the information to conceive and investigate the validity of possible alternatives on a systematic basis. The presence of an occasional legislator who is truly expert in a particular field does not invalidate the generalization. Administrative agencies are unlikely to be very helpful. Once committed to a program, they are not likely to respond creatively to generalized requests for better alternatives. Moreover, they usually consider themselves obliged to defend the proposals in the governor's budget. It is an important strength of the *Analysis* that it is prepared by a full-time staff that can devote much of its resources to conceiving, investigating, and evaluating alternatives.

Analysis of Performance

The *Analysis* increasingly provides both qualitative and quantitative evaluations of the accomplishments of agencies and programs. Release rates from state mental hospitals, parole violation rates, length of stay in prisons, revenue per dollar of cost from audit of tax returns, space utilization measures, and similar data are employed to gauge the effectiveness of operations where quantitative approaches are possible.

As an example of performance analysis, we may cite the discussion of the Department of Mental Hygiene in the 1961 *Analysis*. The examination included data on per-patient and total costs, patient-therapist ratios, content summaries and costs of new programs, increased facilities, administrative inadequacies, sick leave and safety records. A statistical study made by the department was discussed in considerable detail. Although the results of the study were consistent with the assumption that expanded treatment programs had resulted in higher release rates, they also suggested that better treatment had little effect on releases in the case of patients not released within the first two years after admission. The *Analysis* also pointed out that data on readmissions had not yet been analyzed and that the rate of readmissions was important in judging the significance of release rates. It also urged the need to develop rating scales for measuring the degree of recovery of patients.[2] The performance analysis of the Department of Mental Hygiene is not typical, for it is more systematic and searching than that accorded to most departments and programs. It does represent the kind of presentation to which the *Analysis* aspires and the direction in which it has been moving.[3]

No less important than the performance evaluations, is the insistence by the *Analysis* that agencies compile and supply data needed in appraising performance, and that they make performance evaluations themselves. In some instances, the *Analysis* recommends that agencies be directed to report subsequently on the extent to which estimates of savings from changes in operations prove to be correct. Increasingly, the *Analysis* recommends that new programs be implemented on a pilot basis only and that the responsible agency submit a precise plan for evaluation of accomplishments before the program begins. The requirement of an evaluation plan at the outset, frequently coupled with a legislative directive that an evaluation be submitted by a specified date, lays the basis for more informed decisions on subsequent proposals for expansion or curtailment of the program. For example, in 1957 the Department of Youth Authority initiated a psychiatric treatment program for emotionally disturbed and mentally retarded wards. On the recommendation of the Analyst, a research program was established by the agency to test the effectiveness of treatment.[4] A report submitted in 1962 concluded that "it could not be demonstrated that psychiatric treatment had a significant effect on either the personal adjustment or the parole performance of Youth Authority wards judged to need such treatment."[5] The *Analysis* recommended that the program be curtailed "in view of the lack of any substantial accomplishments."

Evaluative studies of existing programs are also recommended from time to time. Frequently, the Analyst lists the questions that the evaluation should attempt to answer and works with the agency in developing the method of the study. By insisting that agencies provide more than general statements and impressionistic judgments as to their accomplishments, the *Analysis* has significantly stimulated increased emphasis on performance evaluation in the budget process.

Examination of Justifications

Justifications of expenditure proposals are subjected to highly critical examination. This scrutiny is based in part on performance evaluations, and in turn provides the basis for the formulation of alternatives. Characteristic questions discussed in the examination of the justification include the following: Should an activity be performed by some other agency, state, local or federal? Are the objectives and scope of a proposed or existing program well-defined, consistent with legislative policy, and properly related to other programs? Is there good reason to believe that the program will in fact achieve the objectives for which it is proposed? Is the workload standard or staffing formula valid; are workload estimates realistic? Where workload standards are not available, are additional positions justified by reason of backlog, excessive overtime, inadequate service, or other specific evidence of need? Can the agency recruit sufficient personnel to fill the new positions requested? Does recent experience indicate that the agency spends most of its funds, or has it been overbudgeting? Is the design of a building consistent with space utilization standards, in line with the average cost per square foot in other similar buildings, and free from excessively luxurious features? Are space requests consistent with established utilization standards? Much of the *Analysis* is concerned with these and similar questions, and its discussion is of substantial assistance to the legislature in judging the need for proposed expenditures and the adequacy of estimates.

Attention to Control

The *Analysis* assists the legislature by providing information and recommendations regarding (1) administrative decisions that deviate from past legislative decisions or from past budget plans; and (2) administrative practices that might distort the budgetary information provided to the legislature. In accordance with the instruction of the Budget Committee, the Analyst points out instances in which the administrative agencies fail to carry out the expressed intent of the legislature. Thus, for example, the *Analysis* severely criticized the Division of Beaches and Parks for organizing its planning activities in a way different from that directed by the legislature through action upon its appropriations.[6] Although clear cases of contravention of expressed legislative intent are infrequent, it is important that they be brought to the attention of the legislature.

The *Analysis* also points out instances in which agencies incur expenditures that, in the opinion of the Analyst, should not be made before they have been reviewed by the legislature. In 1957, for instance, it was noted that three hospitals in the Department of Mental Hygiene were operating "unofficial 'outpatient clinics'" with personnel authorized for other purposes and without legislative sanction.[7]

The *Analysis* strongly objects to budget presentations that suggest a lack of candor. In particular, objection is taken to budgets that show as "authorized positions" those that have been created administratively during the course of the year and therefore have not appeared in earlier budgets reviewed by the legislature. Such positions, it is contended, should be shown as new positions; otherwise, they may escape the special attention that is customarily devoted to new ones.

Defects of the *ANALYSIS*

In the past two decades, the *Analysis* has improved very markedly in the quality of its examination of budget questions. It includes more information about the purposes for which money is to be spent, and less about the objects to be purchased. Reasoning and evidence to support recommendations are more convincing, and it has become less preoccupied with budgetary minutiae. Inasmuch as the paragraphs that follow are critical of the *Analysis* on a number of points, it is appropriate to stress at the outset the significant progress that has been made in making it a more useful aid to legislative review of the budget.

The extent to which the legislature concurs in the Analyst's recommendations for reductions in budget bill appropriations is indicative, in an indirect and approximate way, of the quality of the *Analysis*. In terms of

TABLE 6

Legislative Acceptance of Reductions in Budget Bill Recommended by the Legislative Analyst, Selected Years

Fiscal Year	Total Reductions Recommended	Reductions Accepted by Legislature	Reductions Accepted As Percent of Total Recommended
1952–53....................	$69,963,991	$12,618,753	18%
1953–54[a]....................	27,308,506	19,484,998[b]	71
1954–55....................	10,509,052	2,341,994	22
1956–57....................	23,975,596	2,390,826	10
1957–58[a]....................	13,611,730	4,424,404	33
1958–59[a]....................	39,167,395	24,058,975	61
1959–60[a]....................	33,239,591	4,786,647	14
1960–61[a]....................	13,714,009	2,020,917	15
1961–62....................	67,993,491[c]	19,006,866	28

Sources: *Analysis of the Budget Bill*; *List of Legislative Changes in the Budget Act...Final Report*, published by the Department of Finance; lists of proposed reductions prepared by the Legislative Analyst.

[a] No recommendation was made on certain capital outlay appropriations pending further study; these are excluded from consideration.

[b] Excludes reductions of $3,145,000 offset by special appropriation or reappropriation of prior year balances.

[c] Includes capital outlay projects tentatively recommended for disapproval because of insufficient justification.

dollar amounts, the legislature usually rejects a substantially larger proportion of the recommendations than it accepts. It adopted one-third or less of the recommendations in seven of the nine years studied (Table 6). In the other two years, it adopted 71 percent (1953–54) and 61 percent (1958–59). A single large item accounts for the high proportion for 1958–59; $18.4 million of the $24 million in reductions approved represented a proposed general salary increase. The proportion of all other recommendations accepted was only 27.2 percent.

In any given year legislative acceptance or rejection of recommended reductions depends not only upon the quality of the *Analysis,* but also upon the financial situation, the liberality of the governor's spending plan, the balance of political forces in the legislature, and the strength of interest groups. If the *Analysis* attacks only the most vulnerable items in the budget, the legislature is more likely to adopt a high percentage of its recommendations than if it objects to those that are more soundly based and widely supported. The significance of data regarding the proportion of reductions adopted is limited in other ways—such data do not take into account recommendations that carry no proposed reductions (reorganizations, studies, etc.); they do not measure the extent to which recommendations rejected by the legislature in one year are accepted by the agency, the Department of Finance, or the legislature in a later year; nor do they reflect the extent to which recommendations are accepted by one house, but rejected in the other. When allowance has been made for these limitations, however, the proportion of recommended budget cuts accepted by the legislature has significance as a general indication of the legislature's appraisal of the strength of the evidence and argument for positions taken in the *Analysis.*

What weight is to be assigned to the legislature's appraisal? Certainly, it is not to be taken as conclusive in any given case, for the legislature undoubtedly rejects some recommendations that are very well founded. But it is scarcely reasonable or consistent with the behavior of the appropriations committees in reviewing disputed issues to conclude that the legislature is always or usually misguided when it rejects the recommendations of the *Analysis.*

In sum, the legislature rejects many of the reductions recommended in the *Analysis,* and there is sound reason for assigning substantial weight to the legislative appraisal of the quality of the *Analysis* as indicated by these actions. It must be added that rejection of a recommendation does not necessarily imply a judgment that the recommendation is lacking in any merit whatever, but only that the case for the expenditure is more convincing than the case against it.

Excessive Detail

Formerly the *Analysis* included much information about the details of proposed expenditures and frequently recommended that minor items costing a few thousand or a few hundred dollars, or even less, be deleted. This preoccupation with budgetary minutiae is open to criticism on several grounds. It is not clear that the appropriations committees are better able to make sound judgments on such details than the departments. The committees spent inordinate amounts of time trying to save minor sums—"penny-grubbing," as a former chairman of the Ways and Means Committee called it. Moreover, the consequence was to direct committee attention to objects of expenditure rather than to policy, program objectives, and accomplishments expected from expenditures. Another consequence was that the committees substituted their judgments for those of management regarding detailed questions as to how management should carry out its tasks. Finally, the Legislative Analyst and his staff devoted extensive resources of time and effort to these relatively unrewarding matters, rather than to the more important questions to which the committees should have directed their attention.

In scrutinizing expenditure details, efforts are disproportionate to results. The bulk of personnel services, operating expense and equipment required for state government is provided through the state operations section of the budget bill. Reductions effected on the recommendation of the Analyst in the state operations budget give some indication of the rewards of paring minor items of expenditure. In only one of the nine years

TABLE 7

REDUCTIONS IN BUDGET BILL APPROPRIATIONS FOR STATE OPERATIONS RECOMMENDED BY THE LEGISLATIVE ANALYST AND APPROVED BY THE LEGISLATURE, SELECTED YEARS

Fiscal Year	Reductions
1952–53	$ 3,415,191
1953–54	4,287,863
1954–55	860,844
1956–57	2,082,126
1957–58	2,034,174
1958–59	20,981,558
1959–60	4,001,183
1960–61	1,903,047
1961–62	4,386,507

Sources: *Analysis of the Budget Bill*; *List of Legislative Changes in the Budget Act... Final Report*, Department of Finance; lists of proposed reductions prepared by the Legislative Analyst.

shown in Table 7 did reductions reach $5 million. If the reduction of $18.4 million for a general salary increase in 1958–59 is excluded from consideration, the average annual reduction in the years shown is $2.8 million. Total expenditures for state operations for the same years averaged more than $500 million annually, and state operations account for less than a third of total state expenditures.

Gradually, the emphasis of the *Analysis* has changed. Fewer details are reported, recommendations for minor cuts are less numerous, and analyses of programs, their objectives, and their costs have greatly increased. Some unnecessary detail is still included. We are told by the 1963–64 *Analysis,* for example, that the $67,000 budget for one program includes an increase for personal services of "$285 over the current year due to merit, salary increases and military longevity increases of $374, offset by a reduction of $89 in contributions to the employees' retirement fund." Similar details are given for operating and equipment expense.[8] In contrast, the discussion of an agency estimated to expend the much larger sum of $7.7 million for the same year makes no reference to equipment and operating expenditures, nor to such routine matters as merit salary increases and retirement contributions.[9] The 1963–64 *Analysis* also contained numerous suggestions for small reductions in budgets for travel, communications, printing and the like. It recommended that 0.5 position of food service assistant in one of the Youth Authority institutions be deleted because the additional position would replace ward help with a paid employee. Four wards would be deprived of a half-day work experience.[10] Although it is appropriate for the legislature to establish general policy regarding work opportunities for wards, the determination of whether, in a specific situation, ward help or a paid employee should be used, is better left to the management of the institution.

Failure to Stress Method

A second weakness of the *Analysis* is that it has been too preoccupied with the validity of specific budget decisions and has paid insufficient attention to the manner in which those decisions are made. It is true that many budget requests are opposed because information supplied to justify them is considered inadequate, and that the *Analysis* has recommended, with respect to particular agencies or programs, that certain kinds of information be accumulated to permit better assessment of the requests. The Analyst has also recommended that the Budget Division review equipment requests in the field, that positions of administrative analyst be established in agencies to improve budget preparation, and that a research program be undertaken to provide a better basis for judging the needs of the Department of Mental Hygiene. In important measure, these recommendations imply an assessment of the kind of information the administration had available when it made the decision.

Nonetheless, the *Analysis* could profitably have directed its attention in a more systematic fashion to the manner in which budgets are prepared and reviewed. It might, for example, have attempted to explain why the Budget Division approves many proposed expenditures that the *Analysis* considers unjustified. It might have enquired more extensively into the staffing, organization, and procedures employed by departments in preparing budgets. It might have attempted in a more formal and systematic fashion to establish criteria regarding the kinds and amount of information required at successive levels of review for effective budget decisions. It might, in short, have made greater effort to assess for the legislature the adequacy of the methods employed in the budget process, rather than attempting to judge all of the decisions those methods produced. Just as an audit agency can limit the extent of its examination of transactions if the existing system of internal control is sound, the Legislative Analyst and the legislature can base the amount and kind of review of specific budget decisions upon an assessment of the system for reaching those decisions. No doubt, the Analyst's impressions of the adequacy of the budgeting practices of particular departments have influenced the choice of budget items selected for more intensive review. But, in general, such choices have not been made explicit, nor has the legislature been provided with thorough analyses of budgeting practices as such, except in the case of capital outlay processes.

Narrow Conception of Control

The conception of legislative control advanced by the *Analysis* is unduly rigid. In general, the *Analysis* accepts the necessity for administrative modifications of the budget in the course of execution, although it criticizes changes considered to be unjustified. One kind of change deemed to be absolutely unjustified is expenditure for positions or other specific items denied by the legislature in the past. It is, of course, appropriate that the administration abide by legislative decisions regarding policies and programs. If, however, the legislature deletes money for a clerk or a prison guard or a piece of equipment, should the administration be bound to abide by the decision, as the *Analysis* insists? It is one thing for the legislature to cut the appropriation by an amount equal to a clerk's salary on the ground that the justification is questionable, but to tell the administration that it cannot hire the clerk is to tell management how to do its job and to dilute its responsibility for results. If management determines that, despite the cut in salary and wage funds, the best allocation of resources requires filling the clerk's position, it should have freedom to do so, using savings or reclassifying other positions. If it is of sufficient importance, the decision, like any other in the execution of the budget, would be an appropriate subject of subsequent inquiry by the Analyst or the legislature.

The existing policy of the *Analysis* (and the legislature) lacks an appreciation of limitations on the ability of the legislature to make correct judgments on budgetary details. A more flexible attitude toward budget administration would accord better with the reality that the administrative agency's judgment will often be as sound as the legislature's on this class of questions.

Overemphasis on Prospective Control

The *Analysis* tends to underestimate the potentiality of retrospective control by the legislature, as illustrated by a case that arose in 1959. The *Analysis* took exception to the fact that during the current year 41 positions of psychiatrist in the mental hospitals had been reclassified as medical administrative positions, the estimated annual cost of the higher salaries being $100,000. The department was requesting 17 new positions of psychiatrist as partial replacement of the positions lost through the reclassification, at an additional annual cost of more than $200,000. The total cost of full replacement would be over $500,000 annually. The *Analysis* noted, however, that the legislature had approved the establishment of 16 medical administrative positions (new positions, not reclassifications) in the past two years at certain hospitals and that all of these changes were in accordance with a reorganization recommended by the Division of Organization and Cost Control of the Department of Finance. Nonetheless, while the *Analysis* conceded that it was appropriate that the Department of Finance have authority to reclassify individual positions,

It is not proper to use this means to establish almost three-fourths of a major program. This action represents a bypassing of the whole budget procedure. It reduces the Legislature's control over the budget and provides an easy avenue for implementing programs which might not be approved if submitted to the Legislature.

The reclassification, it added, would result in a lower level of treatment than that authorized by the legislature, since the ratio of psychiatrist positions to patients would decline. The *Analysis* recommended that the 41 administrative positions be returned to their former classifications and salary levels, that the 17 psychiatrist positions be denied, and that thereafter the Departments of Finance and Mental Hygiene submit such proposals through "regular budgetary channels for legislative consideration and review."[11]

Certainly, a change in administrative organization involving sums of this magnitude is an appropriate subject for legislative consideration. But it does not follow that legislative review must take the form demanded by the *Analysis*. The issue is the timing of legislative consideration—must it be prospective in order to ensure adequate legislative control? In this instance, review took place during, rather than before, the year in which the reclassifications occurred. But the legislature was not without remedies—it could, for example, deny the department funds to pay for reclassifications in the coming year or even make deeper cuts. The procedure is, perhaps, an "easy avenue" for initiating programs, but not for continuing them over time, if their implementation requires further appropriations.

Unquestionably, the *Analysis* and the legislature could appropriately ask the department to explain and justify this reclassification, but such an enquiry is properly directed to the merits of the reorganization and the reasonableness of the procedure followed to effect it. It is unduly rigid to stigmatize the procedure as being on its face a breach of legislative control, especially in view of the prior legislative action in approving similar changes in selected hospitals. Control is both prospective and retrospective, and the latter is by no means ineffective because (1) sanctions are available to the legislature and (2) knowledge of the existence of such sanctions influences administrative decisions.

Preoccupation with prospective control is not limited to cases in which large sums are involved. Thus, the 1962–63 *Analysis* objected to the fact that a correctional institution had established a position of personnel officer at the beginning of the 1961–62 fiscal year despite the fact that the budget for that year had not included the position. There was, it said, no emergency that justified establishing the position prior to legislative review. Continuation of such practices would "reduce proper legislative control over the state budget." It recommended that the agency be "directed" to abolish the position during the 1961–62 fiscal year.[12]

Inadequate Analysis

Partly because the *Analysis* has attempted to review comprehensively the decisions in the budget, its treatment of particular issues has often been superficial, illogical, and unconvincing. In 1945, for example, it recommended that appropriations for public health education be reduced from about $30,000 to about $25,000 for the sole reason that "the proposed expenditure is up by 74.2 percent, which is out of line with economic reality."[13] In 1951 the *Analysis* recommended deletion of $25,081 to establish two branch offices of the Division of Narcotic Enforcement. The entire justification for deletion was that the branch offices would provide expanded service to local government and that, "instead of the State assuming direct responsibility for enforcement, the staff of the division should be used to stimulate local police to enforce narcotic laws and to coordinate narcotic enforcement between local departments." The considerations that led the Department of Justice to make the proposal received no mention whatever.[14]

In 1954 the *Analysis* recommended that the costs of board and room for children attending schools for the deaf and blind be charged to their parents on the basis of a means test, and proposed budget reductions accordingly.[15] The legislature did not approve the recommendation, but a study made at its request by the Analyst and the Departments of Finance and Education indicated that maximum returns from adoption of the proposal would be ten or fifteen thousand dollars annually, whereas the Analyst had recommended budget reductions of nearly $200,000.[16]

Although the quality of analysis has improved greatly over the years, some more recent examples may be cited to indicate that further improvement needs to be made. In 1959 the governor proposed legislation and an appropriation in order to establish in his own office a consumer counsel to advise the governor on matters "affecting the interests of the people as consumers and as to methods to increase the competence of the people as purchasers," and to recommend legislation to protect consumer interests. The *Analysis* recommended against the establishment of such an agency. Although the argument is far from clear, the main points appeared to be that there is no justification for giving consumer interests a preferred position by placing a representative in the governor's office, that it is difficult to separate the interests of the people as consumers from their interests as producers, that the proposal offered no "tangible definition of consumer interest which is not under existing legislative and executive processes duly accounted for and properly administered (or for which correction there is not already executive and legislative recourse)" and that failure to establish the consumer counsel would "in no way affect the ability of the Legislature or of the executive to consider the interests of the people as consumers."[17]

It is difficult to believe that the argument was offered seriously. There is no recognition of the underlying reality of the weakness and lack of organization of consumer interests as compared with the power of producer interests and their institutionalized representation in executive agencies. It is highly superficial and formalistic to suggest that the location of the consumer counsel in the office of the governor implies a preferred position for consumer interests; it would be more consistent with political realities to recognize that such location is only a small step toward giving consumer interests some of the influence already enjoyed by other groups. Nor is any interest group likely to relinquish an institutionalized spokesman in the executive branch on the assumption that "executive and legislative recourse" are available. The assertion that a consumer counsel would not affect the ability of the legislature or of the executive to consider consumer interests is not convincing in the absence of any analysis of the potential of such an agency for conducting research on consumer problems, drawing attention to them and suggesting possible solutions, and helping citizens to be more aware of their interests as consumers and to have more informed opinions. Because it ignores political realities, and hence virtually denies that there is any problem of representation of consumer interests in government, the analysis is largely irrelevant.

On two occasions the *Analysis* recommended elimination of state support to child care centers, a program established during World War II to make it easier for women with children to work.[18] The state provides approximately two-thirds of the financial support, while parents provide the remainder through fees based upon ability to pay. In recommending elimination of state support in 1951 and 1958, the *Analysis* contended that the program is fundamentally a local responsibility and benefits primarily large metropolitan areas where most of the centers are located. These areas could afford to support the centers, for which the state spent $4.6 million in 1958–59. In 1958 the *Analysis* failed to point out certain benefits of the program that it had recognized in the previous year, namely that the program helped to ease shortages of school teachers, whose children could attend the centers by paying the full cost of care, and that the centers served mainly needy families and "may" help such families to be self-supporting by permitting the parents to work, thereby reducing state and local welfare costs.[19] In neither year in which the subvention was recommended for deletion did the *Analysis* report how many counties were operating centers, nor has it ever presented definitive information on the effect that elimination of the subvention would have on welfare costs. It predicted incorrectly in 1951 that, if the subvention were made permanent—authorizing legislation contained termination dates until 1957—the state would "ultimately be flooded with demands for centers in every community of the State."[20] In fact, the number of centers declined from 244 in 1957 to 233 in 1963.[21] Recommendations involving a few thousand dollars have often received more thorough analysis than has the recommendation to abolish state support for child care centers, which have cost the state about $5 million annually.

Inconsistent Argument

The arguments offered in support of recommendations in the *Analysis* are sometimes inconsistent. If an institution argues that its staff should be increased to the level of other institutions, the *Analysis* may respond that need rather than the staffing patterns of other institutions should be the basis for justifying positions.[22] This is inconsistent with its general approach, which has been to treat similar institutions uniformly as far as possible, and with specific cases in which the *Analysis* opposed the addition of positions at an institution on the ground that all of the other institutions were getting along without them.[23] Again, the *Analysis* has at various times referred to the experience of other states in order to bolster argument for a recommendation, but discounted the argument of the Division of Fair

Employment Practices that certain positions had been found necessary in similar programs in other states:

> ... the experiences of other states is [sic] undoubtedly of interest, but the actions of other state legislatures regarding budgets of other agencies enforcing other laws in other states is [sic] of questionable validity in justifying the budget request of an agency in California.[24]

By contrast, the *Analysis* of the previous year had presented extensive data regarding fees paid at colleges and universities in other states, had concluded that "in keeping with the student fee policy in other state institutions of higher education, it appears that California students should pay 15 to 18 percent of the total expenditures," and had recommended an increase in fees.[25]

Application of Policy Regarding New Services

In the past, the policy that no new or expanded services should be approved in a budget session year was carried to lengths which tended to stultify the budget process. This policy, adopted by the legislature and the executive when the annual budget session was inaugurated in 1948, was never followed rigidly by either branch, and has slowly been eroded by practice. The rationale for the policy was that the 30-day budget session is too short a time in which to consider major changes in programs and policies, that, with few exceptions, the constitution does not permit statutory changes during a budget session, and that the annual budget should not be allowed to increase the rate of growth in state expenditures. The policy is open to objection, but even if it is accepted, there is little merit in applying it to very minor increases in personnel or equipment, as the *Analysis* has done. For example, the *Analysis* recommended against authorization of one position costing $2,988 annually, for expansion of inspections to enforce statutes which protect the public from unwholesome or otherwise objectionable meat products. It did not contend that the position was unnecessary or undesirable, but only that it was an increase in the level of service and should be deferred for consideration at the general session one year later.[26] With respect to the reclassification of a position costing an additional $600 per year, the *Analysis* contended, among other things, that the request *"represents a basic increase in the level of operations which should be proposed during a general session."*[27]

In 1958 rigorous criteria were established by the Analyst to determine whether equipment requests entailed new services,[28] and many items of equipment were proposed for elimination on this basis. For example, the request of the Division of Industrial Safety for $1,000 to prepare a sound film on shoring of trenches, "especially needed as an educational measure to combat the continuing toll of injuries and deaths to workers from cave-ins of trenches and excavations," was opposed on the basis that it was a new service not based on workload.[29] The *Analysis* never consistently opposed all new services in budget session years, and it usually coupled the no-new-service argument with other objections. Nonetheless, its application led to subtle distinctions and unnecessary argument in an effort to determine whether an item was a new service or based on workload. More important, there is no convincing reason why questions of new service should be excluded from consideration in a budget session year. Perhaps in recognition of this fact, the 1962–63 *Analysis* virtually abandoned this argument in justifying recommended cuts.

SUMMARY

The *Analysis of the Budget Bill* strengthens the legislature's capacity for rational decision-making by providing information in convenient form, by suggesting specific and considered alternatives, by appraising accomplishments of agencies and programs, and by scrutinizing the justification for expenditures. It also assists the legislature to maintain effective control of spending.

Although the value of the *Analysis* as an aid to rational calculation is indisputable, it is subject to criticism on several points. It has been too much preoccupied with details of expenditures, while failing to give enough attention to the methods by which budgetary decisions are made. Its recommendations have sometimes been based on a narrow conception of legislative control of expenditure, one which underestimates the utility of retrospective methods. At times its treatment of budgetary questions has been superficial, illogical, or inconsistent. The policy of no new or expanded services in budget session years has been interpreted too rigidly.

The character of the *Analysis* is a reflection, in part, of the expectations of the legislature and of the state of the budget system. The conception of control and the undue emphasis on expenditure details that we have criticized were not inconsistent with legislative attitudes. And the attempt to pare small amounts may be a result in part of the fact that only one-third of the expenditure program is annually reviewed by the legislature. If appropriations for schools, highways, and welfare were provided in the budget act, minor economies would probably have received less emphasis.

Substantial progress has been made toward the correction of each of the defects to which we have referred. Two objectives deserve high priority in efforts to further improve the *Analysis* as an aid to rational decision-making: (1) strengthening the treatment of program and policy issues and the analysis of accomplishments; and (2) developing ways to assess the quality of administrative decision-making without attempting a comprehensive review of the decisions taken in the formulation of the budget.

[1] *Analysis*, 1957–58, pp. 264–5.

[2] *Analysis*, 1961–62, pp. 416–22, 461–78.

[3] In 1965 the *Analysis* included discussion of "Program Plans" and "A Review of Agency Accomplishments" under each item of appropriation in the support and local assistance sections of the budget. This format was not followed in 1966.

[4] *Analysis*, 1957–58, p. 173.

[5] Quoted in *Analysis*, 1963–64, p. 100.

[6] *Analysis*, 1960–61, pp. 360–1.

[7] *Analysis*, 1957–58, p. 479.

[8] *Analysis*, 1963–64, p. 594.

[9] *Ibid.*, pp. 728–33.

[10] *Ibid.*, p. 120.

[11] *Analysis*, 1959–60, pp. 479–82.

[12] *Analysis*, 1962–63, p. 58.

[13] *Report*, 1945–47, p. 369.

[14] *Analysis*, 1951–52, p. 286.

[15] *Analysis*, 1954–55, pp. 202–4.

[16] "Schools for the Deaf and Blind; Study of Ability of Parents of Children to Pay Costs of Room and Board According to a Means Test," (1955), pp. 2–3 (mim).

[17] *Analysis*, 1959–60, pp. 50–1.

[18] *Analysis*, 1951–52, pp. 499–500; 1958–59, pp. 841–2.

[19] *Analysis*, 1957–58, pp. 996–7.

[20] *Analysis*, 1951–52, p. 500.

[21] *Analysis*, 1957–58, p. 996; 1963–64, p. 959.

[22] See *Analysis*, 1957–58, pp. 88, 118, for examples.

[23] See, for example, *Analysis*, 1956–57, p. 159.

[24] *Analysis*, 1960–61, p. 255.

[25] *Analysis*, 1959–60, p. 289.

[26] *Analysis*, 1956–57, p. 35.

[27] *Analysis*, 1960–61, p. 350. Italics in original.

[28] *Analysis*, 1958–59, p. XVI.

[29] *Ibid.*, p. 385.

Chapter VI

THE LEGISLATIVE ANALYST: PROBLEMS AND PROPOSALS

Three important questions regarding the office of Legislative Analyst remain to be treated: (1) To what extent does the Analyst contribute to budget reductions and increased efficiency of governmental operations? (2) What are the merits of the requirement that the Analyst make public, specific recommendations regarding amounts to be appropriated? (3) How does the Analyst participate in administrative decision-making? The chapter concludes with some proposals for modifying the role of the Analyst.

THE ANALYST'S CONTRIBUTIONS TO ECONOMY AND EFFICIENCY

The Analyst undoubtedly provides information and makes recommendations that are instrumental in achieving economies and in increasing operational efficiency, but it is difficult to establish the magnitude of the savings effected. Table 8 shows for selected years the percentage by which budget bill appropriations were reduced on the recommendation of the Analyst. In only one of the nine years for which data are presented did the reductions exceed $20 million; the annual average was approximately $10 million. Although the absolute amounts are by no means negligible, they are small relative to the total appropriations in the budget bill, which, as has been remarked, normally provides for only about one-third of the total expenditure program. In five of the nine years shown, reductions were less than one percent of the appropriations in the budget bill. In the other years reductions ranged from 2.2 to 4.3 percent.

When compared to the amounts cut from agency requests by the Department of Finance and the governor, or to savings effected in budget execution, the reductions made on the recommendation of the Analyst are small. In 1963 Governor Brown stated that "hundreds of millions of dollars" in budget requests had been eliminated from the budget, and that "average management savings were more than $24 million a year" during his first four years in office.[1]

Although the reductions made on the recommendation of the Analyst give some indication of the extent to which the office is responsible for savings in appropriations, several considerations limit the significance of such data. Some reductions effected in any given year result in savings in subsequent years. When a program is rejected or curtailed, the savings in that year will be repeated annually thereafter. If the program is affected by population increases or is one likely to expand, the annual savings in

TABLE 8

Reductions in Budget Bill Appropriations for State Operations, Capital Outlay, and Local Assistance, Recommended by the Legislative Analyst and Approved by the Legislature, Selected Years

Fiscal Year	Appropriations Proposed in Budget Bill	Reductions Recommended by Analyst and Approved by Legislature	
		Amount	Percent of Proposed Budget Bill Appropriations
1952–53.............	$433,046,918	$12,618,753	2.9%
1953–54.............	451,165,608	19,484,998[a]	4.3
1954–55.............	400,200,504	2,341,994	0.6
1956–57.............	567,948,253	2,390,826	0.4
1957–58.............	746,841,199	4,424,404	0.6
1958–59.............	758,574,915	24,058,975	3.2
1959–60.............	785,853,902	4,786,647	0.6
1960–61.............	913,457,058	2,020,917	0.2
1961–62.............	872,231,648	19,006,866	2.2

Sources: *Budget*; *Analysis of the Budget Bill*; *List of Legislative Changes in the Budget Act...Final Report*, Department of Finance; lists of proposed reductions prepared by the Legislative Analyst.
[a] Excludes reductions of $3,145,000 offset by special appropriation or reappropriation of prior year balances.

future years will be even greater. It is impossible to estimate these cumulative savings, but they are substantial.

On the other hand, some reductions do not result in savings in the long run. The most important case is that of capital outlay projects, whose postponement during a period of rising prices may well result in increased cost. Genuine savings may result, however, if the project is subsequently scaled down or if a less expensive type of construction is undertaken. Of course, postponement may have real advantages in a year when the budget is out of balance, even though the costs of the project will ultimately be incurred.

Deterrent Effect

The knowledge that the Legislative Analyst will scrutinize budgets closely may deter the administration from making requests that would otherwise be included in the budget. Some legislators believe that the chief value of the office of the Legislative Analyst is not that it helps the legislature reduce appropriations, but rather that it encourages the departments to budget more stringently. It is difficult to judge the importance of this deterrent effect. It is true that the Department of Finance has sometimes informed agencies that particular requests must be cut out of the budget because the Legislative Analyst would never approve them, but such statements have usually been an attempt to escape responsiblity for turning down expenditures that the department would not have approved in any case. That the deterrent effect works imperfectly is clear, for every year the Analyst and the legislature find that some proposed expenditures are unjustified.

No doubt the Analyst is a protection against completely unjustified expenditures that may escape the control agencies within departments and in the Department of Finance—the unnecessary travel, the purchase of new office furniture to replace that which is still serviceable, and the like. But the more important question is the effect on requests that have a certain amount of justification. Generally speaking, the governor, the Department of Finance, and departmental executives can discern many ways in which additional funds could be usefully employed; it will not normally be to their advantage to approve or propose waste and extravagance. But there seems to be no reason to expect administrators to delete from the budget items for which there is a certain amount of justification simply because the Analyst will scrutinize them carefully and might recommend against them. Proposals may be more carefully prepared and justified in order to minimize their vulnerability, but they will not be omitted for the sole reason that they will be critically examined. Indeed, inasmuch as the legislature rejects many of the recommendations of the Analyst, the administration may reasonably hope to secure legislative approval of items that the Analyst considers unjustified.

Inasmuch as the Analyst is expected by the legislature to recommend reductions, departments might conclude that padding their budgets would permit this expectation to be met without risk of harm to their programs. Although it is difficult to know whether budgets are padded, it is doubtful that the existence of the Analyst encourages the practice. Large departmental budgets are sometimes recommended for approval by the Analyst without any change whatsoever; hence, it does not appear that the Analyst feels compelled to recommend reductions regardless of the needs of the department. Moreover, legislative rejection of many of his recommendations suggests that an honest budget can emerge unscathed, even if the Analyst should recommend that it be cut.

Special Appropriations

The data presented above do not include legislative actions with respect to the Analyst's recommendations on special appropriation bills. Some observers have felt that the Analyst deters the passage of special appropriation bills by his presentations to the appropriations committees. No doubt he has provided information and argument useful to forces opposing special appropriations. That his recommendations have carried some weight is indicated by the fact that the appropriations committee chairmen sometimes do not invite his oral testimony on bills that they wish to have reported from committee. At the same time, it is obvious that the legislature will not refuse to pass special appropriation bills merely because of the Analyst's recommendation, albeit the amounts and the precise terms of the bills may be influenced by his suggestions. The importance of the Analyst's role in special appropriations is reduced because many originate in the legislature rather than with the executive, and the executive frequently opposes them. The governor himself has often made clear his intention to veto special appropriations, if necessary, to keep the budget in balance. Insofar as external restraints deter the passage of special appropriations, the representations of the executive carry more weight than those of the Analyst.

Program Change and Management Improvement

In order to assess the effect of the Analyst's work upon economy and efficiency, it is necessary to consider not only reductions in appropriations, but also recommendations and studies that lead to improvements in management and organization, and to changes in program. Many improvements are not directly reflected in appropriations. It is beyond the scope of this study to analyze the impact of the hundreds of recommendations, major and minor, that the Analyst has made in the *Analysis* and other reports regarding program and administrative improvements. It would, in any case, be most difficult to discover the importance of the Analyst's influence relative to that of legislative committees, ad hoc commissions, the Department of Finance, and the agencies themselves. That the Analyst has contributed substantially to administrative improvement, especially at the level of changes in procedure and minor reorganization, is clear. To mention only a few examples, the Analyst successfully pressed for the expansion of central automotive pools and curtailment of the practice of assigning automobiles to individuals or agencies; made studies and recommendations that led to greater returns from the investment of surplus state funds;[2] made studies and recommendations leading to the standardization of forms and procedures for the processing of patients in hospitals for the mentally ill;[3] and played an important role in the mechanization of motor vehicle registration and the establishment of a centralized payroll system. In the budget process itself, his insistence upon better justification and upon measurement and evaluation of performance has undoubtedly had salutary effects; significant improvements in capital outlay budgeting were adopted on his recommendation.[4]

To conclude, there can be no doubt that substantial sums have been saved as a result of the Analyst's efforts, and that the value received for funds expended has been increased. To say this is not to suggest that the budget is a great deal smaller than it would otherwise be, nor that an inefficient government has been made efficient through the Analyst's efforts. Administrative improvement depends heavily upon the initative and cooperation of the departments. Nevertheless, the Analyst performs an important service by drawing attention to administrative deficiencies, prodding agencies to act, and strengthening the hand of those within the administration whose efforts to bring about improvement might otherwise be blocked.

Specific Recommendations Publicly Made

The Analyst's recommendations are made in published documents and in committee hearings open to the press and the public. Moreover, as has been illustrated, many of the recommendations deal with questions of policy, and in some instances with major policy. They relate not only to mechanical and instrumental questions, but also to the amounts and kinds of services to be provided by administrative agencies as well as certain aspects of financing those services.

Two principal questions deserve consideration: (1) Why has the legislature been willing to permit the Analyst to make recommendations? (2) What are the consequences for budget review of his doing so? The first question is prompted by the assumption that a staff agency which makes public recommendations on matters of policy is likely to create sufficient resentment over time to endanger its usefulness or even its existence.

In specific cases, the Analyst's recommendations sometimes arouse the ire of individual members of the legislature. An assemblyman who was a strong advocate of state purchase of the Central Valley Project stated that he was "damned tired" of the Analyst's making recommendations on policy, after the latter had proposed the use for other purposes of $9 million earmarked for purchase of the CVP.[5] A resolution sponsored by five senators in 1957 would have prohibited the Analyst from opposing or urging legislation or expressing any opinion regarding the policy of proposed or existing legislation.[6] The principal author believed that the Analyst was "talking too much on policy" and should restrict himself to "finance."[7]

Legislators are sensitive to the impact that recommendations or public statements of the Analyst may have. It is significant that the Budget Committee discourages speechmaking by the Analyst, recognizing that even factual statements may be viewed as affecting party or other interests. Also noteworthy is the recent change in practice of the Ways and Means Committee. Formerly, it systematically secured the opinion of the Analyst regarding the merits of special appropriation and other cost measures; after Assemblyman Jesse Unruh became chairman of the committee in 1959, the Analyst's recommendation was not always invited. Selectivity in calling for recommendations was one of many methods employed in an effort to control the decisions of the committee. It was not of great importance as a method of control, for the leadership of the committee certainly would not be defeated on significant issues by a staff recommendation. But an unfavorable recommendation might provide ammunition for the opposition and make the path less smooth.

Factors in Legislative Acceptance

Several factors explain legislative acceptance of the making of recommendations. The Analyst does not wander at large over the whole range of public policy. His orientation is fundamentally financial and recommendations are offered in a financial context. In practice, important limitations are recognized. With rare exceptions, the governor's budget is accepted as a maximum—increases are almost never recommended. Moreover, on-going, well-established programs normally are not recommended for drastic curtailment, much less for abolition. In general, it is the new program or the expansion of an existing program that the Analyst is most likely to oppose. Finally, the Analyst is sensitive to legislative attitudes and recognizes that there are areas of controversy with respect to which his recommendations are not desired.

Legislators recognize their own spending propensities, and some of them perceive the Analyst as a "devil's advocate" or someone to help them "hold things down a bit." Those who have a special interest in economizing see the Analyst as a valuable ally. When Senator Ben Hulse was chairman of both the Finance and Budget Committees, and dominated the review of the budget in the senate and to a considerable extent in the legislature as a whole, he gave strong backing to the Analyst and used the office as an instrument for keeping the state's finances in what he considered sound condition. The position of the office was less strong after Hulse left the legislature in 1956, but the Democrats, who gained control of both houses and the governor's office in 1958, soon came to see the value of the Analyst as an ally, even though he opposed some of the administration's spending measures. The Democratic leadership in the legislature found that it had to be concerned not only with securing approval of the governor's spending proposals, but also with preventing the passage of appropriations that would throw the budget out of balance. It was helpful to have the Analyst join with the Department of Finance and the governor's spokesmen in opposition to unwanted appropriations.

To some legislators, an independent staff that "calls the shots as it sees them" is an appealing idea. They prefer to have the staff make recommendations according to its own lights, even though the recommendations may be troublesome at times, rather than to have it reflect the policy views of a particular committee or group. In the opinion of one member, if a legislator cannot make a case strong enough to win in the face of opposition from the Analyst, he does not deserve to win.

Finally, it should not be forgotten that the Legislative Analyst is a source of strength for the legislature in its efforts to control administration and to maximize its power vis-à-vis the executive. A legislator can view most of the Analyst's recommendations with detachment because his district and program interests are vitally affected by few of them. He may disagree or be annoyed when a favored agency or program is under attack by the Analyst, but much of the time he can take satisfaction in the fact that the Analyst is keeping an eye on the administrative agencies. In this perspective, the Analyst is a valuable ally of the legislative branch in its struggle to avoid being overwhelmed by the political strength of the executive and the expertise and complexity of the bureaucracy. The Analyst's recommendations can be perceived as directed at another branch of government and hence not only acceptable but highly desirable.

Advantages of Specific Recommendations

The requirement that the Analyst make a specific recommendation on each item of appropriation in the budget bill has three important advantages: (1) It ensures that a limited number of specific, considered alternatives is presented to the legislature. (2) It encourages a more penetrating analysis of the budget than would be likely if no recommendations were made, for the Analyst is required to take a definite position that he must be prepared to defend. The alternative would be for the Analyst to present information, raise questions, advance relevant considerations, and perhaps present arguments on both sides of issues. Under such a procedure there would be less pressure on the Analyst to find weaknesses in the budget and to weigh carefully the evidence and arguments relating to budget issues. (3) The requirement of recommendations provides some protection against covert advocacy, for it frankly abandons the notion that the staff should present objectively all sides of an issue. If the Analyst did not make recommendations, the questions asked, the facts presented, the interpretations placed upon them, the conclusions reached, the arguments offered—all would be influenced by the values and perceptions of the staff.[8] Overt advocacy tends to put the legislator on his guard, and makes him likely to examine the evidence and argument of the staff more closely than if he assumes that the staff is "objective."

Disadvantages of Recommendations

Requiring recommendations also has certain disadvantages. (1) Because the Analyst almost always recommends reductions rather than increases, some legislators tend to discount his recommendations on the ground that the Analyst's role requires him to propose cuts, whether they are justified or not. (2) The role of advocate imposes strains upon the capacity of the staff to take a balanced, relatively objective view of the issues in the budget. It is natural to become personally involved in winning one's case, to overstate it, and to give less than due weight to the arguments and evidence of the opposition. In general, however, the staff maintains a reasonably objective attitude. Moreover, in appropriations committee hearings the departments have ample opportunity to correct any distortion or unfairness that may creep into the Analyst's presentations. (3) The role of advocate invites legislators to bring pressures on the Analyst in an effort to influence his recommendations. Whether this is a serious consequence depends upon the caliber of the staff and the degree to which its independence is supported by the Budget Committee or other power centers in the legislature. Although individual legislators have put pressure on the Analyst at times, the evidence indicates that the staff has been remarkably successful in maintaining a position of independence. For example, the Analyst has taken positions in opposition to the strongly held views of powerful members of the Budget Committee.

Some Conclusions

These considerations suggest the conclusion that under certain conditions it is possible for a legislative fiscal analysis staff to contribute effectively to legislative decision-making on appropriations by making public, specific recommendations. The important conditioning factors during the period since 1941 have been: (1) Most legislators have believed that it was appropriate and desirable for the Analyst to make recommendations. (2) The caliber of the staff has, in general, been high. If the staff had had less respect for facts, or had taken less care to minimize its political role, or had become subservient to individual legislators, committees, or groups, the legislature might have withdrawn or curbed its power to make recommendations. (3) Parties played a very limited role in the legislature during most of this period. Hence, there was little tendency to try to use the office for partisan advantage or to view its recommendations as aiding or injuring the interests of the parties. It remains to be seen whether the growing importance of parties in the legislature will lead to attempts to capture the office for partisan purposes or to limit its recommending function in the interest of party advantage.

On balance, there are no overriding reasons for abandoning the policy that permits the staff to make recommendations. The more important question is whether the staff approaches its tasks with a high degree of objectivity and is able to maintain a position of relative independence. If these conditions are met, making recommendations will not seriously impair legislative confidence in the agency.

THE LEGISLATIVE ANALYST AND ADMINISTRATION

The Legislative Analyst has been drawn into administrative decision-making in a variety of ways. There have been cases in which agencies have asked him to approve proposals and have then used his approval as leverage to secure consent from the Department of Finance. The Analyst has served on interagency committees,[9] and the legislature frequently requests that one or more administrative agencies study a matter "jointly," or "in cooperation," or "in consultation" with the Analyst. Subcommittees of appropriations committees sometimes ask the Analyst, the Department of Finance, and the agency concerned to work out an agreement on a disputed budget issue and to return with a joint recommendation. In specific ways to be discussed in the following paragraphs, the Analyst has participated in the formulation and execution of the budget.

In general, the Analyst has been sensitive to the dangers of putting himself in the position of "clearing" agency proposals or of accepting responsibility for approval of administrative action. Thus, he reported in 1953 that he had denied requests from administrators who had asked his assistance in the preparation of their budgets.[10] Nevertheless, there has been continuing, if changing, participation of the Analyst in administrative decision-making. For the most part, this participation has not been based upon formal authority, but rather upon influence exercised in executive budget hearings and in conferences.

Budget Preparation

Hearings. Until formal executive hearings were abandoned in 1960, the Legislative Analyst and members of his staff attended the hearings at which agencies presented their budget requests to the Department of Finance.[11] Prior to 1953 the Analyst often expressed his views at the hearings, opposing requests considered unnecessary or unwise. His active participation, the Analyst repeatedly made clear, influenced the agencies to submit smaller budgets and encouraged the Department of Finance to reduce or reject spending proposals. Legislative Analyst Vandegrift asserted in 1949 that the information presented by his office in the budget hearings was "material in reducing departmental budgets by many millions of dollars" and that other contacts with departments resulted in "forestalling many requests for appropriations."[12] His successor stated in 1953 that participation in the budget hearings had a "tempering effect" on the members of the executive budget staff and was welcomed by them, for it strengthened their position vis-à-vis department heads, who could "bring political pressure on them." They could justify denial of requests on the ground that the Analyst had shown the requests to be vulnerable.[13] Despite these views, after 1953 the Analyst no longer revealed his attitude on budget requests, although he continued to attend the hearings and to ask questions to obtain information.

As already noted, in 1943 the Analyst took part in private conferences with the Director of Finance and the governor-elect at which budget decisions were made. In 1949, at the invitation of the Director of Finance, he participated in conferences where many final decisions were reached.[14]

Capital Outlay. The Analyst plays an active role in the making of executive decisions regarding capital improvement and equipment expenditures. For a number of years, the Analyst and representatives of administrative agencies have jointly reviewed proposals for minor construction. In 1962 the Analyst reported that he had "gone into" minor construction projects in "complete detail," and had discussed them with the agencies concerned "with a view towards the assurance that only those projects would be included in the budget which could be fully justified as to need and as to adequacy of design and cost estimates." Consequently, he was recommending approval of these projects, with very few exceptions. The total amount in the budget for minor construction was "substantially less than that which was first proposed by the several agencies, partly as a result of the conferences and discussions mentioned above."[15]

The Analyst has also participated in deliberations on major capital improvements. Under the procedure adopted in 1955, extensive conferences are held on proposed construction projects submitted by the departments.

The Analyst reported in 1956 that during the previous year he had participated in "hundreds of conferences" regarding

problems of program, space utilization, space needs, standards of both utilization and construction detail, structural types, site development, utilities developments required by institutional expansions, timing of construction, and many more details too numerous to mention.

These conferences had resulted in final cost estimates for proposed projects that were "satisfactory to all concerned."[16] Subsequently, the Analyst took a less active part in these conferences, although a representative of the office continues to attend them.

Equipment. The equipment requests of some agencies are reviewed jointly by the Department of Finance, the Legislative Analyst, and the agency concerned. On numerous occasions, the Analyst has indicated that his participation in these reviews results in a reduction in the amounts proposed in the governor's budget. For example:

As has now become customary, we reviewed the equipment requests of the division [of Beaches and Parks] with its representatives as well as representatives from the Department of Finance prior to the final formulation of the budget.... The review resulted in a reduction of over 32 percent...[17]

Budget Execution

The Analyst's participation in budget execution has been almost entirely limited to the capital outlay process. In 1944 the legislature created the Post War Public Works Review Board, which was given responsibility for the allocation of funds to local government for construction purposes.[18] The authorizing legislation made the Legislative Analyst a member of the board having "the same duties and powers as the other members of the board to the extent that such duties and powers are constitutionally compatible with his position" as Legislative Analyst.[19] The legislature abolished the board in 1947 and transferred its functions to the State Allocations Board, but made no provision for membership by the Legislative Analyst.[20]

Meanwhile, in 1946 the legislature created a State Public Works Board consisting of the Directors of Finance and of Public Works and the Real Estate Commissioner. This agency has extensive authority in the execution of the capital outlay budget, including approval of preliminary plans, allocation of funds, and determination of the timing of major construction projects of all state agencies. It is also responsible for the selection and acquisition of property needed for new state facilities.

Two legislators from each house "meet with and participate in the work of the board to the extent that such participation is not incompatible with their respective positions as Members of the Legislature."[21] In 1950, the

Director of Finance described to the Budget Committee the role that the Legislative Analyst had played in the work of the Public Works Board.

We asked Mr. Vandegrift to come in as your representative. He did come in on what we called a screening committee prior to the meetings of the Public Works Board, and we were able to obtain his advice and he was able to obtain information on what was going on so he might advise you and the legislative members of the Board. . . .

The screening committee had "read the agenda that was going to be presented to the Public Works Board and carefully reviewed it, making many changes before it went to the Public Works Board." The Legislative Analyst could advise the legislative members of the board of his point of view and suggest changes. "We did make many changes," the director added significantly. On the same occasion, he agreed to a suggestion by the Legislative Analyst that the latter participate in a similar screening committee to review, prior to action by the Public Works Board, the capital outlay appropriations enacted in 1950. He stipulated, however, that the Legislative Analyst would not have "a veto power. . . . He can sit with us and advise, but if the vote is against him we must go ahead."[22]

A representative of the Analyst's office continues to attend meetings of the screening committee and to participate fully in its discussions. One week in advance of the monthly meetings of the Public Works Board, the screening committee meets to review the details of projects on the board's agenda and to reach agreement regarding them, or at least to define and narrow areas of disagreement. Other members of the committee consider seriously and sometimes accept the suggestions of the Analyst's representative, who comments on projects under consideration; he speaks upon his own initiative or the request of the legislative "members" of the board. The legislators have before them the Analyst's written report and recommendation regarding each project on the agenda. Although they do not vote or make motions, the legislators participate fully in the discussion. Legally, they have no veto over board actions, but rather act in an advisory capacity.[23] In practice, board members and legislators almost never find themselves in serious disagreement.

Only on rare occasions has the legislature imposed upon the Legislative Analyst responsibilities relating to budget execution. Appropriations for university and state college residence halls provided in the 1957 budget act were not to be made available for expenditure unless the Director of Finance made certain alternative certifications, one of them being that in the opinion of the director and the Legislative Analyst, federal funds for this purpose would be available at a lower interest rate than proceeds of the sale of state bonds.[24] In approving an agency's request for certain positions in the 1960 budget, the legislature stipulated that a report of accomplishments be submitted and approved by the Department of Finance "in conjunction with the Legislative Analyst."[25] Although the Analyst has recommended in a number of instances that agencies be required to make reports to the Budget Committee, he has avoided recommending that agency action be conditional upon approval of his office.

Objections to Analyst's Participation in Administration

There are important objections to the Analyst's participation in administrative decisions. Admittedly, he may be instrumental in effecting economies at times or in saving the administration from making mistakes, but there is no reason to assume that his influence will always be on the side of the wiser course. Moreover, it is his function to discover and criticize error, not to save the administration from it.

Recently, the state adopted a new form for use of local school districts in requisitioning free textbooks from the state. This form was "devised through the joint efforts" of the Department of Education, the Organization and Cost Control Division of the Department of Finance, and the Legislative Analyst.[26] It is difficult to believe that the Department of Education, with the aid of the central management analysis unit of the state, is incapable of devising an adequate form for requisitioning textbooks. But even if it were, the proper course would be to correct the deficiencies of the administration, not to rely on the Legislative Analyst to come to the rescue on particular management decisions. Such decisions are myriad, and there is no logical point at which to stop the rescue operation. If the Analyst is to help the administration decide how to make forms or what equipment to buy or how buildings should be designed, there is no reason why he should not help it decide what personnel to request or what travel to undertake or what documents to print.

But the more fundamental criticism of the Analyst's participation in administrative decisions is that it tends to undermine the legislature's function of oversight of administration. It is true, of course, that the Analyst's participation in budget decision-making is almost entirely on the basis of influence, not of formal authority. The formal responsibility for decisions remains with the administration. But how is that responsibility to be enforced? The more influential the Analyst is in the making of a decision, the less likely he is to criticize the decision before the legislature. One does not criticize a course that he considers wise; having concluded that it is wise, he is less likely to look for, recognize, and focus attention upon undesirable consequences that may ensue. But the legislature relies heavily upon the Analyst to examine critically the decisions of the administration. That reliance is misplaced insofar as the Analyst's involvement in administrative decisions makes his examination less critical and less disinterested than it would otherwise be.

One may object that it makes little difference whether the Analyst's influence is exercised in direct relationships with administration or in recommendations to legislative committees; in either case, his influence is subject to errors of judgment, and he will be reluctant to criticize his own positions that turn out to be erroneous. There is an important difference, however. Recommendations to committees necessarily draw issues to the attention of the legislature, whereas direct influence upon administrative decisions tends to keep issues out of legislative view. This result would be unimportant if there were perfect correspondence between legislative positions and those of the Analyst, but such correspondence is not to be expected, as is evident from the fact that the legislature rejects many of the Analyst's recommendations.

It is inevitable, of course, that some degree of influence will be exercised by the Analyst and his staff, even if conscientious effort is made to avoid participation in administrative decisions. Even the questions asked in the course of inspecting field installations and gathering information may affect departmental decisions. But differences of degree are often important; minimizing the Analyst's direct influence on administration tends to strengthen legislative oversight and control.

Accommodation of Interests

There is a danger that a legislative fiscal analysis agency will be drawn into activities that are considered to be the responsibility of the executive branch under the prevailing doctrine of the executive budget. Although the California experience demonstrates that this danger is real, it also reveals an accommodation of conflicting executive and legislative interests.

Several factors help to explain that accommodation. The Analyst's participation has been limited to certain kinds of budget decisions and has been based largely on influence, consultation, and advice, seldom on formal authority to make binding decisions. Participation based on influence permits all parties to maintain their commitment to the doctrine of the executive budget and permits administrators to feel that, although they may be influenced, they remain in charge, formally and in fact. Moreover, the relationship of influence is not a one-way street. By accommodating to extensive interactions with the Analyst, administrators can hope to reassure the legislature that its interests are being protected and to gain sympathetic understanding from the Analyst, through the development of personal relationships and by "educating" the legislative staff. Recognition must also be given to the moderate spirit and self-restraint of the Analyst, who has opposed occasional legislative attempts to give him formal authority in budget administration. Finally, legislative-executive relations have been relatively harmonious since shortly after the office of the Analyst was created. Under less auspicious circumstances, it is quite possible that the legislature would have attempted to give the Analyst formal authority to participate in administrative decision-making.

Proposals for Changing the Analyst's Role

There is every evidence that the office of Legislative Analyst is firmly established as an element in the budget system. The broad outlines of its role are well-defined and are unlikely to be changed quickly or drastically. There will be gradual change, in the future as in the past, and it is appropriate to conclude the discussion of the office with some suggestions as to the directions that change should take. The first three proposals arise from earlier discussion, and need only be mentioned; the remaining two require some elaboration.

1. The Analyst's participation in the processes of formulating and executing the budget should be reduced to the minimum consistent with his need for information.

2. Improvements that have been made in the *Analysis* should be carried further. The amount of discussion of expenditure details should be examined critically, and program explanations and evaluations should be strengthened.

3. The *Analysis* should de-emphasize attempts to evaluate budget decisions, and concentrate instead on the methods whereby decisions are made as well as the amounts and kinds of information available to decision-makers.

4. The strategy of a comprehensive review of all proposed appropriations in the budget bill should be replaced by a strategy of (a) examining major program changes and (b) studying in depth selected operations whose improvement would be likely to bring substantial benefits in economy or operating effectiveness.

5. The Budget Committee and the Analyst should assume greater leadership in appraising basic elements of the budget system and in bringing about needed innovation.

Redesigning Strategy

The activities of the fiscal analysis staff have been guided by questionable strategy. The Analyst has been directed to analyze all appropriations in the budget bill; he has tried to scrutinize all increases, large and small, and in recent years to give substantial attention to existing programs. This comprehensive approach has inevitably meant that many expenditures have received less than searching analysis. An alternative strategy would have been to select each year certain agencies, programs, or cost factors for more searching study, and to have conceded frankly the impossibility of making well-founded recommendations on a comprehensive basis. In 1963 the Analyst reported the results of a thorough review of the preparation and serving of food in the hospitals administered by the Department of Mental Hygiene. He concluded that the state "is losing a minimum of $500,000 annually due to the current practices of preparing too much food and inefficiently distributing food. . . ."[27] It may be presumed that these practices had existed over a substantial period of time.[28] If the problem had been studied in some depth a few years earlier, substantial savings would have resulted. But the depth of analysis permitted by the comprehensive approach apparently did not enable the Analyst to make a serious attack on this problem, for it received no significant attention in the *Analysis* during the previous decade.

It is reasonable to assume that investigation in some depth of a few selected, important problem areas in any given year may reveal opportunities for savings and improved operations that are of much greater significance than the discovery of numerous instances in which individual positions, items of equipment, or specific operating expenses are unjustified. If such selective investigations were coupled with an analysis of the major program changes in each budget, legislative review would be directed to important matters. Because such a procedure would recognize frankly that a comprehensive, thorough review of all proposed expenditures in any given year is not possible, there would be less tendency on the part of the appropriations committees to assume that expenditure proposals are sufficiently justified if the Legislative Analyst makes no objection to them. Moreover, selective investigations would provide a better basis for important improvements in management than does the discovery of small, unjustified items, which in many cases have no significant implications for such improvements.

The proposed strategy could be implemented in various ways. The most drastic change from existing practice would be to abandon the requirement that the Analyst make a recommendation regarding every appropriation in the budget bill, permitting recommendations to be made only on those appropriations or components of appropriations that have received thorough review. Another possibility would be for the Analyst to specify in the *Analysis* the expenditures and operations that have been given special attention. In either case it would be possible to examine all agencies systematically over a period of years.

Examining Basic Elements of the Budget System

To a considerable extent, the Budget Committee and the Analyst have missed the opportunity to provide leadership in evaluating and improving the budget system. There is a need for systematic, comprehensive, and thorough study of the way in which budget decisions are made and ought to be made. Goals need to be articulated, policies formulated, implementation planned, and progress assessed. Although the executive necessarily must play an important role in planning and implementing change, there is wide scope for the Budget Committee and the Analyst to assume initiative in raising basic problems and proposing broad solutions.

Reform Suggestions

It is true that the Budget Committee took the lead in establishing an auditing agency responsible to the legislature, a reform of fundamental importance. Moreover, significant changes in the capital outlay process were made on the recommendation of the Analyst. He has urged that the central service functions of the Department of Finance be placed in a separate department in order to permit Finance to concentrate its efforts on budgeting and fiscal control, and he has opposed the enactment of continuing appropriation measures and the creation of additional special funds. He has gradually increased the emphasis upon program and evaluation of accomplishments in the issues and information presented to the legislature, while de-emphasizing concern with objects of expenditure. This change in emphasis has resulted largely from case-by-case criticisms and recommendations, however, rather than from comprehensive study in depth leading to the establishment of broad policy positions and implementation of needed change. Issues are raised at particular times regarding particular budgets: Is the workload standard for particular functions satisfactory? Has this specific treatment program resulted in more rapid rehabilitation? Such questions are entirely appropriate; the case-by-case approach has the merit of avoiding easy, broad generalizations to which more general studies are susceptible. The case approach also permits experimental solutions to limited problems based upon recognition of the peculiarities of different agencies, programs, and situations. But there are also benefits to be derived from searching inquiry into basic elements of the budget system.

Yet, most of the recent basic recommendations for reform of the budget system have come not from the Analyst or the Budget Committee but from other agencies. It was the Division of Organization and Cost Control of the Department of Finance that criticized the Budget Division for having no clear understanding of its own objectives in budget administration, for placing disproportionate emphasis on mechanics and detail and too little emphasis upon programs and their results, for failing to make a coordinated effort to place the budget on a performance basis, for failing to examine on a continuing basis its own internal operations and the budget process as a whole, and for overemphasizing central controls while failing to work to strengthen the fiscal management function in the departments.[29]

Again, as noted in Chapter II, it was an ad hoc committee appointed by the governor that recommended placing the central budget administration function in a proposed Executive Department and giving the operating agencies greater authority to make budget decisions. It is remarkable that neither this fundamental recommendation nor the issues raised in the OCC study of the Budget Division received any significant consideration in the *Analysis*.

Another recent development was a report by the Assembly Ways and Means Committee on the subject of long-range program and budget planning. The report recommended that the budget be accompanied each year by a five-year projection of expenditures and revenues, and a five-year projection of probable program changes and capital improvements, and their costs; that budget planning and presentation emphasize programs and costs with less attention to itemized detail of personnel to be hired and things to be bought; and that electronic data processing equipment be utilized to provide quickly the information needed by the legislature in reviewing the budget, including the financial effects and other implications of possible changes in programs.[30] With respect to the content of the budget document, the committee recommended that "the itemized detail of individual jobs and amounts for materials, supplies and other objects of expenditure" not be published any longer, but rather that the document

concentrate on program, the work units and cost factors which form a realistic basis for deciding the expenditure program of the State and on the indicators of the future which show the consequences of what is being proposed and decided.

It also criticized the budget for "too much verbiage purporting to describe 'program and performance' when in most cases it is but a general description of function, with no data on performance."[31]

Finally, it was the Assembly Committee on Ways and Means that launched a major attack on the problem of special funds in 1961.[32]

These studies are cited to show that in the past few years responsible agencies have believed that basic aspects of the budget system need to be appraised and overhauled. The merits of particular criticisms and prescriptions are not our concern here, nor do we mean to suggest that such studies should be the exclusive concern of the Legislative Analyst and the

Budget Committee. The significant fact is that the Analyst and the committee have not taken the lead in pursuing these questions, all of which would have been appropriate subjects for consideration a decade or so ago. Moreover, when the Legislative Analyst testified before the Ways and Means Committee regarding long-range planning and budgeting, he expressed uncertainty as to the feasibility, limitations, costs, and difficulties that would be encountered in implementing the committee's recommendations.[33] Although the Analyst raised a number of pertinent questions, his testimony did not leave the impression that his office had thoroughly explored the problem of long-range budget planning.

With respect to the proposal of the Committee on Organization of State Government that more budgetary authority be decentralized to operating agencies, the Analyst told a legislative committee that he had talked to some administrators about their problems with the Department of Finance:

Is it simply a matter of administration, or is it a matter of basic responsibility that is causing so many of the administrators to support the idea that they should have greater responsibility in matters of this kind? There were wide differences of opinion, but overall, I think it would be reasonable to say that the main criticism—to the extent that there was criticism—would be in administration, rather than in basic responsibility. They just felt that it was too cumbersome to get across the agency point of view in terms of fiscal control—too much paper work and too much argument with people who were, perhaps, not in a position to make decisions.[34]

Whether the difficulty is in administration or in authority, the problem deserves study, especially in view of the recent insistence of five of seven Agency[35] heads queried that further decentralization of authority is needed.[36]

The cases cited do not, of course, exhaust the problems that the Analyst and the Budget Committee should have studied. Others include (a) organization for budget administration—the internal organization of the Budget Division, the kind of staffing it should have, its relationship with central service functions, organization and staffing of budget functions in the departments, and the appropriate location of the Budget Division; (b) the costs of the budget system, with particular reference to the costs of central controls, preparing budget estimates, and accumulating data required for justification of requests; (c) criteria for determining the extent to which the executive branch should have discretion in the execution of the budget; and (d) the values and limitations of performance budgeting, its implications for budget formulation and presentation, and the practical problems of its implementation.

[1] *Budget,* 1963–64, pp. iii, v.

[2] *Analysis,* 1956–57, p. 329; 1957–58, p. 409.

[3] *Analysis,* 1962–63, pp. 425–6.

[4] *Analysis,* 1952–53, p. 500; 1953–54, p. 462; 1954–55, p. 529.

[5] *San Francisco Chronicle,* March 9, 1954, p. 5.

[6] SCR 62 (1957).

[7] Quoted in *Sacramento Bee,* March 8, 1957, p. A-10.

[8] Cf. Norman Meller, "The Policy Position of Legislative Service Agencies," *Western Political Quarterly,* V (March, 1952), 109–23.

[9] "Report of the Joint Legislative Budget Committee to the Fifty-Seventh Session of the California Legislature," *Senate Journal,* June 20, 1947, p. 3511; *Analysis,* 1961–62, pp. 28, 213.

[10] Statement by Legislative Analyst Post at the workshop on "Legislative Fiscal Analysis" of the Legislative Service Conference, held in New Orleans, September 28–October 1, 1953. (Recording by the Council of State Governments).

[11] Staff members of the Analyst's office have also attended the hearings held by the directors of the Departments of Corrections and Youth Authority on their own departmental budgets.

[12] Letter of January 24, 1949 from Vandegrift to Budget Committee Chairman William P. Rich, attached to the "Minutes" of the Budget Committee meeting of January 25–26, 1949. For other statements making similar claims, see *Analysis,* 1947–48, p. V; 1950–51, p. V; 1952–53, p. II.

[13] Post, see note 10 above.

[14] "Minutes," October 14, 1949, p. 14.

[15] *Analysis,* 1962–63, p. 673.

[16] *Analysis,* 1956–57, p. 612.

[17] *Analysis,* 1960–61, p. 370.

[18] *Cal. Stats.* (1944 4th Ex. Sess.), chap. 47, pp. 196–204.

[19] The Supreme Court held the act constitutional, but made no reference to the Analyst's position. *City of Los Angeles v. Post War Public Works Review Board* (1945), 26 Cal. 2d, 101.

[20] *Cal. Stats.* (1946 1st Ex. Sess.), chap. 145, pp. 187–91.

[21] *Cal. Govt. Code,* sec. 15770, 1963 ed., p. 447.

[22] "Minutes," September 1, 1950, pp. 3–4, 7.

[23] "State Public Works Board—No. 10089," Opinion of the Legislative Counsel, *Assembly Journal,* March 26, 1959, pp. 1827–9. This opinion concludes that the legislators are not "members" of the board and may not vote nor exercise any veto power over its actions.

[24] *Cal. Stats.* (1957), chap. 600, items 448.1, 449.1, 450.1, 451.1, 452.1, 453.1, 454.1, 455.1, 456.1, 457.5.

[25] *List of Legislative Changes in the Budget Act of 1960, Final Report,* prepared by the Department of Finance (1960), p. 16.

[26] Assembly Interim Committee on Ways and Means, *Progress Report on Dedicated Funds and Reports on State Purchasing—Military Leave Pay—Institutional Costs—Lake Earl* (Assembly Interim Committee Reports, 1961–63, vol. 21, no. 8, 1963), p. 63.

[27] *Analysis*, 1963–64, p. 410.

[28] In 1953 the *Analysis* made a passing reference to food waste (p. 318).

[29] *General Management Survey of the Department of Finance*, Survey 852 by the Organization and Cost Control Division of the Department of Finance (1957), pp. 155–65.

[30] *Report on Long-Range Program and Budget Planning*, Assembly Interim Committee on Ways and Means (Assembly Interim Committee Reports, vol. 21, no. 5, 1963).

[31] *Ibid.*, p. 31.

[32] *Report on Dedicated Funds* (Assembly Interim Committee Reports, vol. 21, no. 4, 1961).

[33] "Transcript of Hearing of the Assembly Interim Committee on Ways and Means," July 18, 1962, pp. 6–30 (mim).

[34] "Hearings on Government Reorganization," Assembly Interim Committee on Government Organization, edited transcript, September 22–23, 1961, pp. 30–1 (mim).

[35] An "Agency" is a grouping of departments having related functions and is headed by an "Administrator."

[36] *Findings and Recommendations Concerning Reorganization of the Executive Branch of California State Government,* report of the Commission on California State Government Organization and Economy (1963), pp. 37–8, 40–1, 49–50, 53, 63–4. An extreme example cited by one agency head: an application had to be made to the Department of Finance and approval received before funds listed in the agency budget for purchase of an ordinary table could be spent to purchase a drafting table, p. 53.

Chapter VII

APPROPRIATIONS COMMITTEES AND BUDGET REVIEW

The California legislature has well-defined organization, arrangements, and procedures for reviewing and making decisions upon the expenditure proposals of the governor. These formal arrangements include the office of the Legislative Analyst, already described. The present chapter discusses the organization and procedures of the appropriations committees and examines the manner in which they make budget decisions.

APPROPRIATIONS COMMITTEES

The importance of the Assembly Ways and Means Committee and the Senate Finance Committee in the process of reaching financial decisions can hardly be exaggerated. All special appropriation bills and numerous "implied cost" bills are referred to them after review by policy committees. Major bills calling for new or increased taxes are usually reviewed by them because such bills entail additional administrative costs. Thus, the appropriations committees are in a position to influence policy with respect to expenditures, revenues, and where some cost may be involved, other fields of legislation as well.

Of all the measures introduced into the legislature, a substantial proportion comes under the scrutiny of the appropriations committees. In 1959, for example, more bills were referred to the Ways and Means Committee than to any other committee of the assembly; in the senate, the Finance Committee ranked second. Of the 3161 measures introduced in the assembly, 482 or 15 percent were referred (or re-referred) to the Ways and Means Committee, and 254 or 23 percent of the 1099 senate measures that passed the senate were referred (or re-referred) to Ways and Means. Of the 1644 measures introduced in the senate, 260 or 16 percent were referred (or re-referred) to the Finance Committee.[1]

Membership

Membership on the appropriations committees is highly prized, for it offers exceptional opportunities for participating in review of much of the major legislation that reaches the floor, as well as for directing the flow of funds to programs or projects of particular interest to the member's district. Members of the Assembly Ways and Means Committee are appointed

TABLE 9

PERCENTAGE OF REPUBLICAN SEATS IN HOUSES AND ON APPROPRIATIONS COMMITTEES, 1937–65

Session	Assembly	Ways and Means Committee	Senate	Finance Committee
1937	41%	24%	60%	89%
1939	45	19	55	44
1941	48	76	60	73
1943	55	70	58	82
1945	53	68	68	82
1947	60	60	65	82
1949	56	64	65	82
1951	58	59	70	73
1953	68	69	70	82
1955	59	64	60	64
1957	53	57	50	54
1959	41	36	33	54
1961	41	36	25	38
1963	35	35	33	15
1965	29	38	35	8

Sources: *Final Calendar of Legislative Business* and *Handbook, California Legislature*, 1937–65.

by the speaker, who considers seniority but also seeks to give reasonably equitable representation to the two parties, rural and urban districts, and the northern and southern sections of the state. In making committee appointments, the Senate Rules Committee follows closely the principle of seniority. Normally, the majority party controls the appropriations committee (Table 9). In 1959, however, the seniority rule gave the Republicans a majority on the Finance Committee even though they were outnumbered two to one in the senate. In recent sessions northern and southern representation on the Ways and Means Committee has been closely balanced, but the north has dominated the Finance Committee, as it has done in the senate as a whole.

The members of the appropriations committees have an extremely heavy workload, not only because of the large number of bills processed, but also

TABLE 10

PERCENTAGE DISTRIBUTION OF MEMBERS OF CALIFORNIA APPROPRIATIONS COMMITTEES
ACCORDING TO LENGTH OF SERVICE, 1937–61 [a]

| Year | Sessions of Service on Appropriations Committee [b] | | | | Total Members |
	First	Second	Third	Fourth or More	
ASSEMBLY WAYS AND MEANS COMMITTEE					
1937........................	62%	19%	19%	..%	21
1939........................	52	38	10	..	21
1941........................	81	10	..	10	21
1943........................	43	43	4	9	23
1945........................	32	28	28	12	25
1947........................	44	16	24	16	25
1949........................	40	4	32	24	25
1951........................	41	7	15	37	27
1953........................	..	41	7	52	26
1955........................	25	7	32	36	28
1957........................	11	4	18	68	28
1959........................	18	5	5	73	22
1961........................	14	5	18	64	22
SENATE FINANCE COMMITTEE					
1937........................	44%	33%	..%	22%	9
1939........................	56	33	..	11	9
1941........................	45	36	9	9	11
1943........................	18	45	27	9	11
1945........................	18	18	36	27	11
1947........................	18	9	18	55	11
1949........................	27	..	18	55	11
1951........................	36	..	27	36	11
1953........................	18	9	36	36	11
1955........................	9	9	9	72	11
1957........................	23	15	8	54	13
1959........................	38	..	8	54	13
1961........................	15	..	31	54	13

Source: *Final Calendar of Legislative Business*, 1931–61.
 [a] Components do not always add to 100 percent because of rounding. In a small proportion of cases service was discontinuous.
 [b] Sessions of service refers to regular sessions only, including budget sessions but not extraordinary sessions.

because the budget bill requires many days of deliberation each year. They do not have fewer committee assignments than do other legislators, however. In 1965 most members of the Ways and Means Committee served on three other committees; most Finance Committee members held four or five other committee posts. As a result, the appropriations committee members are often well-informed on various fields of legislation, but their responsibilities on other committees reduce the time and attention they can give to budgetary questions.

The appropriations committees are among the largest in the respective houses. In 1965, the Ways and Means Committee had 21 members, more than one-fourth of the assembly; the Finance Committee had 13, about one-third of the senate. Committees of this size can represent a wide range of interests, viewpoints, and specialized knowledge, and, if united, can have a strong influence on house decisions by sheer weight of numbers.

A low rate of turnover can be expected to improve the quality of budgetary review by the appropriations committees. Experienced members will be more familiar than newcomers with committee procedure, departmental programs, and budgetary materials and methods. In each regular session from 1949 through 1961 at least 60 percent of the members of the Finance Committee and 50 percent of the Ways and Means Committee had two sessions or more of experience on the committee (Table 10). In each session from 1953 through 1961, each committee included several members having six or more sessions of committee service.

Members of the appropriations committees tend to have long tenure in the legislature as well as on the committees. In 1959 and 1961 all of the 12 members of the senate having greatest house seniority were members of the Finance Committee. Of the 22 members of the Ways and Means Committee in 1961, 16 had served six years or more in the assembly and nine had served at least 10 years. Seniority is not necessarily correlated with ability, of course; some of the junior members of both committees have been able and effective.

Chairmen

Custom requires that the speaker appoint as chairman of the Ways and Means Committee a member named by the governor, or at least acceptable to him.[2] The governor looks to the Ways and Means chairman to defend his financial policies in the committee and on the floor of the lower house, but the chairman does not consider himself obliged to defend the budget in every detail.

The chairman of the Senate Finance Committee is not normally considered to be the governor's spokesman, although the governor has sometimes been consulted regarding the appointment. In 1939 Democratic Governor

Olson was allowed to name the chairman even though the Republicans controlled the senate, but two years later Senator Mixter, a Republican not acceptable to Olson, was made chairman.[3] When the Democrats took control of the senate in 1957, they gave the chairmanship to Democrat James J. McBride, although the incumbent governor was a Republican. McBride continued to serve as chairman during the Democratic administration of Governor Brown, but he was not the governor's spokesman on financial legislation. He opposed Brown's tax program in 1959, and in the following two years supported proposed tax reductions to which the governor objected.

A skillful chairman can exercise great influence over the decisions of the committee. He appoints subcommittees, schedules hearings, and presides at committee hearings. He presents and defends the committee's budget bill recommendations before the house, and he almost always serves on the conference committee on the budget bill. He directs the small committee staff, formerly only a secretary or two, but now including one or two administrative assistants. In the assembly he is consulted regarding appointments to his committee. He can build support and exercise some control over subcommittee actions by judicious selection of subcommittee chairmen and members. The chairmanship of a subcommittee of Ways and Means having responsibility for the conduct of an interim investigation (the Finance Committee is inactive during the interim) is especially prized, for it enhances prestige and affords opportunities for publicity. The power to schedule bills for hearing, potentially a source of considerable influence, is greatly limited by the unwritten rule that the author of a bill has a right to a hearing—a rule that is seldom broken. Nevertheless, the chairman can determine when a bill is heard, and by delaying the hearing until late in the session can reduce its chances for passage. As the presiding officer at committee meetings, the chairman can sometimes determine the outcome of voice votes, and he may fail to hear a request for a roll-call vote. He may be able to influence the committee's decision by requesting—or failing to request—that the Legislative Analyst or the Department of Finance give their views on a bill or budget item under consideration, although the informality of committee procedure permits any committee member to make such a request. Exercising persuasion outside of the committee room, seeing to it that members are present when their votes are needed, and helping a member of the committee to get favorable action on a bill are other techniques of influencing decision.

Yet another significant power of the chairman is his control over timing of action on the budget bill itself. Special appropriation bills may not be passed in either house before the budget bill has been signed by the governor, unless they are certified as emergency measures by him. If the chairman delays reporting the budget bill until late in the session, authors of special appropriation bills must seek the governor's certification or risk loss of the bill in the closing rush. Moreover, so long as the budget bill remains in committee, a member must consider the possibility that projects in the budget bill of particular interest to him may be eliminated if his voting record is not satisfactory to those who control the committee.

Subcommittees

The detailed and systematic examination of each appropriation in the budget bill is performed by subcommittees. In 1961 the Finance Committee employed four subcommittees, each having three members; the Ways and Means Committee, six subcommittees of seven members. In general, special appropriation bills and implied cost bills have been processed by the full committees, although in 1961 the Ways and Means Committee appointed several subcommittees to make recommendations on groups of related bills.

Hearings

Each house has a fixed schedule of committee meetings. The Ways and Means Committee meets two afternoons, and the Finance Committee one morning per week, either for subcommittee or full committee meetings. In 1961 the Ways and Means Committee began in early May to hold two night meetings a week, and numerous special meetings were called during the last three weeks before the legislature adjourned on June 16. Prior to the abolition of the 30-day constitutional recess in 1958, the committees met during most of the recess, thereby gaining a period for uninterrupted work and escaping the distractions and competing claims of the session. Although the abolition of the mandatory recess during general sessions deprived the committees of a valuable period for work, a month's recess has been available during the budget session since 1956.

Normally, a decision is taken by committee vote immediately after a budget bill item or other bill has been explained at the hearing. Hearings, however, are open to the public and the press, and the Finance Committee sometimes "takes the matter under advisement," meaning that the decision will be taken privately. Some important and controversial issues are the subject of informal consultation among committee members in advance of the hearing. Such consultation permits members to find out how the vote will go, and to influence their colleagues.

In Congress the hearings of the House Appropriations Committee are closed, while most of the Senate hearings are public; both committees take decisions in executive session. The House committee considers that open hearings would delay the proceedings, deprive the committee of off-the-record testimony,[4] and "intensify the assault on the public money."[5] It is undoubtedly true that committee deliberations in California consume more time because sessions are public and members feel constrained to direct to the audience and the press comments which would not be made in closed sessions. Witnesses and members are probably less frank than they would be in executive sessions. Perhaps, too, the necessity for committee members to vote in public makes them more susceptible to pressures to spend. The custom of public hearings and decisions is so well established in the legislature, however, that there is little likelihood of their abandonment. Votes may be arranged in advance, members may absent themselves to avoid difficult issues, voice votes may be taken so that members do not have to go on record, but the form of a public hearing and, on most issues, public decision will be retained.[6]

Joint Hearings

A 1953 survey found that joint hearings are held on at least some appropriation measures in 34 states.[7] Although permitted by the rules,[8] joint hearings are almost never held by committees of the California legislature. Joint hearings on the budget bill and other measures would reduce the time spent by legislators in presenting bills or items before the committees, would be much more convenient for citizens desiring to be heard (several trips to Sacramento may be required if one testifies before the subcommittee and full committee in each house), and would save the time of department heads and other high-level agency personnel, the Legislative Analyst, and the Department of Finance. But joint hearings presumably would not save time for the appropriations committee members themselves and might even take more of their time, for the interests of the two committees differ and each might have to listen to the airing of questions which would not be raised in its own hearing. Joint hearings might also lead to better understanding between the two houses and reduce the number of conflicts to be resolved in conference, although it is unlikely that the need for a conference on the budget bill would be removed.

Although California legislators recognize some of the advantages of joint hearings, they doubt their feasibility. They fear personality conflicts, interhouse rivalries, and a breakdown of the check of the second house. They believe further that joint interim committees have been less successful than single-house committees. The combined membership would be too large and unwieldy, and the necessary changes in committee schedules would be difficult to arrange. The drastic reduction in the use of joint interim committees effected in 1959 suggests that the trend is away from formal arrangements for inter-house cooperation.

Reports

The appropriations committees do not prepare written reports explaining and justifying their recommendations regarding the budget bill or other appropriation bills. Prior to consideration of the budget bill on the floor, the Department of Finance prepares a list of changes made by the committee, showing in detail the amounts and positions added or deleted, but this document throws little light on the program effects of committee decisions and contains no explanation whatever of the reasons for them. Committee proceedings are not recorded verbatim—few records of any kind are kept—but even if a record of proceedings were available, few members would have time to study it. The legislator who is not a member of the appropriations committee must rely for information upon informal communication or floor discussion.

A brief report on the budget bill, summarizing the principal recommendations and reasoning of the appropriations committee would be useful to other members of the legislature and to the public. The value of such a report, however, must be weighed against the costs in time and effort of its preparation. The budget bill is usually sent to the floor shortly before adjournment. At that stage members have little time to prepare or read reports, for workload is near its peak. Much of the work of drafting a report and securing agreement could be performed by committee staff, and if sections were prepared as decisions were reached, the report would be largely completed by the time the budget bill was sent to the floor. Some members would make little use of it, but others would find it a useful guide to major budget issues.

In their reports to the full committee, subcommittees list the positions or other expenditure items recommended for deletion or addition; some reports include brief explanations. The reports are read to the full committee or made available in written form. In many cases, there is almost no explanation or discussion of the subcommittee report before it is approved by the full committee.

Inspection in the Field

The appropriations committees have made little attempt to supplement with observation in the field the information obtained through documents and hearings. Some members visit state institutions and installations on their own initiative or in the course of interim investigations undertaken by other committees, but organized inspections by the appropriations committees are rare. The committees have the benefit of the field observations of the Legislative Analyst, and departmental field personnel sometimes testify in budget hearings, but such second-hand information is not a substitute for personal inspection. Field trips are subject to abuse and can be singularly unenlightening if improperly planned, but the shrewd observer can learn much from them. If judiciously used, they would strengthen the committees' ability to make informed budget decisions.

Jurisdiction

The legislature has established an effective system to ensure that the appropriations committees review all bills which might result in substantial costs to the state. The committees must scrutinize not only bills that carry appropriations, but also those which would require substantial expenditures for implementation, either currently or in the future. This system is of fundamental importance, for it places upon a single committee in each house the responsibility for coordinating spending decisions and encourages consideration of the relative benefits to be derived from alternative uses of available resources. It helps to ensure that a realistic appraisal of present and future costs will be made, and it provides a safeguard against the bias of the policy committees, many of whose members naturally desire to expand programs and benefits in the fields of their own concerns.

Although sound in concept, the system presents problems in operation. The assembly rules require reference to the Ways and Means Committee of

any bill which would require the expenditure of additional state moneys in any manner, including any bill which creates any additional state agency or office, or adds any functions, duties, or responsibilities to an existing agency or office. . . .[9]

The Legislative Counsel, who has been given the task of examining all bills to determine whether they must be referred to Ways and Means under this rule, has interpreted the provision to mean that any bill which adds functions, duties or responsibilities must be so referred even if no additional expenditure would result. Hence, the committee is required to process many bills that entail only nominal costs or none at all. Although usually disposed of in a few minutes, such bills are numerous enough to increase substantially the committee's workload. From the standpoint of the author of a bill, the Ways and Means review is a nuisance because it delays the bill's progress, usually requires the author to spend time presenting it to the committee, and may result in the bill's being amended or even killed.

Formerly the senate rule was identical to that of the assembly, but in 1957 it was amended to require that only bills involving "substantial" costs need be referred to the Finance Committee.[10] While the change reduced the committee's workload, it retained a reasonable safeguard, although the criterion of "substantial" expenditure is open to interpretation. The chairman of the Finance Committee, with the aid of cost analyses prepared by the Legislative Analyst, examines bills to ensure that those carrying important costs do not escape committee scrutiny.

Attempts to amend the assembly rule have been unsuccessful. In 1957 the house defeated on a party-line vote a proposal which would have retained the requirement that bills creating agencies or offices be referred to Ways and Means, but would have eliminated the reference of bills merely adding functions or duties to existing agencies.[11] The proposal stemmed from dissatisfaction with some of the policy positions taken by the Ways and Means Committee.

Policy Determination by the Appropriations Committees

The implementation of the rules of both houses gives rise to questions concerning the proper role of the appropriations committees in reviewing measures approved by policy committees, whether they carry appropriations or merely imply additional cost. There is a general disposition to distinguish the financial aspects of bills from their substantive policy and to exclude the latter from the purview of the appropriations committees. The chairman of the Ways and Means Committee assured the house in 1955 that only the cost factors were considered in reviewing bills not containing express appropriations,[12] but the house seemed unconvinced, for it adopted a resolution instructing the committee to limit itself to the financial aspects of such bills.[13] In presenting bills before the appropriations committees, authors often say, a bit wistfully, that they assume the committee is interested only in the cost factors, and the committee members frequently remind each other that substantive policy should not be considered. Usually, such injunctions are unnecessary because the committee has no interest in the policy of many of the minor bills that come before it, but opponents of controversial bills often discuss policy, while supporters insist that it is improper to do so.

The appropriations committees do in fact make policy determinations which go beyond financial aspects of the legislation. In 1955 the Ways and Means Committee bottled up a fair employment practices bill, and the house took the unusual step of withdrawing it. The chairman of Ways and Means conceded that the committee had not limited itself to the financial aspects of the bill and supported the motion to withdraw.[14] In 1961 a minimum wage bill was amended by the committee to exclude farm workers.[15] At the same session the committee refused to approve, but subsequently reported in amended form, a bill to prevent discrimination in housing, the basic issue obviously being the policy rather than the cost of the measure.[16] The Senate Finance Committee made drastic changes in a fair employment practices bill in 1959,[17] made substantive changes in the 1954 measure to reform alcoholic beverage administration, and in 1961 killed a bill to require employers of farm workers to provide washing and toilet facilities in the field during harvesting of crops.[18]

There seems to be no solution to the problem of invasion of the policy field by the appropriations committees. A partial safeguard is the provision in the rules of both houses that a majority of the entire membership can withdraw a bill from committee. Although members dislike such a drastic remedy, they occasionally resort to it.[19] Amendments proposed by the appropriations committees can be rejected by the house, and occasionally it may be possible to amend into another bill the provisions of a measure killed in committee.[20]

Possible Changes in Procedure

The assembly could expedite consideration of those cost bills which do not carry appropriations. Referral to Ways and Means could be limited to those entailing costs greater than a specific amount; cost estimates could be provided by the Legislative Analyst, and if desired, by the Department of Finance.

The legislature of Wisconsin requires that, upon introduction, the title of every bill affecting revenue, making an appropriation, or increasing state costs must incorporate an estimate of the amount of money involved. If amendments change the fiscal effects of the proposal, the joint committee on finance may include a revised estimate in its report on the bill.[21] Under the Wisconsin procedure, the financial effects of a bill are readily apparent to all who read it and at every stage of its consideration (assuming that estimates are revised to reflect amendments). In California the financial effects of a bill are available on a systematic basis only to the financial committee (and two or three others who have asked the Legislative Analyst to provide estimates on all bills referred to them). Not until a bill has cleared the policy committee and has been referred to the appropriations committee does the Analyst prepare a cost estimate. Although the cost is likely to be discussed on the floor, there is no report or fiscal note accompanying the bill and stating its cost.

On the other hand, the Wisconsin procedure would result in some wasted effort if applied in California, for it would be necessary to estimate the effect of every cost bill introduced, including bills that would never be heard or would die in the policy committee. Moreover, if amendments were adopted in the policy committee, re-estimates for the appropriations committees would be required. Nevertheless, the Wisconsin procedure suggests two possible improvements that deserve consideration in California. (1) The Analyst might be requested to provide the policy committee with an estimate for any bill that is scheduled for hearing, and (2) Estimates might be transmitted with bills reported to the floor from the financial committees.

COMMITTEE REVIEW OF THE BUDGET

Participants

In addition to committee members, participants in committee review include representatives of the Department of Finance, the Legislative Analyst, and the department concerned. Lobbyists and citizens appear infrequently on budget items, more often on special appropriation or other cost bills. Legislators who are not committee members often appear in behalf of their bills and occasionally urge changes in budget bill items, usually augmentations. The Director of Finance attends the first meeting of the committee each year to outline the governor's policy and summarize important changes in the state's expenditure program. At subsequent hearings, the Department of Finance is represented by the chief of the Budget Division, an assistant director of the department, or, in some subcommittee hearings, by a senior budget analyst. Departments are represented by officers responsible for department-wide budgeting, and in many cases by the director of the department and the heads of component units. When controversial matters are under consideration, waiting witnesses and spectators often fill the hearing room to capacity.

Alternatives

Many members of the appropriations committees tend to perceive their role as judicial in character. They see themselves as judges, hearing the briefs of contending parties and ultimately deciding which side has the better of the argument. Hearings are adversary proceedings in which the Legislative Analyst is pitted against the Department of Finance and the administrative agency (joined sometimes by representatives of clientele groups). At times, however, Finance and the Analyst find themselves allied in opposition to augmentations sponsored by departments, legislators or interest groups. In general, the committees do not seek out controversies; like courts, they wait for disputes to be brought before them. Nor do the committees conceive it to be their responsibility to make a comprehensive review of the expenditure program; rather their task is to render decisions on specific controversies. In other words, the committees do not make a systematic search for courses of action alternative to those proposed in the budget.[22] Consequently, the extent to which they achieve the goal of rational decision-making depends upon the range and kinds of alternatives arising from controversies that come to their attention.

The leading supplier of alternatives is the Legislative Analyst, but legislators, departments, and interest groups also offer them, usually in the form of proposed augmentations to the amounts recommended by the governor. Departmental requests for augmentation are infrequent, and are more likely to come from independent agencies than from those under the governor's control. Interest groups occasionally make direct appeals to the committees, but more often their alternatives are reflected in the proposals of legislators. Although legislators supply hundreds of alternatives in the form of special appropriation bills, their proposals for changes in the budget bill are far fewer than those of the Analyst.

As explained above, the Analyst's alternatives almost always involve reductions in budgeted amounts for programs or resources for programs, and many deal with budgeted increases rather than with existing programs and levels of resources. A substantial proportion of the alternatives propose small reductions. Legislators, interest groups, and departments usually propose program augmentations or capital outlay projects. The result of reliance on these agencies for setting the agenda is that the committees have given insufficient attention to existing programs and levels of resources and, so far as the budget bill is concerned, have devoted much time to small items of expenditure.

Several factors help to explain the failure of the committees to make a wider search for alternatives. The legislature has institutionalized search processes in the office of the Legislative Analyst, and the committees tend to assume that if the Analyst finds no basis on which to recommend a reduction in a budget, they are not likely to be able to do so either. Just as the Analyst specializes in the search for budget-reducing alternatives, legislators specialize in producing—or relaying from departments and interest groups—budget-increasing alternatives in the form of special appropriation bills, as well as other measures that affect costs. The committees operate on the assumption that, if there is a need for additional expenditure, their attention will be drawn to it by these agencies.

Justification for scrutinizing proposed increases rather than existing levels of expenditure is based on the belief that the latter have been reviewed and approved by the legislature in the past and therefore may be presumed to be acceptable. Morever, there is no great incentive for seeking budget-reducing alternatives, for representations from interest groups almost always favor particular increases; the occasional proposals for budget reduction received from such groups as the Chamber of Commerce are couched in general terms. When the governor or the Analyst recommends curtailment of existing programs, the clientele groups concerned are likely to shower the committee with telegrams and letters and to appear at hearings to oppose the recommendations, whereas opinion is almost never mobilized in favor of specific cuts. The committees correctly perceive that, at least so long as the budget is kept in balance without additional taxes, the political advantages of additional expenditures outweigh those of budget cuts. Finally, the limitations of time and information under which committees operate preclude extensive search for alternatives. They do well if they can find the time to give due consideration to the alternatives that are thrust upon them.

These considerations suggest that it is unrealistic to expect the committees to extend greatly their search for alternatives. An unlimited legislative session, a general session every year, or a reduction in committee assignments would give the committees more time to engage in search. There are political obstacles to all of these changes, although it seems almost certain that annual general sessions will be adopted sooner or later.[23] The problem is not only one of time, however, but also of motivation and the committees' conception of their role. Given motivation, the committees could under existing conditions reduce the time devoted to minor items of expenditure in favor of more attention to existing and proposed programs.

Prerequisites for Change

Before such a change in emphasis can occur, certain conditions must be met. The committees must become convinced that "penny-grubbing" is relatively unrewarding as compared with program analysis. This view is difficult to accept because scrutiny of expenditure details is believed to be necessary to promote efficiency. Such scrutiny is unlikely to produce political repercussions, whereas program reductions often do. However, the volume and complexity of policy and program questions that arise as the state grows and the public sector expands, can be expected to push the committees willy-nilly toward greater emphasis on such questions. Second, the committees must recognize more fully than they do now that the existing programs need to be reviewed from time to time in the light of changed conditions. As new demands are made upon limited resources, the relative benefits of existing resource allocations need to be reexamined. Third, the perceived payoff for program curtailment needs to be greater if existing allocations among programs are to be scrutinized and altered. The exhaustion of the reserves built up during and after World War II resulted in a general tax increase in 1959. Nevertheless, pressure on available resources will be heavy for the foreseeable future, and further tax increases may be required. Consequently, there will be stronger motivation in the future than there was in the forties and fifties for serious reexamination of existing programs.

As partisan influences have become more important in the legislature, fiscal policy has emerged as one of the prime battlefields. In the context of narrowly balanced budgets and the threat of increased taxes, the parties may come to perceive political advantages in scrutinizing existing expenditure programs. They will, of course, face the same pressures to spend, but they can also reallocate resources with political profit, if they "correctly" judge that such reallocation, by avoiding increased taxes, will win more support than it loses. Unlike the committee members, individually or collectively, the parties can mobilize support for such a policy, thus helping to ensure that their judgment will be "correct."

Consideration of Consequences

A prime purpose of the committee hearings is to discover the consequences associated with the alternatives that find their way onto the agenda. Sources of information include the *Analysis,* the budget, oral testimony, and statements of the members of the committees. The departments do not submit to the committees written justifications for their budgets. In subcommittee hearings, an opening statement summarizing major features of an agency's budget is presented by the agency or, in many cases, by the Analyst. Representatives of the Department of Finance generally leave the defense of budgets to the agencies, although they step in from time to time to clarify questions and to help the agency out of a difficulty.

The practices of the appropriations committees impose limitations upon the ability of members to secure information about the consequences of alternatives. Members do not question witnesses in turn, but rather intervene whenever they desire, usually but not always, securing the recognition of the chairman in advance. Consequently, lines of questioning are interrupted, members jump from one subject to another, and searching examination of witnesses is infrequent. Too often, members break off their interrogation before they have obtained the information they seek, either because of a failure of communication or because of unresponsiveness of the witness. Sometimes the committees proceed to a vote even when the discussion of an issue is clearly inconclusive, preferring to risk an "incorrect" decision rather than to incur the costs of a further search for information. In some cases the Analyst and the representative of the Department of Finance are called upon by the chairman or a member directs a question to one of them; occasionally they volunteer their views, but at other times they are not heard from at all. In part, this flexible procedure reflects the fact that the outcome of some issues is determined before the committee meets; there is no need to waste time by hearing from the agencies. In part, it is a matter of tactics—the chairman does not want negative views on a bill that he wishes reported out of committee. And in part it is the result of a haphazard approach to the committee's task.

Where important interests are at stake, the committee may not be interested in information at all, because, as the chairman of Ways and Means stated on one occasion, "we all know what we are going to do with this." The committee members have all the technical and political information they need to know what position to take. Such was the case in 1954, when it was proposed that one-half of the revenues earmarked for fairs and expositions be diverted to the general fund. The hearing was scarcely underway before a motion was made to refer the proposal to a joint legislative committee for study, despite the fact that, as one member pointed out, the question had been studied "for years and years and years."[24] The motion passed after a brief discussion in which one member stressed the complexity of the problem, a second asserted that it would be a waste of time to have testimony, another expressed confidence that the numerous representatives of local fairs in the audience would be glad to go home without being heard, and a Sacramento assemblyman added that they could enjoy the beauties of Sacramento ("We're not going to give them anything, but we'll be glad to take anything they leave").

Usually, the committees make no attempt to examine exhaustively the facts involved in an issue, but rather by selective probing attempt to judge the soundness of the conclusions of facts presented by the interested parties. Sometimes the vigorous statement of a conclusion of fact is all the committee asks as the basis of its decision. For example, the Legislative Analyst contested a proposed position on the ground that improvements in procedures would render it unnecessary. After the chief of the Budget Division declared that it was justified on the basis of a well-recognized staffing formula and that he could not see how there could be any question about its justification, the committee approved it without delving into either the formula or the procedural changes which the Analyst thought would make it unnecessary. Failure to probe deeply is in part a reflection of the fact that the consequences of decision regarding small sums will not be of great importance one way or another.

Paradoxically, however, smaller expenditures sometimes receive a more thorough review than do large sums. Near the end of the 1961 session, the Ways and Means Committee added various items amounting to $7.5 million to the budget bill at the request of the Department of Finance after perhaps 30 minutes of consideration, despite the fact that, as the Legislative Analyst pointed out, the committee had labored throughout the session to produce cuts of only about $4 million. Parkinson's Law of Triviality works imperfectly—the time spent in deliberation is not always inversely proportional to the amount involved—but at times there is a serious disproportion between time spent and the amount at stake.[25]

Why are members willing to spend considerable time processing small expenditure items? Some committee members believe that it is necessary in order to prevent unjustified increases in personnel and other costs. Moreover, the issues involved are likely to be relatively easy to grasp, and even if they are complex, no great harm would result from an "incorrect" decision. Larger amounts are likely to involve imponderables and to be more far-reaching in their implications. An exhaustive examination of them would be impossible, and a more limited one would soon show sharply diminishing marginal returns in terms of more accurate predictions of consequences. In any case, political considerations may dictate a particular course on larger expenditures, making an examination of other consequences largely irrelevant.

By questioning witnesses, committee members regularly seek certain kinds of information, such as:

1. the basis for expenditure estimates. Members are particularly attentive to estimates which appear arbitrary on their face and are usually reluctant to approve appropriations that are not supported by a detailed plan of expenditure. For example, members of the Ways and Means Committee complained in 1954 that a $100,000 appropriation to establish a commission to study alcoholism was, in the words of one member, "putting out a gift" because there was no "line-item" justification of the amount.

2. the need for further expenditures. Committee members attempt to secure commitments that a proposed expenditure will accomplish the purpose for which it is undertaken. Such commitments are not always forthcoming, because administrators are understandably reluctant to foreclose future requests.

3. the source of financing. Members want to know from which fund an expenditure is to be made. If it comes from the general fund, the question is whether that fund can afford it. If it comes from a special fund, members want to be sure that the fund is not being "raided" for a purpose they disapprove. There is a definite tendency to apply less rigorous standards in judging the need for a special fund appropriation than in judging general fund requests. Members may remind each other that "it's all taxpayers' money," but not infrequently they succumb to the idea that the special fund "belongs" to the agency or interest group which benefits from it. Thus, an assemblyman stated in 1954 that "we're not going to save any money" by denying a request for an expenditure for the state fair because the money would come from the Fair and Exposition Fund and would in any case be used for some purpose relating to fairs. And a senator argued in the same year that, because the Highway Patrol is supported from a special fund derived from motor vehicle user revenues, it was entirely appropriate to take action to solve the problem of the patrol's communica-

tion system without regard to the effects on the operation of other departments.

4. identity of opponents and supporters. Members are interested in knowing who supports or opposes special appropriation bills and other measures that come before them. On many issues they know without being told, but they sometimes ask, "Who gave you this bill?" or "Who would benefit by this bill?" The positions of the governor, the Department of Finance, and the department concerned, as well as of interest groups, are often a matter of keen interest.

Strengths of the Review Process

For all of its limitations, the committee review process has important strengths. Members receive an "education" in administrative programs and problems through service on other committees and annual examination of the budget. They need not rely on hearings or documents to provide many of the facts that are helpful in judging the consequences of alternative courses of action. For example, in opposing augmentation of nursing services at hospitals for the mentally defective in 1954, the Legislative Analyst's representative pointed out that one of the hospitals had the highest ratio of staff to patients for personal care. Committee members quickly pointed out that (1) all of the inmates of that hospital were children and consequently could not render institutional services, whereas other hospitals benefitted from inmate help; and that (2) the ratio was misleading because the hospital was new and population had not yet reached maximum capacity. To some extent, members accept the judgment of colleagues who are known to be well-informed in particular fields, rather than attempting to obtain all of the facts for themselves. An outstanding example of a committee member who is an acknowledged authority is Senator Randolph Collier, chairman of the Committee on Transportation and co-author of the Burns-Collier highway financing act of 1947. In the 1954 hearing on the budget of the Highway Patrol, he took the lead in raising a number of questions regarding performance and problems:

1. What was the patrol doing to reduce the 18-months' delay in the completion of its statistical reports?

2. What had been the results of establishing "super-inspectors" and what was their relationship to responsible field officers?

3. Did the patrol have enough cars of the right quality?

4. What was being done regarding the unsatisfactory status of the patrol's communication system?

5. How much time was being spent on traffic accidents?

6. What was the role of the patrol in incorporated areas, and what was its relationship to local police?

7. How many uniformed men were being used for office work rather than in the field?

A second strength of the review process is that the committees give considerable attention to the performance and problems of agencies. Typically, this review is less searching and extensive than in the case of the Highway Patrol. Nevertheless, some department heads take the opportunity presented by the budget hearings to explain general objectives, specific features of the proposed budget, and problems faced by the department.

Moreover, the subcommittees give systematic attention to specific problems raised by the *Analysis of the Budget Bill,* and they often take action to implement suggestions and correct deficiencies discussed therein.

For example, in 1960 subcommittees recommended: (1) that the Department of Finance initiate a study of the organization of the Department of Natural Resources; (2) that the Department of Natural Resources provide information regarding its plans for forest and fire research, and that in the future the budget document indicate the history and results of research programs; (3) that the Department of Mental Hygiene report at the next legislative session the results of its safety program, after-care clinics, and convalescent leave program; (4) that the Legislative Analyst report the following year on deficiencies in the program of assistance to local mental health agencies; (5) that the university provide certain information requested by a subcommittee the year before; (6) that representatives of the Academic Senate of the university be requested to give testimony regarding the use of faculty time for research and classroom activities; (7) that the university submit data to support more fully its expenditures for out-of-state travel; (8) that the Board of Equalization report the following year regarding the criteria used in establishing, continuing, and discontinuing field offices; (9) that the board report on its use of "undercover" cars; (10) that the Department of Finance study the workload of the Division of Oil and Gas to ascertain the proper staffing formula; and (11) that a procedure for budgetary review of promotions in the Military Department be worked out jointly among the department, the Analyst and the Department of Finance. All of these recommendations arose from questions in the *Analysis,* and all involved study and reports.

Another technique is to criticize agencies for failure to comply with past directions from the committees and for deficiencies in their operations. Thus the Public Utilities Commission was severely criticized in 1960 for continuing to maintain a handwritten record that duplicated records on typewritten cards. In 1958 members criticized a "messy situation" in the state narcotics bureau's San Francisco office, one of whose agents had been convicted of giving heroin to an addict. The Department of Corrections came under attack in 1954 for having placed a condemned murderess in

San Quentin prison because of apprehension lest she be attacked by gang-land enemies if she remained in the women's prison at Corona. The Ways and Means Committee eliminated $16,000 from the agency's budget, the annual cost for the salaries of women guards required for custody of the prisoner. The Director of Corrections explained that the Corona facility was an open prison lacking guard towers, and it was feared that prison personnel and other inmates might be injured in an attack from outside the prison. After he had outlined in secret session the reasons why such an attack was feared, the committee reversed itself and allowed the funds.

A third strength of committee review is that members generally avoid arbitrary and precipitate action. Punitive budget cuts are rare, even when considerable provocation is offered.[28] When the committees are unsure of criticisms directed toward agencies, they often call for a study and report, before directing that particular changes be made or cutting the budget. Moreover, expenditures are sometimes made conditional upon further review and approval by the Department of Finance. Another device is to approve expenditures for personnel or other items for a limited period. Thus, a position may be allowed for one year, with the understanding that if it is proposed for continuation it will be shown as a new position and justified on that basis. New programs are often approved with the condition that a report of their accomplishments be made by a specified time.

CONCLUSIONS

The appropriations committees play a crucial role in determining the components of the expenditure program and its aggregate size. Empowered to review all legislation having substantial expenditure implications, they concern themselves with substantive policy in a significant number of cases. Their heavy workload limits their ability to review the budget in penetrating fashion, and it has been suggested that the Ways and Means Committee burden could be slightly lightened by not reviewing bills having only negligible costs. The disadvantages of public hearings and failure to employ joint hearings have been noted, but there is little prospect for change in these practices. On the other hand, there are no convincing reasons why the committees should not make brief reports to the house on the budget bill and special appropriation bills of major importance. The committees benefit by having many senior legislators among their members and by dividing work among subcommittees. Although the overlap of membership with policy committees enhances the expertise of the appropriations committees, it also reduces the time and attention their members can devote to financial legislation. Fewer committee assignments would give committee members more time for budget review, but such a reduction is unlikely; members believe that the prestige and influence resulting from service on several committees are essential to their political welfare.

An analysis of budget review by the appropriations committees reveals a number of devices and practices conducive to rational decision-making. In the office of the Legislative Analyst the legislature has institutionalized processes for discovering and analyzing alternatives to the governor's budget recommendations, as well as for investigating the consequences of the alternatives presented to committees. Although the alternatives presented by the Analyst generally seek to prevent or minimize increases in spending, other agencies propose expenditures over and above those sponsored by the governor.

Much useful information about the consequences of alternatives is available to the committees in the budget document, the *Analysis,* and the statements of witnesses and committee members. When the committees deem it necessary, they seek additional information about the basis for expenditure estimates, the need for future expenditures to accomplish given purposes, funds affected, and sources of opposition and support.

In analyzing consequences, members may draw upon information they have accumulated through budget review in previous years and through service on other committees. By giving considerable attention to the performance and problems of administrative agencies, the committees increase their store of information, and stimulate the development of future alternatives and additional information by their requests for studies and reports. Committee avoidance of arbitrary or hasty action indicates a disposition to base decisions upon an analysis of consequences.

The rationality of the committee review process could be enhanced by certain changes that appear to meet the test of feasibility. The committees could search for and consider a wider range of alternatives, rather than limiting themselves so closely to those offered by the Legislative Analyst and other sources. In particular, they might give more attention to existing programs and the allocation of resources among them. They might also analyze more thoroughly the performance of administrative agencies— their accomplishments, the problems they face, and the administrative improvements they have made. Such analysis is likely to be a fruitful source of additional relevant alternatives.

Rationality would be served by reducing the time and effort devoted to relatively small items of expenditure, in favor of more attention to program and to the methods of arriving at budget decisions within the administration. This is not to say that considering and deciding expenditure details is necessarily irrational. Understanding policy issues and maintaining control of policy sometimes require attention to detail.[27] But committee decisions on positions and equipment are often directed at questions of efficiency, rather than issues of policy. An analysis of the problem of the distribution of committee time and effort between questions of efficiency and questions of resource allocation is presented in Chapter XI. That analysis examines possibilities for controlling administrative efficiency by methods other than committee decisions on the budget.

Finally, rationality could be increased by the adoption of hearing procedures that would encourage more orderly consideration of the consequences of alternatives. In particular the committees might establish a definite order in which they would hear from the Legislative Analyst, the Budget Division and departmental representatives, and other witnesses. Members of the committee might also be given the floor in turn, so that each would have the opportunity to pursue lines of questioning without interruption.

[1] *Final Calendar of Legislative Business, 1959.* "Measures" includes bills, constitutional amendments, and all resolutions except house resolutions.

[2] When Republicans and anti-Olson Democrats took control of the assembly during the latter part of Governor Olson's administration, a bitter opponent of the governor, Seth Millington, was named chairman of Ways and Means. Robert E. Burke, *Olson's New Deal for California* (Berkeley and Los Angeles: University of California Press, 1953), pp. 68, 153.

[3] Interview, Senator Arthur H. Breed, Jr., November 27, 1957.

[4] George B. Galloway, *The Legislative Process in Congress* (New York: Thomas Y. Crowell Company, 1953), p. 128.

[5] Clarence Cannon, Chairman of the House Appropriations Committee, as quoted in the *San Francisco Chronicle,* January 19, 1958.

[6] In 1959 the governor recommended that a subsidy to counties to support certain services to veterans be discontinued. When the issue of restoring the funds came before the Ways and Means Committee, the chairman announced that there were not sufficient votes to prevent restoration of the funds. He refused to permit a roll call vote: "I'm not going to let this become a political football and have some of us made heroes and others goats." The appropriation was restored on a voice vote. *Sacramento Bee,* May 7, 1959, p. A 10.

[7] Taxpayers' Federation of Illinois, "Control of the Purse Strings—Part II: What Other States Are Doing" (Springfield: 1953), p. 25 (process).

[8] Joint Rule 3.

[9] Assembly Rule 64.

[10] Senate Rule 28.5.

[11] HR 18, *Assembly Journal,* March 11, 1957, p. 1341. Favoring the change were 29 Democrats and 3 Republicans; 38 Republicans and 4 Democrats opposed. For other proposals see HR 14 (1956 1st Ex. Sess.), p. 141 and HR 118 (1960 1st Ex. Sess.), p. 389.

[12] *Journal,* April 4, 1955, p. 2100.

[13] *Journal,* April 11, 1955, p. 2451.

[14] *Sacramento Bee,* May 11, 1955, p. 10. Hereafter referred to as *Bee.*

[15] *Bee,* May 25, 1961, p. C1.

[16] *Bee,* April 18, 1961, p. 1 and May 19, 1961, p. 1.

[17] *San Francisco Chronicle,* April 3, 1959, p. 1. Hereafter referred to as *Chronicle.*

[18] *Bee,* June 1, 1961, p. A20.

[19] Of eight contested efforts to withdraw bills from assembly committees in 1959, three were successful.

[20] This was done in 1955, for example, in the case of a bill that had received the unanimous approval of the Fish and Game Committee but had been killed by the Finance Committee. *Bee,* June 7, 1955, p. 14.

[21] M. G. Toepel, "Putting a Price Tag on Legislation," *State Government,* XXXI (May, 1958), 88–91.

[22] The search for alternatives and the search to discover consequences of alternatives are treated by James G. March, Herbert A. Simon, and Harold Guetzkow, *Organizations* (New York: John Wiley and Sons, Inc., 1958), pp. 140–2, 178–80.

[23] See note 3, Chapter II, above.

[24] *Chronicle,* March 12, 1954.

[25] C. Northcote Parkinson, *Parkinson's Law* (Boston: Houghton-Mifflin Company, 1957), p. 24.

[26] According to informed legislators, a slash in the budget of the State Disaster Office in 1959 was the result of failure by the head of the agency to consult legislators on appointments.

[27] Cf. Robert Ash Wallace, *Congressional Control of Federal Spending* (Detroit: Wayne State University Press, 1960), pp. 12–17.

Chapter VIII

HOUSE DELIBERATION ON THE BUDGET

Most decisions regarding the composition of the expenditure program are taken in committee and are ratified by the house without review. By the action of party agencies, individual legislators, regional blocs, or interest groups, a few issues are selected for consideration by the house. In general, these issues are more controversial and have greater political implications than the vast majority of those aired in committee. The analysis of the consequences of alternatives is usually more searching in committee than on the floor of the house.

The following sections examine the procedural framework within which house deliberation takes place, the structure and function of the conference committee, and the nature of debate.

The Legislature's Floor Procedure

The assembly usually acts upon the budget bill earlier than the senate. The senate frequently adopts amendments unacceptable to the assembly, and one or more conference committees are named to iron out the differences. In each house the budget bill is considered under a special order requested or moved by the chairman of the appropriations committee. The special order simply establishes the time at which the budget bill will be taken up; it does not place special limitations upon amendments or debate. The purpose of the special order is to avoid the delay which might result if the budget bill awaited its turn on the calendar, to put everyone on notice as to the time for its consideration, and to schedule it at a convenient hour.

The committee of the whole is a device that permits non-members to give testimony or be questioned, and provides greater informality and wider latitude in debate than prevails under ordinary procedure.[1] In the past, both houses made use of the committee of the whole for consideration of the budget bill—the Legislative Analyst and the directors of several departments were heard in committee of the whole in 1945[2]—but this device has not been employed in recent years. Under present procedure the Legislative Analyst and the Director of Finance (or his representative) sit beside and advise the appropriations committee chairman during consideration of the budget bill, but they may not speak except through the chairman.

The senate permits a member to speak as long as he wishes, although he may not speak more than twice at the same stage of a bill without leave.[3] Assemblymen may speak only once for five minutes on any one question on the same day and at the same stage of the proceeding, except that the author of a bill or the mover of a question has 10 minutes to open and five minutes to close debate.[4] Members are often granted extra time to speak, and it does not appear that the time restrictions impair the quality of debate on the budget bill. Members desiring to speak on a question request a place on the list maintained by the speaker, who arranges to have someone on the list move the previous question, when, in the speaker's judgment, the question has received sufficient discussion. Frequently, a motion for the previous question is unnecessary because few members wish to be heard. In both houses a majority of the members present may cut off debate.

CONFERENCE COMMITTEES

In the period 1937–61, there were only five occasions (all prior to 1949) when it was not necessary to appoint a conference committee on the budget bill. Two conference committees were required in 1941 and in 1953. In 1958, six committees were necessary to break a deadlock on the appropriation of construction funds for water development, in the absence of a constitutional amendment clarifying water rights. In the budget session, the report of the third committee on the budget bill was rejected only a few minutes before the expiration of the 30 days permitted by the constitution. The governor called an extraordinary session, and three more conference committees were required before agreement was finally reached.

Conference committees consist of six members, three appointed by the assembly speaker and three appointed by the Senate Rules committee. Two members from each house must have voted with the majority on the bill, the third with the minority.[5] By advance arrangement, one of the members slated to serve on the committee votes against the budget, not because he opposes the bill, but in order to make himself eligible for appointment to the conference committee. Appointments are made in consultation with the chairman of the appropriations committee. Conferees are almost always members of the appropriations committee, and at least two (rarely, all three) from each house are members of the majority party.

A conference committee has unrestricted authority to recommend; it may include provisions rejected by both houses, delete those approved by both, or add entirely new ones. By contrast, Congress prohibits conference consideration of matters not in dispute, although conferees sometimes violate the rule.[6] In 1956 the California senate adopted a resolution to prohibit conferees from adding appropriation items to the budget bill and to restrict their authority to increase items, but the proposal died in the assembly.[7] Items not approved by either house are seldom placed in the budget bill in conference, but items approved by both houses are occasionally eliminated if the conferees consider them to be unjustified.

Conference committees deliberate in private, although they sometimes hear legislators, officials, or even private persons regarding issues in dispute or proposals for adding new items. The only formal report made by the committee on conference is a lengthy list of recommended amendments to the budget bill. The Legislative Analyst prepares a written summary of the committee's actions which is distributed to the members of the house, and the conference committee chairman explains the conference report and answers questions on the floor.[8]

A conference report must be approved by two committee members from each house and is not subject to amendment. If agreement cannot be reached or if either chamber refuses to adopt the report, a new committee may be appointed, but no more than three committees are permitted on a single bill.[9]

HOUSE CONSIDERATION OF THE BUDGET

House consideration of the budget bill begins with a brief statement, perhaps five minutes in length, by the chairman of the appropriations committee, who indicates the principal changes made by the committee, the size of the total expenditure program, and the resulting condition of the general fund. He urges the house to accept the committee recommendations and, in the senate, usually suggests that any members who have amendments to propose should present them to the conference committee. The Ways and Means chairman reminded his colleagues in 1959 that the budget bill was not the entire "spending package" and that chances of passing any special appropriation bills would be diminished if the house augmented the appropriations recommended by the committee. In 1958 he stressed that almost all of the members of the Ways and Means Committee were senior legislators, that the budget bill had the approval of all but two, and that every dollar taken out on the floor would reduce the taxpayer's burden, while every dollar added would increase it.

Amendments

More often than not the senate complies with the request of the Finance Committee chairman that the budget bill not be amended on the floor; sometimes amendments are not even proposed. When no amendments are offered, the budget bill is disposed of very quickly; it passed in less than 10 minutes in 1960, without a word of debate.[10] In 1954 the chairman of the Finance Committee noted that there was one proposed amendment—to restore funds cut from the Recreation Commission budget—and offered "reluctantly" to ask that the restoration be made by the conference committee if the author would withdraw the amendment. The author graciously consented, remarking that 24 senators had agreed to support the amendment and that the chairman would therefore enjoy "a strong position" in pressing the amendment in the conference committee. It is considered good form in the senate for the author of an amendment to pass the word in advance if he has the votes to get it adopted, in order that his colleagues may be spared from casting politically inexpedient votes that will be futile because they fall on the losing side. In recent years the only sizable sums added on the senate floor were for armories ($2.5 million in 1952) and for pay increases ($4 million in 1956 and $18.4 million in 1958). It is noteworthy that each of these augmentations occurred in an election year. The author of the 1958 pay increase amendment noted that "There are a lot of State Employees," and the chairman of the Finance Committee explained: "A panic hit the Senators. The fellows are running for reelection."[11]

Floor amendments are offered every year in the assembly and usually some are adopted. A trend toward greater partisanship, which began in the 1950's, received new impetus after the Democrats took control of the governorship in 1959. The Democratic majority crushed all efforts in 1959 and 1961 to change the budget bill on the floor. In 1960, however, many Democrats voted with Republicans to amend $17 million in pay increases into the budget bill, much to the dismay of the Ways and Means chairman and the governor.

Various types of amendments are offered. In some years, they are designed to reduce the aggregate size of the budget. Proposals to increase capital outlay expenditures for armories, parks, and institutional facilities and to provide pay increases for state employees have been offered on a number of occasions. Until reserve funds were exhausted at the end of the 1950's, a recurring issue was whether and to what extent to use reserves. Some amendments propose to allow (or cut out) particular projects or programs eliminated (or added) by the appropriations committee. Across-the-board percentage cuts and unallocated reductions are rarely proposed.

Debate in the Assembly

Because there is usually little or no debate on the budget bill in the senate, most of the following discussion is applicable only to debate in the lower house. The chairman of the Ways and Means Committee plays the leading role in debate. He is recognized to speak on each amendment, and he resists all efforts to change the committee version of the bill, whether to increase or decrease. Members of Ways and Means are often especially active in proposing amendments and in debate, but other members of the house also participate freely.

Debatable questions include amendments, passage to the other house, concurrence in amendments of the other house, and adoption of the report of the conference committee. Serious and extensive debate usually occurs only at the amendment stage. In recent years it has been assumed that there will be a conference committee on the budget bill, and refusal to concur in the amendments of the other house has usually been routine. Conference reports have been the occasion for intensive debate on some occasions, notably in 1958, when many hours were devoted to consideration of a series of six conference reports. The debate on final passage is usually not intensive or extended because it takes place only after all proposed amendments have been considered. Because all specific proposals for change have been settled one way or the other, and the money to operate the state must be provided, passage of the bill is usually not an issue.

However, the requirement that the bill pass by a two-thirds majority of the membership[12] permits a minority to block passage even though it cannot muster the necessary majorities to secure adoption of the amendments it desires. Such a situation arose in the assembly in 1962 when the Republican minority was unable to prevail on its amendments, and the Democrats were unable to muster a two-thirds majority. Normally, however, final passage is an occasion for registering dissatisfactions and justifying one's vote rather than for discussing alternative action. Members are likely to say that the bill contains questionable expenditures or omits desirable ones, or that the total expenditure program is too high, but that it is probably as good a bill as can secure approval. Rarely, the amount of expenditure in a member's district may be cited as a reason for supporting the budget.

In the debate upon proposed amendments, the merits of particular expenditures are the center of attention, but the effect of the amendment on total expenditures is also considered. Although it is usually pointed out that the budget bill contains only one-third of the total expenditure program, members recognize that the most significant expenditure figure is the total provided by both the budget bill and continuing appropriations. In general session years members do not know precisely how much spending will be authorized in special appropriation bills after enactment of the budget bill, but they are aware of any major spending proposals that have good prospects for passage.

There is little effective discussion of the distribution of appropriations among major functions and agencies, although members sometimes state that one expenditure is more meritorious than another. Two factors discourage significant deliberation directed to finding the optimum allocation of resources. Members may be committed to party positions, to the governor's program, or to the idea that committees should not be overridden. But the fundamental difficulty lies deeper. At bottom, the question of optimum allocation deals with values, such as safety, health, economic progress, and education. Because it is highly unlikely that members can agree on the relative importance of these and other values, there is little prospect of establishing a common basis for judging whether the allocation of resources reflected in the budget bill approaches the optimum or not.

Rather than addressing themselves to overall resource allocation, members talk in terms of the need or justification for an expenditure considered as an isolated issue: How much increase is being allowed this year, and what increases have been made in the past? How efficient is the agency? Is the agency doing a "good job"? Have expenditures been increasing more rapidly than workload? Is the program "desirable" but not "essential"?

The content of debate is determined by the issues that are considered relevant. The members have little interest in a general discussion of broad policy issues, such as the aggregate size of the budget, the sources of its financing, and the adequacy of its provision for the long-range needs of the state, unless specific proposals are offered relative to such issues. But even when such general policy issues are raised, the debate tends to be brief and superficial. The assembly debate on the 1954 budget bill provides an instructive case study. Governor Knight's budget for 1954–55 provided for a lower percentage increase in state operations than almost any other since the executive budget was adopted in 1922. Capital outlay expenditures, except for highways, were drastically reduced from the 1953–54 level and for most functions were below that of 1952–53:[13]

Function	Percentage Decrease from 1953–54
Corrections	64%
Education	59
Fiscal Affairs	44
Mental Hygiene	66
Natural Resources	41
All other (except highways)	54

Yet, it was known that future population growth would require extensive additions to state mental institutions, prisons, state colleges, the University of California, and other facilities. For example, the Department of Finance estimated that there would be an increase of 31,000 (about 100 percent) in state college enrollment in the following ten years.[14] Despite the governor's stringent expenditure policy, a current general fund deficit of $76 million was anticipated, and the budget was proposed to be financed from surplus and from reserves earmarked for other purposes. Furthermore, the budget was presented in the midst of an economic recession. In the senate there was no discussion of these policy questions during floor consideration of the budget bill. An oblique attack on the governor's policy was made by the assembly Democrats, who caucused and agreed to propose amendments to (1) augment capital outlay by some $14 million, mainly for state colleges, and (2) oppose use of the school bond retirement fund to balance the budget, preferring to dip into the "rainy day" fund or the $9 million that had been earmarked for purchase of the Central Valley Project.

Although a limited amount of information concerning the extent of future needs for capital outlay was offered in debate, and the assembly approved most of the capital projects sponsored by the minority, the governor's capital outlay policy did not receive thorough, systematic consideration. The possibility of raising taxes to avoid using reserves or to finance a higher level of expenditures was scarcely mentioned, and the relationship of the budget to the economic situation received only passing notice by two members. Nor was there consideration of the possible alternative of dipping more deeply into reserves to finance a larger expenditure program. The only issue that evoked anything approaching an adequate discussion was the question of which reserves should be used to balance the budget.

Why did the other important questions implicit in the governor's policy receive so little consideration? It may be assumed that the members considered them largely irrelevant. The alternative of increasing taxes in an election year to support a higher level of expenditures was so undesirable that it did not deserve consideration, even though the governor's policy might be short-sighted. It was assumed that no disastrous consequences would result, or at least that serious adverse consequences would be experienced at a later time, whereas political repercussions of increased taxes would be felt in the next few months. Failure to consider using more reserves to finance a larger capital outlay program rested in part on the hope, specifically expressed by the chairman of the Senate Finance Committee, that tax increases could be avoided for two or three years, if remaining reserves were husbanded for future budget balancing. There was no point in decrying the governor's policy if no one was prepared to offer basic alternatives—and no one was.

Limitations on the Quality of Debate

The ability of the house to have a reasoned, objective, well-informed discussion of budget issues is limited by several factors. On many issues, most members know how they will vote before any discussion takes place. Party commitments, identification with particular group or sectional interests, attitudes toward state expenditure generally, or preexisting knowledge of the merits of the issue—one or several of these may predetermine a member's position. There is little incentive to demand or provide a thorough discussion of the issues if most minds are assumed to be made up— and the generalization that debate seldom changes many votes is frequently heard in Sacramento.

Some contributions to debate aim neither to persuade nor to inform other members. They seek rather to place a member on record and to communicate with the voters in the district or with members of interest groups.

Some issues are complex and difficult to manage. A good example is the question of salary levels for the faculties of the university and state colleges, discussed in the assembly in 1958, 1959, and 1960. In each case, the debate was unsatisfactory because (1) there was disagreement regarding the criteria which should determine salary levels; (2) dubious statistics were cited comparing salaries at California institutions with those elsewhere and in private industry; (3) attempts were made to demonstrate general propositions by citing particular cases; (4) specific and convincing evidence of alleged recruitment difficulties was lacking; and (5) inconclusive arguments were offered regarding the effect upon private colleges of salary levels at public institutions. The issue is of interest to large numbers of voters, of course, and the effect of alternatives upon the results of the next election was uppermost in the minds of many members. But even if political considerations had been put aside, adequate analysis of other consequences would have been extremely difficult.

Finally, whereas the primary aim in committee is to secure information and develop understanding of issues, the predominant objective in floor deliberation is to persuade. Most contributions to debate aim to gain support rather than to analyze problems or communicate information impartially; arguments are liberally sprinkled with emotionally-toned words and phrases, "red herrings," and irrelevancies. For example, in 1961 assembly proponents of budget reduction used such phrases as "empire building," "ever-expanding bureaucracy," "grown like Topsy," and "Parkinson's Law at work"; the opposition urged rejection of these "butcher knife," "meat axe," or "fly-specking" amendments.

A clinching argument for a proposed reduction of $335,000 in an agency budget was the statement that the budget reestablished a position of information officer which had been abolished by legislative action in 1955. A proposal by a Republican assemblyman to "cut out some brass" by eliminating a brigadier general position from the Military Department was opposed by the Democratic chairman of the Ways and Means Committee. One of his arguments was that no Republicans and only one Democrat had supported a proposal in committee to save over $200,000 annually by eliminating 30 days' military leave pay received by state employees performing military service. Another dubious argument was that an amendment to hold the budget for the governor's office to the level of the prior year "transgresses the division of authority under our Constitution."

Values of Floor Debate

In spite of its limitations, debate does serve the important function of informing members about the judgments of respected colleagues or of other officials presumed to be authoritative. Numerous appeals are made to the authority of the appropriations committee, the governor, the Department of Finance, and the Legislative Analyst. Amendments that have been refused adoption in committee are resisted on the ground that they have been thoroughly considered at the committee stage. An appeal to the authority of the Legislative Analyst formed the basis of a series of reductions proposed on the assembly floor in 1961 and in 1962. The author of the 1961 amendments not only cited pages in the *Analysis of the Budget Bill* where the Analyst had recommended the proposed cuts, but also referred to the "well-reasoned arguments" of "our very competent Legislative Analyst," and insisted that "we can rely on his conclusions in this respect." He suggested that perhaps the opposition of the chairman of the Ways and Means Committee to the amendments indicated a belief that the office of the Legislative Analyst should be eliminated, and concluded that, unless the Analyst's recommendations received more acceptance, the office probably should be abolished. The chairman acknowledged the authority of the Analyst as a financial expert and noted that recommendations of the Analyst amounting to $6 million had been accepted by the committee, but declared that he is "not always right."[15]

While appeal to authority is not altogether satisfactory as a basis for making rational decisions, especially when authorities are in disagreement, legislators inevitably rely heavily upon each other, committees, and other agencies thought to be worthy of confidence. Consideration of the views of authorities enhances rationality if members properly evaluate the special viewpoints and the past performance of authorities.

The key to understanding floor deliberation lies in the political character of the consideration of the budget at this stage. Personal or party fortune at the next election becomes a critical factor in decision. Whether a party or a bloc seeks to make a record for economy, or an individual seeks a project for the district, or the supporters of the governor try to uphold his budget policies, political advantage is implicit in almost every sentence spoken and every vote taken. Ostensibly, there is an effort to carry on a reasoned discourse, but political consequences are so heavily weighted that there is little interest in searching, objective examination of other important consequences of alternatives. To make a record, to discover the alignment of forces, to decide—these are the aims, and their realization does not require a great deal of time nor extensive discussion.

Consequences of the Deliberative Style

One of the consequences of the style of house deliberation on the budget is that the potential value of legislative debate for informing and shaping the opinions of interested publics is not fully realized. It must be added that the absence of a verbatim record and the failure of the press to report debates in any depth severely limit the possibility of significant communication to those publics, although an optimist might hope that more effective debate would encourage better reporting and perhaps even persuade the legislature that a more complete record of its proceedings would be worth keeping. A second result is that long-run consequences of budgetary decisions are given little explicit consideration and are greatly discounted. A third consequence is that the legislature neglects an opportunity to create more favorable public attitudes toward itself and to strengthen its position vis-à-vis the executive. Insofar as the legislature fails to perform its function of raising, clarifying, and deciding the most important issues of public policy, the influence of the executive and the bureaucracy in shaping policy is enhanced. Individuals will judge the desirability of these consequences in the light of their own preferences, but legislators, as well as interested publics that evaluate legislative actions, should be aware of these consequences if they wish to realize their own objectives.

CONCLUSIONS

House debate on the budget bill focuses on specific proposals offered as amendments. Normally few amendments are offered in the senate, and consequently there is little debate.

In the assembly, there is scant discussion of broad policy issues relating to the budget, unless they are the subject of specific proposals. Perhaps because the value questions that underlie allocation problems are so difficult to handle, there is little effective discussion of the distribution of appropriations among major functions and agencies.

Estimates of political consequences shape house deliberation. Members recognize that what is done and said may influence personal and party prospects for electoral success. They also know that their votes may affect their relationships with party or house leaders, with the governor, and with interest groups. Such political considerations influence the selection of alternatives and the manner in which consequences are discussed. Certain factors limiting the assembly's capacity for well-informed, reasoned discussions of budget issues are directly related to the political character of deliberation: minds may be made up in advance; interventions may be intended to place the member on record rather than to inform or persuade; and canons of logical discussion are often violated in the effort to win support or justify positions. Another obstacle to rational decision-making is the complex character of some issues confronting the house.

The style of deliberation has three important consequences: (1) opportunities to shape and inform the opinions of interested publics are not fully exploited; (2) long-run consequences tend to be neglected; and (3) the legislature's role in the determination of public policy is diminished.

Change in the character of house deliberation depends largely on recognizing the interests of the legislature as an institution in sharing fully in the shaping of opinion and policy. Potentially, the parties are an important source of change in the character of deliberation. They can become powerful instruments for identifying alternatives, forcing attention, examining consequences, and mobilizing support for those preferred. In particular, the party that does not control the governor's office will normally have an interest in examining critically the governor's policies and searching for alternatives. To be sure, there is no certainty that alternatives will be proposed and discussed in responsible fashion, but the irresponsibility of one party is an invitation to a rational defense of its policy by the other. Thus far, however, the parties have developed little in the way of bureaucratic support for their efforts. The identification and responsible analysis of alternatives and consequences require staff assistance on a partisan basis. This need is greater in the case of the party not in control of the executive, for the governor and his supporters have extensive resources in the administration itself. The plight of the party out of power is suggested by the fact that its attempts to reduce the budget bill in 1961 and 1962 were based almost entirely upon recommendations of the Legislative Analyst. It lacked resources of its own for developing and exploiting issues intelligently. Although the parties can obtain significant aid from the Analyst in the form of information and suggestions for budget cuts, the Analyst is restricted by the necessity to maintain a position of neutrality between the parties.

The parties need assistants who, under the supervision of party leadership, can map campaigns, mobilize support, evaluate alternatives from a partisan standpoint, and work closely and continuously with the leadership.

In the assembly there is a tradition of party organization and action, although both parties have been plagued by disunity until very recently. There remains a need for clarification of leadership roles. Historically, the majority floor leader has been the de facto representative of the speaker, his role being that of making motions and otherwise aiding in the processing of the business of the house. He has not been recognized as the leader of the majority party. The position of minority leader is somewhat more clearly defined, although the leadership has been divided between the caucus chairman and the floor leader since the Republicans became the minority in 1959. Both parties have made extensive use of the caucus in recent years.

Although partisan considerations play a role in senate voting and the election of the president pro tempore, there is no party organization. The senate is characterized by a club-like atmosphere and a strong sense of institutional loyalty. It has a distaste for fighting its battles on the floor, preferring maneuvering behind the scenes. Senators feel decidedly superior to the assembly, which they sometimes refer to as the "Cave of Winds," and which they consider to be unpredictable and slightly undignified. Attempts of the "corner office"—the governor's office—to exercise influence are received coolly, for the senate is determined to maintain its prestige and independence of gubernatorial control. These characteristics are not auspicious for the development of party organization in the upper chamber. There are, however, some younger senators who are less than fully committed to the senate style, who cautiously recognize the claims of party to the extent that prevailing sentiment permits, and who may in time find ways to establish effective party roles. In the meantime, budgetary decisions will be left mainly to the Finance Committee, whose membership includes a number of the most influential senators.

[1] Arthur A. Ohnimus, *The Legislature of California* (Assembly, 1962), p. 82.

[2] *Bee,* May 11, 1945, p. 1 and May 12, 1945, p. 1.

[3] Senate Rule 35.

[4] Assembly Rule 116.

[5] Joint Rule 28.

[6] George B. Galloway, *The Legislative Process in Congress* (New York: Thomas Y. Crowell Co., 1953), pp. 316–24.

[7] SCR 7 (1956). ACR 6 (1958 2nd Ex. Sess.) was a similar proposal.

[8] A brief explanation of the conference report was printed in the *Senate Journal,* March 26, 1960, pp. 357–62.

[9] Joint Rule 29.

[10] *Berkeley Daily Gazette,* March 25, 1960, p. 1.

[11] Quoted in the *Chronicle,* March 26, 1958, p. 8.

[12] *Cal. Const.,* Art. IV, sec. 34a.

[13] *Budget,* 1954–55, p. A-40.

[14] *Analysis,* 1954–55, p. 186.

[15] In both 1961 and 1962 all of the proposed reductions were refused adoption on votes that largely followed party lines.

Chapter IX

DETERMINATION OF THE AGGREGATES

The manner in which a budget system provides for determination of the level of total spending and total revenue, and the resulting relationship between these aggregates, are of fundamental importance. The traditional commitment to balanced budgets, the economic effects of taxing and spending, and the intensity of attitudes concerning questions of taxation make the level of aggregates and their relationship an overriding political issue. The limited capacity of states to influence the level of economic activity tends to remove the question of compensatory fiscal policy from serious consideration in decisions on aggregates; however, the alleged discouragement of enterprise by taxation figures prominently in discussion of the level and kind of taxation and, hence, of the level of expenditure. The belief in the desirability of the balanced budget, often reinforced as in California by constitutional limitations upon the creation of debt, is more influential in state and local than in national fiscal policy.

DIFFUSION OF RESPONSIBILITY

Whatever one's attitudes about the proper scope of governmental activity, the appropriate level of expenditures, or the merits of deficit financing, it is clear that the budget system should encourage policy-makers to decide issues regarding aggregates in a methodical deliberate fashion rather than a haphazard one. Previous chapters have shown that an elaborate system exists for reaching decisions on the components of the expenditure program. The argument of this chapter is that responsibility for the making of decisions regarding aggregates is diffused. Certain proposals for procedural or organizational reform are considered, but it is concluded that they fail to meet the test of feasibility. Rather, it is argued, the aim should be to provide the various decision-making centers with more information about long-run consequences of decisions on aggregates and to increase the ability of the legislature to adjust aggregates annually. In order to provide a basis for discussion of reform and to indicate the nature of the process of determining aggregates, attention is directed to the extent to which the legislature accepts the governor's recommendations concerning total expenditures, to the use of the veto power, and to the recent history of the process of reaching decisions on basic budget policy.

THE AGGREGATE EXPENDITURE PROGRAM

The legislature makes hundreds of changes, both increases and decreases, in the details of the expenditure program each year, but the level of total authorized expenditure is usually about the same as the governor proposes. In nine of the 17 fiscal periods shown in Table 11 the net change was less than 2 percent and, except for the war and immediate postwar period, it was as high as 5 percent in only one year (column 8). The legislature increased the total expenditure program in every case save two. One exception (1960) involved a reduction so small as to be negligible; the other (1948) occurred only because of vetoes by the governor and the replacement of a budget bill appropriation by a deficiency appropriation in order to make funds available in the current fiscal year. The governor often recommends expenditures above the amounts included in the budget. Thus, of the $96 million in special appropriations enacted in 1957, $51 million were requested by the governor.[1] He also recommends augmentations to the budget bill, usually a few million dollars at most, but occasionally more. Nearly all of the $37 million increase in the 1959 budget bill was recommended by the governor.[2]

The impact of the legislature on the expenditure program is not fully revealed by the percentage changes made in the total expenditure program, two-thirds of which is made up of continuing appropriations. A better indicator of the legislature's influence is the extent to which it changes budget bill appropriations. It is noteworthy that there have been several years in which changes in the budget bill did not exceed one percent (Table 11, column 5), and nearly half of the largest percentage change (10 percent in 1953) resulted from the provision of funds in separate appropriation bills instead of the budget bill. Almost without exception, the reductions in the budget bill made by the legislature are more than offset by special appropriations. Thus, although the change in the composition of the expenditure program resulting from legislative increases and decreases is substantial, the total program is usually close to the amount proposed by the governor.

The aggregate expenditure program is the result of a series of decisions by the governor, the policy committees, the appropriations committees,

TABLE 11

LEGISLATIVE CHANGES IN BUDGETED EXPENDITURES, 1943–45 TO 1961–62

Fiscal Period (1)	Expenditures Proposed By Governor		Net Legislative Changes in Budget Act[a]		Special Appropriations Enacted[a] (6)	Net Changes in Total Expenditure Program (Col. 4 + Col. 6)	
	Total (2)	From Budget Act Appropriations (3)	Amount (4)	Percent (5)		Amount (7)	Percent (8)
1943–45	$ 463,947,005	$157,803,176	−$13,835,766	− 8.8%	$101,584,458	+$ 87,748,692	+18.9%
1945–47	683,710,643	202,003,999	+ 11,984,824	+ 5.9	48,026,248	+ 59,011,072	+ 8.6
1947–48	641,599,026	381,360,134	+ 3,651,565	+ 1.0	126,245,372	+ 129,896,937	+20.2
1948–49	919,943,287	265,024,801	b	b	b	− 16,682,277[b]	− 1.8
1949–50	1,060,187,939	414,746,140	− 24,257,746	− 5.8	43,098,595	+ 18,840,849	+ 1.8
1950–51	971,615,944	310,018,014	+ 1,881,606	+ 0.6	4,674,725	+ 6,556,331	+ 0.7
1951–52	1,016,883,002	335,640,448	+ 7,349,416	+ 2.2	22,950,690	+ 30,300,106	+ 3.0
1952–53	1,185,397,270	433,046,918	+ 3,531,348	+ 0.8	11,069,000	+ 14,600,348	+ 1.2
1953–54	1,326,851,805	451,165,608	− 46,239,335	−10.2	113,087,934	+ 66,848,599	+ 5.0
1954–55	1,423,345,648	400,200,504	+ 8,487,260	+ 2.1	100,000	+ 8,587,260	+ 0.6
1955–56	1,529,768,426	474,378,668	− 423,052	− 0.1	21,229,142	+ 20,806,090	+ 1.4
1956–57	1,736,112,983	567,948,253	+ 42,893,517	+ 7.6	30,430,224	+ 73,323,741	+ 4.2
1957–58	1,947,964,993	696,841,119	− 33,482,333	− 4.8	96,365,372	+ 62,883,039	+ 3.2
1958–59	1,984,476,603	628,854,249	+ 15,346,380	+ 2.4	1,280,665	+ 16,627,045	+ 0.8
1959–60	2,188,377,635	724,062,092	+ 36,567,291	+ 5.1	23,418,321	+ 59,985,612[c]	+ 2.7
1960–61	2,476,176,827	913,457,058	− 944,747	− 0.1	642,310	− 302,437	d
1961–62	2,492,364,068	772,311,195	+ 2,900,963	+ 0.4	2,352,912	+ 5,253,875	+ 0.2

Sources: *Analysis of the Budget Bill, 1948–49*, p. 8; *The Tax Digest*; Department of Finance, *List of Legislative Changes . . . Final Report* and "Summary of Financial Legislation . . .".

a Net appropriations after reductions by governor's veto.

b Changes in the 1948–49 budget:

Net increases by legislature.............	+ $32,335,249
Reductions in budget bill by governor's veto......	− 11,432,500
Budget bill appropriation replaced by deficiency appropriation......	− 30,000,000
Other net decreases in budget...........	− 7,585,026
Net Change...............	− $16,682,277

c Revised estimates, carryover appropriations, and fund transfers resulted in further augmentation of authorized expenditures by $47,912,717.

d Less than one-fiftieth of one percent.

and the legislature as a whole. It is the appropriations committees that take the lead in the legislature to ensure that the aggregate expenditure program is consistent with available resources. When funds are short, the committees can be ruthless in killing appropriation bills, even those providing for expenditures that are conceded to be desirable. It must be added that committee members are sometimes generous with colleagues requesting projects for their districts, even on the same days they find no money for expenditures having more general benefits. Nonetheless, the appropriations committees and the legislature have shown themselves capable of acting to control the total budget when faced with a choice of increased taxes or stringent controls on spending. The governor proposed taxes in 1949, 1953, and 1955, and in each year the legislature effected cuts in the budget bill, cuts of substantial magnitude in 1949 and 1953.[3]

The Governor's Veto

The governor accepts responsibility for ensuring that the budget is balanced, not only in making budget recommendations to the legislature, but also in exercising influence upon legislative decisions. He has employed the veto and the threat of veto to curb any tendency of the legislature to authorize expenditures in excess of available financing. In 1949 Governor Warren placed an upper limit of $15 million on special appropriations from the general fund; appropriations in excess of that amount would be vetoed unless financed by additional taxes.[4] After the assembly passed a $50 million school aid bill in 1951, Warren announced that if the measure received legislative approval, he would veto it because the general fund could not afford the cost.[5] In 1957 Governor Knight stated, after passage of the budget bill, that he would approve only those special appropriations which were required by a "real emergency to the state."[6] A few days later he noted that $147 million in special appropriations had passed one house or the other and urged the legislature to avoid a "financial crisis that could do irreparable damage to the economy of California":

If the legislature fails to keep spending in check, I shall have to assume the responsibility alone through exercise of the executive veto. I want to prepare the legislature and the people for some sharp vetoes.[7]

Governor Knight found it necessary to veto $43 million in special appropriations.

After the assembly went on a spending spree in 1960, adding $17 million to the budget bill in floor amendments, Governor Brown warned that he would keep the budget in balance "if I have to wear out a dozen blue pencils and a couple of veto pens."[8] He sent a letter to newspaper publishers asking their support in keeping the budget down,[9] and threatened to veto revenue-reducing measures which were pending in the legislature.[10] Brown took the unusual step in 1961 of promising in his budget message to use the veto if necessary to keep the budget in balance.[11]

The Department of Finance and chairmen of the appropriations committees also call for restraint in approving special appropriations. The department usually tabulates the amounts contained in all special appropriations bills introduced and issues a press release to emphasize their magnitude, usually at least $200 or $300 million in general session years.

It is impossible to measure the effect of the governor's threatened vetoes on the actions of the legislature. His willingness to take responsibility for keeping the budget in balance could encourage the legislature to "pass the buck" to the governor. In general, however, the legislature has not taken this course. The governor's supporters naturally dislike the prospect of placing the onus for eliminating expenditures upon him, and both parties seek to maintain an image of "fiscal responsibility." Moreover, many members feel a personal sense of responsibility for maintaining a balanced budget.

The Item Veto

The governor's power to eliminate or reduce items of appropriation in the budget bill without vetoing the entire bill removes the possibility that he will have to accept unwanted appropriations in order to obtain financing for state operations, but the item veto is more important for its potential effect than for its actual use to reduce budget bill appropriations. The governor eliminated or reduced items in only six of the 19 budget bills passed in the period 1939–61, and the amounts were small:

	Amount (millions)
1948	$11.4
1952	5.0
1958	0.2
1959	0.7
1960	4.9
1961	0.2

Substantial reductions in special appropriations have been effected, however, through both the item veto and the regular veto. General fund appropriations were reduced or vetoed in the amount of $25 million in 1947,[12] and a deficiency appropriation for school construction was reduced by $15 million in 1948. The governor reduced or vetoed special appropriations in the amount of $6.7 million in 1949, $9 million in 1951, $22.4 million in 1955, and $43 million in 1957.[13]

By 1960, the legislature had overridden the governor's veto only once since the administration of Governor Olson (1939-43) —and the measure was an appropriation bill.[14] The unusual event occurred during a special session in 1946 convened by Governor Warren to consider, among other things, a $154 million program to construct state buildings and facilities. The legislature appropriated $90 million in wartime surplus funds to aid counties and cities in the construction of local public works. Warren denounced this "division of the spoils" in his veto message, but to no avail.[15] Normally, however, the governor's veto is virtually absolute, and he can scale down the total expenditure program if he wishes to do so.

FINANCING THE EXPENDITURE PROGRAM

The greatest challenge to the governor in the postwar period was to persuade the legislature to accept his policies for financing the expenditure program. The recurrent issue was whether taxes should be increased or whether reserves accumulated during World War II and the Korean War and from tidelands oil revenues should be used to balance the budget. On four occasions a governor proposed major increases in taxes and resisted use of reserves; in 1949 and 1953 he failed completely, in 1955 he achieved minor success, and in 1959 he secured approval of most of his tax program.

Warren and the Reserve Funds

Governor Warren proposed in 1949 to finance a current general fund deficit of $112 million by using $27 million of surplus and by increasing taxes. In lieu of new taxes, the legislature preferred to use the reserve funds established during and after World War II to finance repair and expansion of the state's capital plant, which had been neglected during the depression and the war. Warren opposed using reserves for two reasons: (1) normal capital outlay requirements should be financed from current revenue, and (2) the amount of reserves available was sufficient only to cover deficiencies accumulated in the past.

His supporters in the Assembly Ways and Means Committee defeated budget bill amendments that would have dipped into reserve funds. After the bill was reported, the governor emphasized that he was "unalterably opposed" to using the reserves. He was supported by the Director of Finance, who said that a budget financed by reserves would be a "false budget," and by the Ways and Means Committee chairman, who charged that it would be "just kidding the public."[16] Nevertheless, amendments to make use of the reserves were adopted on the assembly floor, an action denounced by Warren as "thoroughly unsound budgeting" and "an effort to avoid facing stark realities,"[17] but concurred in by the senate. Cuts were made by both appropriations committees, on the assembly floor, and in the conference committee. By using reserves, deferring $13 million in capital outlay, and making other reductions, the legislature avoided tax increases, although it concurred in Warren's recommendation that tax rates, temporarily reduced during and after the war, should revert to the 1943 level. (The return to the 1943 rates did not solve the problem of the deficit, for Warren's budget had assumed that this action would be taken.) An attempt by the chairman of the Ways and Means Committee to secure additional taxes by attaching a rider to a school apportionment bill was defeated by the assembly.[18] In the opinion of the Legislative Counsel, such a rider could legally be attached to an appropriation bill.[19]

In 1953 Governor Warren estimated that general fund expenditure in 1953-54 would exceed current revenue by $91 million. Although prior-year surpluses and use of reserves for some capital outlay would reduce the deficiency to $25 million, he estimated that there would be a deficiency of $111 million in 1954–55 and $132 million in 1955–56. He urged that the legislature enact a $50 million tax increase in order to bring revenues and expenditures into a more equal relationship. The legislature chose to reduce appropriations in an amount sufficient to avoid a deficit in the 1953–54 budget. As Warren had predicted the 1954–55 budget was presented on a deficit basis, although the gap between revenues and expenditures was less than he had estimated, partly because Governor Knight, who succeeded Warren in October, 1953, curtailed capital outlay drastically. The legislature accepted Knight's recommendation that $28 million from the school bond retirement fund be used to meet the deficit.

Knight and the Rainy Day Fund

Warren's expectation was also fulfilled by the 1955–56 budget, which estimated general fund revenues to be $100 million less than expenditures. Knight waged a vigorous campaign in behalf of his budget, which proposed to meet the deficit by (1) using a prior-year surplus of $30 million, (2) increasing taxes on distilled spirits, beer and horse racing, and (3) imposing a new levy on cigarettes. He also sponsored a bond issue for financing capital outlay expenditures to ease the financial problem in subsequent years. The legislature accepted the bond proposal, but could not resist the temptation presented by the $75 million "rainy day" fund. The fund had been created at Warren's behest as insurance against two contingencies: (1) disaster and (2) a revenue deficiency (i.e., failure of revenue to meet budgeted estimates with consequent inability to finance the expenditure program authorized by the legislature).

As in 1949, the budget bill was amended on the assembly floor, this time to provide for use of $40 million from the rainy day fund to balance the budget. Knight charged that, as neither house had acted on his tax proposals, the assembly decision to use this reserve was "a parliamentary maneuver to defeat the administration's tax program by subterfuge and without a hearing on its merits." It was "against the best interests of the state to delay balancing the budget and to force the state into insolvency." Moreover, the rainy day fund was a very small reserve, considering that it amounted to only five percent of a single year's expenditures.[20] Subsequently, the house reversed its decision, supporting the governor by a wider margin (47–24) than that by which he had lost on the original vote (27–41).

The senate voted to use the rainy day fund, despite another strong statement from Knight insisting that use of this reserve to balance the budget was playing "fast and loose" with state finance and was "conceived in desperation."[21] The senate view prevailed, and although Knight made further efforts to save his tax program, he obtained only a $14 million annual increase in the levy on distilled spirits.

Knight's defeat at the hands of the legislature was made less serious by a sharp upturn in the economy, which produced revenue greatly exceeding 1955–56 budget estimates and removed the necessity of resorting to the rainy day fund that year. The resulting surplus and a $200 million bond authorization for capital outlay, approved by the voters in 1956, helped to finance expenditures until Knight's term ended in January 1959, and he sought no more tax increases. Nevertheless, in the election year of 1958, Knight submitted a budget showing a general fund current deficit of $110 million and proposing use of the rainy day fund and other reserves to balance the budget—thus reversing the policy he had espoused in 1955, albeit under different economic circumstances.[22]

Brown and the Investment Fund

When Governor Brown took office in January 1959 the day of reckoning so often predicted by his predecessors seemed to be at hand. Revenue for 1958–59 had not fulfilled expectations because of an economic recession; a general fund deficit of $68 million was in prospect. The outlook for 1959–60 was even less auspicious. A deficit in excess of $200 million was expected, and Brown found it necessary to propose a $202 million tax program.[23] He rejected the only other large source of financing to which he might have had recourse, the investment fund. The latter had been created to receive Long Beach tidelands revenues and subsequent oil royalties and was estimated to have a surplus of $172 million as of June 30, 1959. The governor believed strongly that this fund should be used exclusively for development of the state's water resources, and the appropriations included in his budget for that purpose would reduce the surplus to $120 million by the end of 1959–60.

Opponents of the governor's tax program suggested certain other funds as possible sources for budget balancing. Even before the governor submitted the budget, Senator McBride, chairman of the Finance Committee, released a tabulation showing that $214 million could be obtained from various funds, including the investment fund.[24] Various groups objected to tax increases in general or to specific features of the governor's proposals. The State Chamber of Commerce announced its opposition to any tax increases and called a meeting of 25 or 30 business and industry lobbyists to discuss strategy, although no decisions were reached.[25] The AFL–CIO supported a proposed new oil and gas severance tax and increases in the bank and corporation franchise tax, the income tax, and the inheritance and gift tax, but bitterly opposed the cigarette tax and an increase in the beer tax.[26] The California Manufacturers Association opposed the tax program generally. Objecting to one or more of the tax measures were the race tracks, malt beverage industry, Associated Farmers of California, the oil industry and a segment of the oil unions, some county boards of supervisors and county assessors (opposing the oil severance tax), the Pacific Gas and Electric Company and the Southern Counties Gas Company.

In a joint caucus of Republicans of both houses, a majority decided to oppose the tax program,[27] and Joseph C. Shell, Republican floor leader in the assembly, denied the need for taxes on many occasions during the session. The chairman of the Senate Committee on Revenue and Taxation, Republican Nelson S. Dilworth, expressed opposition to the tax program.[28] Finance Committee chairman McBride repeatedly made clear his unwillingness to support tax increases, and he abstained from voting when the tax measures were considered by the senate.[29] In addition to objections to particular taxes or rates, opponents of the tax program argued that the governor's estimates of future revenues were too pessimistic. The chairman of the Republican caucus in the lower house, Walter I. Dahl, said that the tax program was unnecessary: "What the governor has his eye on is a fat surplus in state funds in the campaign year of 1960."[30] This allegation of political motivation for the tax program was made by other Republicans as well.

Tax Program Strategy

The strategy of the administration embraced several important elements. Perhaps the most important was the decision to propose a tax "package" which, in the opinion of the administration, would maintain a "reasonable balance" between taxes falling directly on the consumer and those "which place an added burden on industry."[31] The package included increased rates in personal and corporate income taxes, the inheritance tax, the excise tax on beer, and taxes on horse racing. It also imposed two new taxes: an excise on tobacco products and a severance tax on oil and gas. To permit legislators to maintain impartiality as between regressive and progressive taxes, the several measures were taken up in pairs in committee and on the floor: the personal income and tobacco taxes, the corporate income and horse racing taxes, and the inheritance and beer taxes. Having adopted what he considered to be an equitable tax program, the governor announced again and again that there would be "no retreat" on any part of it.

A second basic element in the strategy was the decision of the administration to exercise restraint on the expenditure program. Not only did the administration submit a "tight" budget,[32] but also it moved vigorously to prevent an expected general fund deficit of $68 million in the 1958–59 fiscal year. By these measures the administration gave evidence of that "fiscal responsibility" which became its watchword and reduced the persuasiveness of charges that the tax measures would be unnecessary were it not for an overgenerous expenditure program.

In order to remove the investment fund from consideration as a source for budget balancing, the administration promptly pushed through a bill to dedicate the fund to water resources development, meanwhile delaying action on the tax measures. The bill gained the support of the Democrats in both houses, as well as a majority of the Republicans in the senate and a substantial minority in the assembly. Although the dedication of the investment fund did not necessarily indicate that the legislature was prepared to accept a tax program—the need to use this money for water development could be recognized without conceding that the tax program was necessary—the practical consequence was to remove any possibility of financing the budget deficit from reserve funds. Opponents of the tax program were then thrown back upon the final weapon in their arsenal—the argument that the governor had been unduly pessimistic in estimating revenues.

The administration strategy in the face of this argument was simply to insist that its estimates were sound. In particular, it declared again and again that its estimates had anticipated the improvements in the economy that were taking place in the spring of 1959.[33]

Finally, the governor, his staff, and the Department of Finance waged a vigorous campaign to secure approval of the tax program. Not only did the governor defend his revenue measures in many statements, speeches, and a two-day tour of the state at mid-session, but he and his staff also conferred frequently with legislative leaders regarding timing and other aspects of strategy in the legislature. When his legislative lieutenants had difficulty in securing the necessary votes, the governor's assistance was sought to bring members into line. He warned legislators that he would

veto special appropriation measures if reductions in his tax program resulted in insufficient revenue to provide a balanced budget.[34]

Only one measure in the governor's program failed to pass—the severance tax. The senate scaled down the tax rates on horse racing and beer.
Despite these actions, the governor's victory was impressive, for the total
program enacted was estimated to produce $183 million of the $202 million
originally proposed.[35] The governor received the support of important
groups, including the California Teachers Association, the County Super-
visors Association, the California Congress of Parents and Teachers, the
California State Employees Association, the AFL-CIO (except on consumer
taxes), and the (elected) State Board of Equalization. The California Bank-
ers Association and the Bank of America agreed not to oppose an increase
in the bank and corporation franchise tax if other parts of the program
were enacted. Within the legislature the governor's party enjoyed substantial majorities (27 to 13 in the senate, 47 to 33 in the assembly) and was
more cohesive on the tax measures than the Republican minority.[36] Although a majority of the Republicans in each house voted against all six
tax measures (except one in the senate), assembly Republicans supplied
votes essential for passage on four of them.[37]

In 1960, 1961, and 1962 the budget aggregates were the subject of continuing partisan debate. The 1960–61 budget anticipated a surplus in the
general fund of about $74 million as of June 30, 1960. The governor pro-
posed to use the surplus, rather than bonds, to finance capital outlay.[38] The
Republicans of both houses caucused and agreed to press for tax reductions
of some $55 million and the use of an equal amount from bonds to finance
capital outlay.[39] The tax reduction effort failed when the Assembly Committee on Revenue and Taxation, voting on party lines, killed various tax
reduction measures.[40] Seventeen million dollars in augmentations, mainly
for salary increases, were added on the assembly floor, but almost all of
them were eliminated by the Senate Finance Committee, the conference
committee, and the governor.

In 1961, the Republicans favored tax reduction to assist recovery from
the recession of 1960–61, but only minor tax cuts were approved by the
legislature. In the following year the governor proposed to use a small
surplus to balance the budget and to finance $141 million in capital outlay
from bond sources. The governor proposed a $270 million bond authoriza-
tion for capital outlay, as well as a total of $550 million for veterans' farm
and home loans, acquisition of land for beaches and parks, and loans for
school construction. Administration strategy called for placing the school
bonds and state construction bonds on the primary ballot in June, the
others on the general election ballot in November. The Republican caucus
in the assembly agreed to insist that all of the bonds appear on the Novem-

ber ballot, in order that the voters might review the entire bonding program and be apprised of the spending policies of the administration.[41] The Republicans offered 24 amendments on the assembly floor to cut the budget by $15 million, but all were turned down on party-line voting.[42] When the conference report was presented, however, the assembly Republicans stood united and denied the majority the necessary two-thirds vote required for its adoption. The budget session ended without passage of the budget bill, and a special session was called. The Democrats ultimately agreed to place all of the bond issues on the primary ballot, and to accept about $4 million in reductions in the budget bill.[43]

Multiple Decision Centers

The foregoing discussion of some recent history of decision-making with respect to aggregates omits many details of the process of reaching such decisions, as well as many fascinating political sidelights. Certain general propositions emerge, however. Perhaps the most important is that these decisions are reached as the result of a complex interplay of political and institutional forces. The decision on aggregates is not made on a single occasion, in a single arena, or by a set procedure. Crucial decisions may be made in committee or on the floor, in the appropriations committees or in the revenue committees, on review of the budget bill or in considering other legislation. An example of the last was the earmarking of the investment fund for water development in 1959.

The party arena has assumed greater importance in recent years, especially in the assembly. The minority party, however, has had difficulty in holding its ranks together to a degree that gave it decisive leverage, and even in 1962, when the Republicans were strongly united, their victories were modest. Although the attempt in 1962 to dramatize the spending proclivities of the Democrats failed to produce the rejection of their party at the polls that the Republicans predicted, it seems very likely that the parties will grow in importance as instruments for raising and deciding issues regarding aggregates and their relationships.

Influence of the Governor

A second general proposition is that the governor is deeply involved in decisions regarding aggregates in three of his roles, as legislative leader, chief executive, and head of his party. No single legislative figure or committee rivals his importance. Indeed, our review of recent history suggests that the governor's policy prevails much of the time. On aggregate expenditures his influence is almost always decisive; he has succeeded in obtaining legislative acceptance as to when and to what extent to use bond financing for capital outlay. When he has chosen to dip into reserves, the legislature has gone along. On the other hand, so popular and influential a leader as Warren failed twice to win acceptance of increased taxes as an alternative to depleting reserves, and Knight largely failed in his own attempt to obtain tax increases.

Brown succeeded where the others had failed, partly because he had just won an election by an impressive margin, partly because of the loyalty and unity displayed by his party, and partly because he vigorously used all of the influence at his command to gain support from interest groups and the legislature. It was true, of course, that the handwriting was on the wall in 1959; yet the legislature could have chosen to use the investment fund to avoid tax increases for one more year, perhaps two if it had chosen to exhaust the bond authorizations for capital outlay in 1960–61. Although reserves had been relatively larger in 1949, 1953, and 1955, the handwriting was on the wall in those years as well, and it was only the extraordinary revenue expansion that resulted from the Korean War and the vigorous expansion in the economy beginning in 1955 that permitted a general tax increase to be so long delayed. Looking back in 1959, the legislature might have counted on a similar stroke of good fortune.

STRENGTHENING COORDINATION IN THE DETERMINATION OF AGGREGATES

The existing process—determination of the aggregates by a series of decisions in varying decision-centers—has, if nothing else, resulted in a "balanced budget" in the past two decades. The state has not, however, been meeting normal capital outlay needs from current revenues," but since 1957 has partially financed capital outlay by bond sales. The question is not only one of balancing the budget, however, but also of striking a balance at the "correct" level of expenditures and revenues. It is necessary to ask whether legislative organization and procedure are well designed for making decisions regarding aggregates in as rational a fashion as possible—that is, giving due consideration to relevant alternatives, analyzing their consequences, and making choices in the light of preferences prevailing in the legislature.

Serial Decisions

By imposing upon the governor the duty to propose a plan of all expenditures and sources for financing them, the constitution provides for a single point of decision and responsibility in the executive branch. The legislature, by contrast, is so organized that no single agency has similar responsibility. Only the legislature as a whole has the responsibility, which it fulfills through a series of decisions. It does not decide by a single legal instrument to establish specified levels of revenue and expenditure, with consequent deficit, surplus, or balanced budget. Rather, it acts upon an omnibus appropriation bill, a series of special appropriation bills, and a series of revenue bills. Moreover, responsibility for most revenue bills is, in the first instance, the responsibility of one committee in each house, while appropriations are the responsibility of another. Still other committees are involved, for in the senate, measures affecting beer, liquor, and horse racing revenues are referred to the Committee on Governmental Efficiency, and those affecting the gasoline tax go to the Committee on Transportation. Consequently, organization and procedure do not in themselves ensure that appropriate consideration will be given to total revenue and total expenditure in relation to each other.

Review by Appropriations Committees

There are certain mitigating factors. All appropriation bills and significant cost bills are reviewed by the appropriations committees, which work diligently to keep appropriations at a level consistent with expected revenues. Moreover, because revenue bills usually entail some costs, they are often reviewed by the appropriations committees after being reported from the revenue or other committees. In 1959 most of the governor's major proposals were re-referred to the appropriations committees; the Senate Finance Committee, after making a careful review of revenue estimates, amended the beer tax bill to provide for an increase of two cents per gallon instead of five cents. Although reference of tax measures to the appropriations committees permits them to scale down revenues in line with appropriations decisions, it does not ensure that they will review all decisions that may be of crucial importance. Bills to raise additional revenue will not be referred to the appropriations committees if they are killed by the revenue committees.

Overlapping Memberships

A second qualification arises from overlapping memberships in the appropriations and revenue committees. From 1947 to 1961, nearly one-half of the members of the Finance Committee were members of the Committee on Revenue and Taxation, and from 10 to 20 percent of the members of the Ways and Means Committee served on the assembly revenue committee. In a number of years the overlapping members included one or both of the chairmen of the fiscal committees. When overlapping membership is as extensive as it has been in the senate, it undoubtedly tends to bring about consistency in the decisions of the two committees.

Consideration of Related Totals

To a certain extent the legislature recognizes the desirability of considering total expenditure and total revenue together. Whenever tax increases or tax reductions are proposed, it is argued that committee or house action should be delayed until the budget bill is passed and expenditure requirements are known. Because the budget bill is usually passed late in the session, however, proponents of tax legislation risk defeat if they accede. Moreover, political strategy rather than concern for proper fiscal procedure often lies behind such argument, for opponents of tax legislation seek delay.

It is significant that in 1959 Governor Brown favored action on his revenue measures before the budget bill had been reported from committee or passed, whereas in 1960 he criticized a senate committee for recommending tax reductions (which he opposed) prior to passage of the budget bill, arguing that "reducing taxes before we see what we need is not good government."[45] Republicans, on the other hand, thought the budget bill should be passed before consideration of tax increases in 1959, but preferred the reverse order in 1960 when they were urging tax reduction.[46] The argument that tax legislation should await determination of expenditure needs is not to be taken very seriously, for legislators can estimate rather closely the size of the expenditure program that will be enacted. There is a practical reason for proponents of tax legislation to await passage of the budget bill before taking up tax increases, however, for legislators feel that constituents will look more favorably upon votes for taxes if the size of the expenditure program has been determined first.

Problems of Reform

Appropriations committee review of some revenue measures, overlapping membership, and recognition of the need to consider aggregates in relationship to each other, do not solve the problem of dispersion of decision-making authority and lack of a single occasion for determining aggregates. Certain changes in organization and procedure offer partial solutions to the problem, but each is open to serious objection on grounds of feasibility: (1) a single fiscal committee in each house; (2) a joint committee on the budget, consisting of all four fiscal committees and having the duty to make recommendations regarding aggregates; (3) a budget bill embracing both revenue and appropriations provisions. A single fiscal committee having jurisdiction over both revenues and expenditures would help to secure consistent policies on aggregates at the committee stage, which is often decisive in the California legislature. Such a reorganization is unlikely because it would fly in the face of tradition, would reduce the number of important chairmanships, and would impose a crushing work-load on the appropriations committees, which already have more work than they can handle well. Only if the number of committee assignments of members of the fiscal committees were substantially reduced would the change make sense. But members are reluctant to give up their committee assignments. Furthermore, the proposal would be resisted because it would place great power in the hands of a single committee.

Congress created a Joint Committee on the Budget by the Legislative Reorganization Act of 1946. Composed of the members of the four taxing and appropriations committees, the committee was directed to study the President's budget and to recommend early in each session a ceiling on appropriations, the ceiling to be adopted by Congress in the form of a resolution. In 1947 the resolution died in conference, and the following year appropriations exceeded by $6 billion the ceiling approved in the resolution.[47] The most fundamental of the various explanations offered for the failure of the "legislative budget" emphasizes the dispersion of power in Congress and its inability to generate effective leadership.[48]

Power is not as highly dispersed in the California legislature as it is in Congress. Seniority is less important, especially in the assembly, committee chairmen are not as powerful, and the agenda is not controlled by a rules committee. Nevertheless, there is sufficient dispersion of power to present obstacles to a reform patterned on the "legislative budget." It is question-able whether the appropriations and revenue committees of the state legislature would conform to house decisions regarding aggregates. In addition, there are other objections to the proposal. A general debate in each house on a proposed expenditure ceiling would not be very meaning-ful, unless a binding decision were the objective. But members are not likely to be willing to establish a firm ceiling until there has been commit-tee review of both revenue and expenditure proposals. Even if a ceiling were adopted, there would be a temptation to make it unrealistically low.[49] The procedure would soon lose meaning if the legislature succumbed to this temptation. Moreover, a committee composed of the members of the four fiscal committees would be too large for effective study and delibera-tion. The total number of members, adjusted for overlapping memberships as they existed in 1961, would be about 50.

Finally, the problem is less acute in California than in the federal government. Whereas the latter has frequently experienced large deficits, the former has no need of a ceiling to prevent deficits, assuming that a ceiling could do so. The relationship between federal expenditures and revenues affects the economy in important ways, but state budget policy is highly inflexible because deficit financing must be authorized by the elec-torate,[50] and in any case, the impact of the relationship between aggregates in a single state has minor significance for the economy. The crucial question for the state is the level at which a balance is struck between income and outgo, and it is doubtful that the legislative budget would make for more rational determination of the level. Because the problem is less far-reaching in the state, the legislature is unlikely to adopt such a procedure.

An omnibus bill providing both appropriations and revenues would be a marked departure from custom. Moreover, the constitution requires a two-thirds vote for passage of the budget bill.[51] If this provision were retained, revenue legislation would require an extraordinary majority rather than the simple majority of the elected membership applicable to most revenue legislation. Again, the governor's veto power would be weakened if the item veto were not made applicable to revenue provisions as well as appropriations. Although the bill could be referred to both the revenue and the appropriations committee of each house for simultaneous consideration, either committee could hold up consideration of the bill by delaying its report. If the decisions of the fiscal committees were inconsistent, the bill would have to be rewritten by amendments from the floor, a difficult task for the house to do well. Essentially the same difficulty can arise under existing procedure, however, if expenditures recommended by the appropriations committee exceed revenues recommended by the tax committee. The house must then scale down expenditure or find additional sources of financing.

Combining revenue and appropriations provisions in a single bill might encourage earmarking of particular revenues for particular expenditure purposes. It would also increase the number of issues embodied in a single measure and might result in delays greater than those to which the budget bill and special appropriation bills are now subjected. Opponents of revenue provisions might seek to have one or more handled in a separate bill, on the grounds that the omnibus measure should not be delayed pending resolution of issues.

Continuing Appropriations and Long-Range Projections

In sum, there are a number of objections to the reforms suggested, the most important being that they involve major departures from the accustomed way of doing things and for that reason are not likely to be accepted. A reform less vulnerable to this objection and one that might have even greater benefits is based on a different approach to the problem. Instead of trying to tinker with the legislative machinery to ensure that aggregates are considered in relationship to each other at a specified point, this approach would aim to change the perspective in which aggregates in any given year are reviewed at whatever point they receive attention. Specifically, this calls for action on two fronts, (1) continuing appropriations and (2) long-range projections of programs, expenditures, and revenues. Consideration of aggregates has limited significance so long as two-thirds of the expenditure program is governed by continuing appropriations. A way needs to be found to give the legislature and the governor greater flexibility in adjusting the total expenditure program annually. That continuing appropriations are a serious problem is widely recognized in the legislature, and it is within the realm of possibility that substantially greater flexibility can be achieved. This problem receives further attention in the following chapter. It needs only to be emphasized here that, although the greater portion of continuing appropriations is subject to legislative control through statutory changes, the present system does not require positive decisions each year regarding the appropriate level of continuing appropriations in relation to others and to aggregate expenditures and revenues.

Aside from the question of continuing appropriations, present organization and procedure do not give adequate assurance that decisions on aggregates will be made in the light of longer-run consequences. There is a strong tendency for both the governor and the legislature to view the budget in the perspective of a single year, or at most in the perspective of the period until the next election. It is true that the departments plan programs for several years ahead; in some cases important indices of expenditure and workload are projected for decades (e.g., enrollment in institutions of higher education). And, as indicated above, a moving five-year plan for capital improvements is maintained and published from time to time. Yet there is no provision for regular and comprehensive publication of projections for the state government as a whole, including the requirements for subventions to local government, which make up more than half of the total expenditure program. As mentioned in Chapter VI, the Assembly Ways and Means Committee has recently recognized the need for regular and systematic presentation in the budget document of information on program plans, expenditures, and revenue for five years beyond the budget year.[52] Aside from assuring that all departments engage in planning, the proposal would have the primary purpose of encouraging the governor, the legislature, and interested publics to view present issues in terms of longer-run consequences. Any decision-center in the legislature, whether committee, party caucus, house, or bloc, would then have the benefit of more complete information about the future, and those groups opposed to shortsighted expedients would be provided with authoritative information to support their position.

Political Consequences

In a penetrating article, Wildavsky has pointed out that changes in the budget system have political consequences, and it is appropriate to assess long-range planning from this perspective.[53] Obviously, long-range projections do not ensure that the legislature or the governor will give due consideration to the long run. The legislature (and the governor, for that matter) may wish to sacrifice long-run to short-run interests, but they ought to have as accurate an estimate as possible of the nature and magnitude of the sacrifice. Moreover, interested publics may be more ready to accept a long-run view if better information is available and disseminated through the mass media, party channels, letters to constituents, speeches, and interest group organs. As a result, legislators might give less credence to the proposition that increased taxes almost inevitably bring retribution at the polls. It is not at all clear, however, that the effect of long-run projections would encourage higher levels of expenditure by making higher levels of taxation more palatable. In hearings before the Ways and Means Committee, an official of the Department of Finance doubted the wisdom of publishing projections of total revenue and total expenditure. He argued that when such projections have been made for internal use of the department, they have shown shortages of future revenue, shortages which often failed to materialize because expenditures are subject to some control.[54] To publish the projections would make the governor, his party, and supporters of his spending policies in the legislature vulnerable to political attack. It would also encourage the governor, however, to consider spending proposals very carefully in order to minimize the projected revenue gap.

Another consequence of long-run projections would be to encourage the legislature to look more carefully at the basis of revenue estimates and to devote more of its time and attention to programs. If it wished to take account of future estimates in making budget decisions, the legislature would need (1) to assure itself that revenue estimates were soundly based and (2) to analyze future costs and relative benefits of program changes planned for the budget year or later. The result would be a strengthening of the legislature vis-à-vis the executive and the bureaucracy, for the legislature would be basing its decisions upon a more thorough analysis of the consequences of policies urged by the governor and administrative agencies. It might often be possible for the opposition party to criticize the governor on the basis of his own estimates. Certainly, arguments against particular expenditures would be more telling if based on the governor's own prediction of a future revenue gap, rather than being based upon general, unsupported allegations that the governor's policy is leading the state into bankruptcy. Similarly, a governor who failed to ask for taxes or made undue use of bond financing would be more vulnerable to effective attack if his own estimates indicated that he was not facing future requirements honestly.

Within the legislature, the projections would strengthen the ability of each house to judge the wisdom of the recommendations of its committees and would provide a common framework for the development of party positions and political dialogue. Although much futile partisan debate could arise from disputes over the validity of the estimates, especially the revenue estimates, raising such issues would be healthful if it led to more thorough consideration of longer-run consequences of decisions.

[1] "Preliminary Summary of Legislative Action on 1957 Budget Bill and 1957–58 State Expenditure Program," Legislative Auditor (1957), p. 1 (mim).

[2] "Summary of Final Legislative and Executive Action on the 1959 Budget Bill and Major Revenue and Special Appropriation Bills at the 1959 General Session," Legislative Analyst (1959), p. 4 (process).

[3] The substantial increase in the *total* program in 1953 is accounted for by an increase in highway taxes, resulting in an additional $80 million for highway expenditures. The governor also proposed other increases in taxes, which stimulated efforts to cut the budget bill. Highways aside, a net reduction was effected in the total program. The $33 million cut in the budget bill of 1957 resulted entirely from failure of northern and southern factions in the legislature to reach agreement on a basis for state water development, rather than from any threat of increased taxes.

[4] *Bee,* June 18, 1949, p. 1.

[5] *Bee,* June 15, 1951, p. 1.

[6] *Bee,* May 31, 1957, p. 1.

[7] *Bee,* June 11, 1957, p. 1.

[8] *Berkeley Daily Gazette,* March 24, 1960, p. 2.

[9] *Chronicle,* March 25, 1960, p. 10.

[10] *Berkeley Daily Gazette,* March 25, 1960, p. 2.

[11] *Budget,* 1961–62, p. vi.

[12] Frank H. Thill, "State Appropriates $771,000,000," *The Tax Digest,* 25 (October, 1947), 336.

[13] "Summary of Financial Legislation . . ." Department of Finance, and John M. Peirce, "State Budget Outlook," *The Tax Digest,* 35 (December, 1957), p. 211.

[14] James W. Wiggins, "The Governor's Veto in California" (Unpublished M.A. thesis, University of California, 1960), p. 72.

[15] "The bill divides this $90,000,000 in half, precisely as one would cut a melon. It then gives a $45,000,000 slice to the counties of the State—not on any basis of the need of any particular county, but entirely according to an arbitrary formula based on population and road mileage.

"In view of the known needs of our State and particularly in view of the fact that our State is still growing, I find it difficult to understand the logic of the action which caused this bill, after five weeks of the special session, to be the first bill to reach my desk. It arrives in solitary conspicuousness ahead of a long list of bills providing for State needs.

. . . .

"The bill is obviously predicated on the assumption that because there is a war-created reserve now in the State Treasury, a division of the spoils is in order. It was enacted before any state needs were determined." *Assembly Journal,* February 8, 1946 (1st Ex. Sess.), p. 575.

[16] *Bee,* May 24, 1949, pp. 1, 4.

[17] *Bee,* May 31, 1949, p. 1.

[18] *Bee,* June 21, 1949, p. 1.

[19] *Bee,* June 8, 1949, p. 4.

[20] *Bee,* May 11, 1955, p. 10.

[21] *Bee,* May 19, 1955, p. 12.

[22] In his budget message, Knight defended his decision:
"In view of the present economic situation this is no time to impose additional tax burdens. Your 1957 Session wisely provided for a comprehensive study of the State's tax structure and expenditure trends by a committee which will make a report at your 1959 General Session. At that session there should be sufficient time for a very complete consideration of the report in face of the then current conditions. Economists advise us that the current business lag will have run its course by that time so that your reexamination of the revenue system can be made in light of normal business conditions. Meanwhile the use of the Revenue Deficiency Reserve ["rainy day"] Fund, in my judgment, is a sound action and in keeping with the basic purpose of establishing the Fund. The time of revenue deficiency unfortunately has arrived." (*Budget,* 1958–59, p. X.)
It is difficult to square this interpretation of the purpose of the Revenue Deficiency Reserve with the language of the statute (*Cal. Stats.* (1947), chap. 958) or with Warren's statement that it "was established as a cushion against a drop of revenues *below budget estimates* which a business depression would produce" or for "disaster relief in case of an extreme national emergency such as an atomic attack." *Budget,* 1953–54, p. vi. (Emphasis added.)

[23] *Budget,* 1959–60, pp. xx–xxiii. On a full-year basis, the tax program was estimated to produce $257 million.

[24] *Bee,* January 21, 1959, p. A-6.

[25] *Chronicle,* February 5, 1959, p. 1. Democrats protested that the Chamber of Commerce had supported Republican Governor Knight's proposed tax increases in 1955. *Ibid.,* December 14, 1958. (Want Ad Sec. p. 10) "Sacramento Scene."

[26] *Chronicle,* January 29, 1959, p. 6.

[27] *Chronicle,* March 20, 1959, pp. 1, 8.

[28] *Bee,* March 7, 1959, p. A-5.

[29] *Bee,* January 15, 1959, p. A-8, January 29, p. A-10, April 8, p. A-6, May 19, p. A-6. See also *Chronicle,* May 27, p. 8, reporting that, although opposed to taxes, McBride abstained on two of the tax measures because he would be the manager of the budget bill in the senate.

[30] *Berkeley Daily Gazette,* May 15, 1959, p. 3.

[31] *Budget,* p. xxi. See note 23, above.

[32] In an address to the California Taxpayers' Association, Director of Finance Levit declared that the budget was "a tough, tight budget," and that the administration had cut agency requests for new services from $21.5 million to $3.5 million. Glenn E. Coolidge, Republican and former chairman of Ways and Means, said that the budget was "probably the tightest in many years." *Bee,* March 9, 1959, p. A-6.

[33] Events tended to confirm the expectations of critics of the administration, for the general fund ended the 1959–60 fiscal year with a surplus of $129 million, even though the severance tax failed to pass. According to an informed Democratic legislator, strategists of his party in the legislature were determined to obtain sufficient additional revenue to cover requirements for the remainder of Governor Brown's term, that is, until 1963. In this they were successful, although it was necessary to secure voter approval of a new bond issue in 1962 in order to finance part of the capital outlay program for 1962–63.

[34] *Chronicle,* May 16, 1959, p. 1. Legislators received an object lesson when a Ways and Means subcommittee deleted a single item from a list of water projects totaling $80 million. The deleted project was in the district of Republican Assemblyman James Holmes, and the deletion occurred a few hours after Holmes voted against the bill to dedicate the investment fund to water development. Governor Brown denied

Holmes' charge that he had instigated the subcommittee action, although confessing that "it was done in support of a principle in which I believe." The governor stated that he had called Holmes following the committee action "to ask him his ideas about water," and had said that he "couldn't understand why coming from a district in need of water, he voted against this water legislation. I know Jim Holmes well, and I have called up many legislators." Holmes' version of the conversation, monitored and recorded by his secretary, was that the governor had inquired whether he was interested in the project in question, and after being assured of Holmes' interest, had said: "Well, you didn't go along with us on the vote yesterday. You've got to make some fast, hard decisions up here, Jim, and you've got to go along." A spokesman for the governor stated that the subcommittee action had been engineered by the chairman of the Ways and Means Committee, Jesse Unruh, and the majority floor leader, William A. Munnell, an allegation that they denied. *Chronicle*, March 25, 1959, pp. 1, 8. Subsequently, the governor announced that he supported restoration of the deleted project, and the subcommittee reversed itself. *Ibid.*, March 25, 1959, p. 1.

[35] "Summary of Financial Legislation Enacted by the 1959 Legislature," Department of Finance (1959), Schedule 9.

[36] Rice indices of cohesion on revenue and other measures in the 1959 session are reported by William C. Johnson, "The Political Party System in the 1959–60 California Legislature," (M.A. thesis, University of California, 1960), pp. 76–8.

[37] A majority of the elected membership is necessary to pass any bill, and the bank and corporation franchise tax measure required a two-thirds vote of the elected membership. *Cal. Const.*, Art XIII, sec. 16.

[38] *Budget*, 1960–61, pp. vii–viii.

[39] *Chronicle*, March 3, 1960, p. 6. A minor portion of this amount was apparently a reduction in federal, rather than state taxes; it consisted of benefits to be derived from declaring the cigarette tax to be a consumer tax and hence deductible.

[40] *Berkeley Daily Gazette*, March 11, 1960, p. 1.

[41] *Chronicle*, March 12, 1962, p. 6 and March 13, 1962, p. 5.

[42] *Fresno Bee*, March 31, 1962, pp. 1A, 7A.

[43] A partisan dispute ensued as to the size of the cuts effected as a result of Republican pressure. Republicans claimed cuts of $28 million, but the biggest item ($18 million) arose from a provision that, if federal money became available for construction of facilities in higher education, it would be used in lieu of state appropriations. The administration contended that it would follow such a course in any case, and that federal money was unlikely to be available in time to be used in 1962–63, even if Congress did decide to offer such aid. The Republicans took credit for an $8 million saving as a result of a provision requiring the Department of Finance to realize that amount in "unidentified savings." Since the budget contemplated $6 million in unidentified savings, it seems more accurate to credit the Republicans with a $2 million saving on this item. *Chronicle*, April 29, 1962, p. 26.

[44] The Legislative Analyst estimated in 1960 that normal requirements in the next 20 years would be $125 to $150 million annually for projects other than highways, water development, and certain other purposes not supported from general fund sources. *Analysis*, 1960–61, p. VII. Yet, estimated and actual general fund expenditures from current revenues for capital outlay averaged less than $22 million annually in 1961–62, 1962–63, and 1963–64. *Budget*, 1963–64, p. XV.

[45] Quoted in *Berkeley Daily Gazette*, March 8, 1960, p. 1.

[46] *Bee*, May 8, 1959, p. A-10; *Chronicle*, March 23, 1960, p. 8.

[47] George B. Galloway, *The Legislative Process in Congress* (New York: Thomas Y. Crowell Co., 1953), pp. 104–5.

[48] Victor Jones, "The Political Framework of Stabilization Policy," in Max F. Millikan, ed., *Income Stabilization for a Developing Democracy* (New Haven: Yale University Press, 1953), pp. 605–7. For other explanations, see Galloway, *op. cit.*, pp. 130–1.

[49] Senate Finance Committee Chairman James J. McBride "hoped" in February, 1958 that the budget could be cut by $50 to $90 million. *Chronicle*, February 6, 1958. His hopes were dashed, for the legislature increased the budget by about $16 million.

[50] *Cal. Const.*, Art. XVI, sec. 1.

[51] *Ibid.*, Art. IV, sec. 34a.

[52] *Report on Long-Range Program and Budget Planning* (Assembly Interim Committee Reports, vol. 21, no. 5, 1963).

[53] Aaron Wildavsky, "Political Implications of Budgetary Reform," *Public Administration Review*, XXI (Autumn, 1961), 183–90.

[54] "Transcript of Hearing of the Assembly Interim Committee on Ways and Means," July 8, 1962, pp. 36–7 (process).

Chapter X

LEGISLATIVE CONTROL OF SPENDING

The idea that expenditures should be "controlled" can be accepted by everyone, but upon analysis the ambiguity of the concept of control becomes apparent. To illustrate, some of the meanings that come to mind with mention of "legislative control of expenditure" include:

1. that the legislature is legally empowered to authorize expenditures through appropriations and to determine the purposes and manner of spending;

2. that the actual application of funds is in accordance with the appropriation acts and other provisions of law governing financial transactions;

3. that an effective system of fiscal control exists in the executive branch, including allotment procedure, preaudit of expenditures, and adequate accounting systems;

4. that expenditures are postaudited by an agency independent of the executive and, preferably, responsible to the legislature;

5. that the legislature in fact determines in detail the manner in which funds are applied, through detailed itemization of appropriations, through participation in execution of the budget, or other means;

6. that the aggregate size of the expenditure program is not "excessive";

7. that the budget as authorized by the legislature is in balance; or that in execution the budget is in balance; or that an "unduly" burdensome debt is avoided;

8. that the legislature has authority to determine, or does determine, on an annual basis, the manner in which all of the available resources of the government will be allocated among agencies and programs—that is, that there are no continuing appropriations, no earmarked funds, and no prior year commitments to limit the flexibility of action in any given year;

9. that expenditure programs are not unduly distorted by the availability of grants for specified purposes from other levels of government; and

10. that legislative decisions to spend money are made with adequate knowledge of the consequences of those decisions.

This listing illustrates not only the ambiguity of the concept of control itself, but also the vagueness of some of the terms used to indicate the presence or absence of control. It can be determined objectively whether spending is legally permitted without a legislative appropriation, and whether continuing appropriations, segregated funds, and prior-year commitments exist; but some of the other criteria are so indefinite as to be of little use. When is spending excessive? How burdensome does a debt have to be to be "unduly" burdensome? How does one measure the "effectiveness" of the executive system of fiscal control? What is "adequate" knowledge of consequences?

It becomes clear that a definitive appraisal of the extent to which the legislature "controls the purse" presents formidable difficulties, if all or most of the criteria suggested are included in the analysis. Although such an appraisal is beyond the scope of this study, some tentative conclusions and selected problems of control are discussed in this chapter. Excluded from consideration is the difficult question of the impact of grants-in-aid. For reasons indicated in Chapter I, we prefer to treat the adequacy of knowledge of consequences as an aspect of the problem of rationality.

SURVEY OF LEGISLATIVE CONTROL

Control of Appropriations

By providing that no money may be drawn from the treasury except through appropriation made by law,[1] the constitution safeguards legislative control of appropriations, with the exception that certain appropriations are required by the constitution itself. The actual application of funds corresponds closely to legal requirements. The Controller, the Legislative Analyst, the Audits Division of the Department of Finance, and the Auditor General all exercise functions designed, among other things, to ensure this result. Fiscal controls within the executive branch are well developed and in general quite effective.

Independent Postaudit

With the establishment in 1955 of the Joint Legislative Audit Committee and the office of Auditor General, the legislature removed a fundamental defect in its system of control of the purse. Although some legislators have expressed doubt regarding the manner in which the Auditor General has performed his functions, it is clear that the agency is rendering useful service in bringing about improvements in accounting systems, internal control, and reporting practices. The biennial report of the Joint Legislative Audit Committee for the period ended December 31, 1962, noted that three-fourths of nearly 300 improvements recommended by the Auditor General during the biennium had been accepted by the administrative agencies concerned, and others were under consideration.[2] The committee has established the procedure of referring the Auditor General's reports to the respective administrative agencies for comment; agencies are asked to include explanations of any reasons they may have for disagreement. Neither the committee nor the Auditor General has the authority to enforce acceptance of its recommendations, of course, although they can recommend changes in law.

Control of Application of Funds

Appropriations are made in lump sums, but practice ensures a high degree of legislative control over the application of funds. Each support appropriation contains a schedule of two items showing the amount available for (1) salaries and wages and (2) operating expenses and equipment. Each subitem is an upper limit on expenditures. Capital outlay appropriations frequently have a schedule of projects, and each item in the schedule is a limitation on expenditure for that project. However, the budget act regularly empowers the Director of Finance to allow transfers between projects or object categories under any item of appropriation. A quarterly report of such transfers must be made to the Joint Legislative Budget Committee. The State Board of Control may, with the approval of the Director of Finance, permit transfers between items of appropriation for support of institutions within the Departments of Corrections, Youth Authority, Education, and Mental Hygiene.[3]

Legally, then, there is wide discretion in the execution of the budget. In practice, however, control is more strict, for it is understood that the administrative agencies will not normally spend money for specific positions, items of equipment or operating expenses deleted by the legislature. If a new secretarial position, a replacement of a desk, or printing of a bulletin is disallowed by the legislature, the secretary will not be hired, nor the desk bought, nor the bulletin printed. Only under the most exceptional circumstances would it be permissible to spend funds for an item specifically disallowed. On the other hand, expenditures which have not been specifically approved may be undertaken if funds are available from administrative savings, the emergency fund, or, in the case of special fund agencies, deficiency authorizations. It is expected, however, that such administrative adjustments will not be made arbitrarily, but will reflect changes in conditions not anticipated when the budget was reviewed by the legislature: an unexpected increase in workload, an unusually bad fire season, or an outbreak of disease. These understandings are rarely violated.[4]

On the whole, these arrangements avoid the disadvantages of detailed itemization of appropriations: inflexibility, additional accounting and control costs, and lack of incentive to allocate available funds to maximize benefits. At the same time, they do not give the administration uncontrolled discretion to depart from the budget presented to the legislature.

Control of the application of funds may be exercised through restrictions placed in the appropriation act, committee resolutions or directions, and legislative participation in budget execution. Restrictions appear in the budget act infrequently. They usually express policy concerning the purposes of expenditures, or the manner in which funds are spent. For example, the budget act has regularly provided for a number of years that no automobile may be purchased unless the Department of Finance has investigated and established the necessity for it; that all automobiles must be of the "light class" unless for constitutional officers or excepted by the Director of Finance on the basis of unusual requirements; and that no rugs or carpets may be purchased for any state office except those of elective officials or department heads.

More numerous and important than budget act restrictions are the directions and restrictions imposed by the appropriations committees. These include requirements that studies be made, often with a report to the Joint Legislative Budget Committee or to the next legislative session; that expenditures not be made until further review has been made by the Department of Finance or the agency concerned; that budgets be presented in a prescribed way in the future; and that positions be approved for one year only or on the condition that they be used in a specified way. In 1961 the Senate Finance Committee resolved that no additional field offices be established by the Board of Equalization without prior approval of the legislature through budget review.[5]

The qualified "membership" of legislators on the Public Works Board and the activities of the Legislative Analyst in execution of the budget were discussed in Chapter VI. An even more formal kind of participation in the application of funds is the membership of four legislators on the State Allocations Board, which allocates funds for school construction from proceeds of bond sales. Since 1949 the constitution has provided that legislative members of the board "shall have equal rights and duties with nonlegislative members to vote and act. . . ."[6] Three members of each house have qualified membership on the Wildlife Conservation Board, which consists of the Director of Finance, the Director of Fish and Game, and the President of the Fish and Game Commission. The board administers funds provided by a continuing appropriation ($750,000 per year) for acquiring and developing land for the preservation and production of wildlife.[7]

The senate rules require that before any funds may be expended for capital outlay for agricultural facilities at state institutions, the agency "shall" first submit such proposals to the Senate Fact Finding Committee on Agriculture for review and recommendations. The Department of Finance "shall consider the recommendations of the committee in approving or disapproving any such expenditures."[8] (Prior to its abolition in 1959, the Joint Committee on Agricultural and Livestock Problems had similar responsibilities.) After the budget bill has been enacted, the committee visits the state institutions, considers the proposed projects, and submits a formal report recommending approval or disapproval.[9]

The Level of Expenditure

The preferences of individuals will determine their answers to the question of whether spending is excessive, but two kinds of data suggest that the state is not rushing headlong toward bankruptcy. In the first place, although there is a slight upward trend in total expenditures in relation to personal income (Table 12), the rate of increase seems modest enough when viewed in relation to the problems associated with increasing urbanization and population growth (from 7.6 million in 1943 to 19.3 million in 1966).[10] Of course, population growth is reflected in both expenditures and personal income, but population growth and accompanying urbanization intensify and make more complex the social problems with which the state must deal—problems of metropolitan transportation, air and water pollution, public health, crime and delinquency, intergroup relations, social welfare, recreation, and others. The result is an increase in expenditures disproportionate to the rate of population growth. Moreover, the population increase from 1950 to 1960 was greater in age categories that had lesser earning power and drew more heavily upon state resources for services and assistance (Table 13). The number of persons in the five to 18 age bracket nearly doubled, greatly increasing the state's costs for school apportionments, while the principal earning group (25–64) increased by only 32 percent. There was also a disproportionate increase in the number of persons 65 years of age or older, a group that directly affects welfare costs.

Secondly, in comparison with other states, the rate of increase in California taxes in relation to income has been modest. From 1951 to 1961 the rate of increase in the ratio of taxes to personal income for all states and for the major industrial states was greater than that for California. For all states, taxes per $100 of personal income were $3.96 in 1950–51, $4.75 in 1960–61: an increase of 19.9 percent. The change in California was from $4.88 to $5.16, or 5.7 percent. Thirty-six of the states showed a greater relative increase than did California. Moreover, all but one of the other nine major industrial states experienced greater relative increases (Table 14).[11] These data are reflected in the fact that, whereas in 1953 California ranked

TABLE 12

State Expenditures and Taxes in Relation to Personal Income
Selected Years, 1938–39 to 1966–67

Fiscal Year	Expenditures Per $100 of Personal Income	Taxes Per $100 of Personal Income
1938–39	$5.63	$4.64
1943–44	2.20	3.11
1948–49	5.02	4.17
1953–54	5.19	4.56
1958–59	5.19	4.74
1963–64	5.77 [a]	5.49
1966–67	6.35 [a, b]	5.71 [b]

Sources: *Budget*, 1963–64, pp. A–19, A–41; *State Support and Local Assistance Budget*, 1965–66, p. A–55; 1966–67, pp. A–17, A–53; *Capital Outlay Budget*, 1965–66, p. xi; *Capital Outlay Budget and Five-Year Construction Program*, 1966–67, p. xvi.
[a] Computed from data in source.
[b] Estimated.

TABLE 13

Population Growth by Major Age Groups, 1950–60

Age Group	1960	Increase 1950–60	
		Number	Percent
Under 5	1,745,799	646,687	58.8%
5 to 18	3,914,992	1,924,477	96.7
19 to 24	1,182,586	269,727	29.5
25 to 64	7,497,623	1,808,891	31.8
65 and over	1,376,204	481,199	53.8
Total	15,717,204	5,130,981	48.5

Source: *Budget*, 1963–64, p. A–39.

19th from the top among the states in the ratio of tax collections to aggregate personal income, it had dropped to 31st by 1962.[12] Although it is true, as Table 14 indicates, that in 1960–61 California ranked well above the average among the 10 industrial states in ratio of taxes to income, being exceeded only by Michigan, the data given above show that the relative position of California improved during the decade of the 1950's.

Balanced Budget and Level of Debt

Since the early 1940's, California has had a balanced budget, in the sense that specific plans have been made to finance the expenditure program in full, and actual expenditures have been kept within available resources.

TABLE 14

Change in State Taxes Per $100 of Personal Income, Industrial States, 1950–51 to 1960–61

	1950–51	1960–61	Change	
			Amount	Percent
All States.....................	$3.96	$4.75	$ .79	19.9%
10 Industrial[a].................	3.45	4.24	.79	22.9
California...................	4.88	5.16	.28	5.7
Connecticut.................	3.21	3.44	.23	7.2
Illinois.....................	2.62	3.31	.69	26.3
Indiana.....................	3.98	3.94	− .04	− 1.0
Massachusetts..............	3.77	4.04	.27	7.2
Michigan...................	4.19	5.32	1.13	27.0
New Jersey.................	1.93	2.37	.44	22.8
New York..................	3.26	4.45	1.19	36.5
Ohio.......................	3.25	3.82	.59	17.5
Pennsylvania...............	3.02	4.53	1.51	50.0

Source: *Budget*, 1962–63, p. A–22.
[a] Leading industrial states as measured by personal income derived from manufacturing.

TABLE 15

Net Long-Term Debt, Selected States, 1955 and 1965[a]

	Per Capita Amount		Percent Change	Amount of Debt Per $100 Personal Income		Percent Change
	1955	1965		1955	1965	
All States— Average......	$ 59.21	$116.59	97%	$3.35	$5.02	50%
California.......	34.07	127.92	275	1.58	4.24	168
Illinois.........	30.17	93.70	211	1.40	3.13	124
Indiana........	73.96	89.60	22	4.03	3.57	− 11
Massachusetts...	157.41	306.15	94	8.19	10.35	26
Michigan.......	70.95	108.28	53	3.52	3.99	13
New Jersey.....	157.06	147.97	− 6	7.08	4.99	− 30
New York......	62.96	171.04	172	2.91	5.46	88
Ohio...........	56.18	69.86	24	2.83	2.68	− 5
Pennsylvania....	107.67	135.94	26	6.03	5.26	− 13
Texas..........	15.50	46.39	199	0.98	2.15	119

Source: U. S. Bureau of the Census, *Compendium of State Government Finances...*, 1955, 1965.
[a] Ten leading industrial states as measured by value added in manufacturing.

Debt has been incurred for capital plant, including school construction, and for self-liquidating programs, such as veterans' housing. Borrowing for capital outlay is generally accepted practice and represents a breakdown of control only if the amount becomes unduly burdensome in terms of the resources available for servicing the debt.

California's net long-term debt increased from $426 million to $2.4 billion in the decade 1955 to 1965.[13] Nevertheless, in relation to population and personal income, California's debt in 1965 was lower than that of four of the leading industrial states, and in respect to personal income, was lower than the average for all of the 50 states (Table 15).

PROBLEMS OF CONTROL

Continuing Appropriations

The ability of the legislature to control spending and adjust allocations on an annual basis is limited by the use of continuing appropriations and segregated funds. The 1966–67 budget provided estimated expenditures of $4 billion, of which $2.6 billion, or about 63 percent, was authorized by continuing appropriations.[14] Major components of the continuing appropriations were:

	Millions
Apportionment to public schools	$1,076
Highways	410
Debt service	103
Revenues shared with local government	457
Health and welfare	499

Debt service and most of the apportionment to public schools are charges fixed by the constitution; the remainder are fixed by statute and, although subject to modification by the legislature, do not require any positive legislative review or action on an annual basis. All proceeds of a $1.75 billion bond issue approved by the voters in 1960 are appropriated for state water development.[15] This continuing appropriation is not reflected in the above figures.

In the opinion of the Legislative Counsel the legislature has the power to restrict the amounts made available in any given year, although it may not use the bond money for purposes other than the development program specified in the bond act.[16] Through budget bill items, the legislature has limited the total amounts available to the Department of Water Resources for salaries and wages and for equipment and operating expenses. A similar attempt to limit the total available for capital outlay expenditures was vetoed by Governor Brown in 1961.[17] A statute enacted in 1961 made clear that the Department of Finance has budgetary authority over the Department of Water Resources with respect to the expenditure of bond proceeds.[18] The continuing appropriation of the water bond money was virtually a political necessity, for important interests in the state were unwilling to support the bond measure if sectional disputes in the legislature could prevent the expenditure of the funds.

Leaving aside debt service, which represents a moral obligation, continuing appropriations exist because benefitted groups desire to protect themselves against unfavorable legislative decisions; they recognize that it is more difficult to secure positive action to appropriate the desired sums through the budget bill each year than it is to prevent the passage of a bill or a constitutional amendment that would deprive them of some or all of the funds provided by continuing appropriations. Because each of the major components of continuing appropriations is of interest to powerful pressure groups, any attempt to eliminate or reduce them faces formidable obstacles, although their impairment of legislative control is widely recognized and often deplored by legislators and others.

The Legislative Analyst examined the problem of continuing appropriations in a realistic statement to an assembly committee in 1958. He pointed out that there is only a limited amount of flexibility in the state's expenditure program, regardless of formal restrictions on control.

The bulk of the State's expenditures are for all practical purposes fixed, but it is this very fact which makes it absolutely essential that there be some element of flexibility in, if not all state expenditure programs, at least a sufficient number that the Governor and the Legislature annually will be placed in the position of being able to carry out their constitutional responsibilities for establishing a politically responsible balance between state income and outgo. The very fact that the effective margin of controllability of costs is inherently narrow emphasizes the necessity for broadening the base of expenditures which are subject to such limited control.[19]

The Analyst recognized, however, that it is not realistic to think that the legislature would or should drastically curtail support to local government for schools and welfare programs. Local resources are inadequate to the need, and major curtailment in any one year would disrupt local programs. Nor does it seem likely that the legislature would be willing to undertake the onerous and politically delicate task of adjusting the formula for school apportionments during 30-day budget sessions in even-numbered years.[20] In view of these considerations, the Analyst suggested that a separation be made between "those elements of a program which could reasonably be varied from time to time as a matter of fiscal policy" and those which as a practical matter are beyond the reach of annual adjustment. Appropriations for the former would be made through the annual budget act, while the latter would be provided through continuing appropriations as at present. In the case of school support, for example, a distinction might be made, on the one hand, between minimum requirements for teachers' salaries and operating costs, and on the other hand, program costs of a less essential nature, such as pupil transportation, driver education, education of exceptional pupils, and adult education.[21]

Although realistic, the approach suggested by the Analyst fails to provide criteria for separation of essential program elements from those that might be adjusted on a year-to-year basis, perhaps for the very good reason that general criteria for establishing such a separation are unlikely to be found. Rather, progress in reducing continuing appropriations will depend upon the strength of the legislature's desire to increase annual control and its ability to reach essentially political agreements on what is more essential, what less. To be sure, there are some programs involving relatively minor costs (when compared with school support, highways, and welfare) that can scarcely be considered so essential as to warrant support from continuing appropriations: agricultural fairs, the wildlife conservation board, and small craft harbors.[22] But no important inroads can be made on the problem until something is done about highways, public schools, and welfare, which account for the vast bulk of continuing appropriations.

In the case of welfare programs, the Legislative Analyst has recommended that a "maximum average grant" be established by law for each program, and that appropriations be provided through the annual budget act, based on the amount of the maximum average grant and the estimated caseload for the budget year. Transfers between appropriations for categorical aid programs would be permitted, with the approval of the governor, in order to cover unanticipated caseloads in any one program. If requirements could not be met through transfers, deficiency appropriations could be requested when the legislature meets several months before the end of the fiscal year.[23]

The Assembly Ways and Means Committee has suggested two possible ways of alleviating the problems that tighter annual control would present for local government: (1) the state might make commitments one year in advance; or (2) the scheduling of fiscal decisions of state or local governments, or both, might be adjusted to ensure final action by the state before local governments were required to adopt their expenditure programs.[24] These suggestions apply equally to the school support program and the social welfare program.

The problem of highway expenditures presents no difficulties with respect to local government operation, for almost all of the continuing appropriations are spent by the state. Rather, the defense of continuing appropriations for highways is in terms of the "pork barrel" politics that might result if they were controlled annually by the legislature. So long as highways continue to be financed by earmarked revenues collected from motor vehicle users, adjustment of overall expenditure totals and of allocations among functions will not be helped by annual appropriations. On the other hand, annual appropriation would provide an opportunity for regular review of the performance of the State Division of Highways and the State Highway Commission. Under present provisions, there is no review whatsover of the highway budget, not even of expenditures for administration, although a statute limits expenditures for maintenance and general administration to not more than the net revenue from one cent of the fuel tax.[25]

Regular review of performance and control of administrative expenditures would be ensured by enactment of legislation similar to the bill that passed the assembly in 1961, but died in the Senate Finance Committee. This measure would have made all highway expenditures, including capital outlay other than for highway construction, subject to annual legislative review and control.[26] Such legislation would largely avoid the "pork barrel" problem while providing the basis for regular and more effective oversight of the highway program. Perhaps it would provide increased access for attempts to influence highway locations, but such attempts are made at present, and the Highway Commission has shown itself to be very adept in treating with legislators.

Segregated Funds

Legislative control of expenditures is further impaired by the existence of more than 150 separate funds, many of which are dedicated to particular purposes.[27] The 1966–67 budget estimated that "special fund" spending during the fiscal year would amount to $1.1 billion or 27 percent of the total expenditure program of $4 billion.[28] By far the largest single component of special fund expenditure was that for highway construction and maintenance and regulation of motor vehicle use.

Special funds and dedications of revenues restrict legislative control of spending in three fundamental ways:

1. Available financial resources cannot be allocated to alternative uses in accordance with needs.

2. Special funds often have idle balances that cannot be employed when and where needed.

3. There is a tendency to apply different standards in judging the justification for expenditures, depending on whether the source is the general fund or a special fund, and on whether a special fund has ample resources or is being depleted.

In addition, legislative control is indirectly impaired because special funds complicate budgeting and accounting, make it more difficult to present comprehensive statements of the state's financial operations and condition, and increase administrative costs.[29]

That segregated funds present a serious problem has long been recognized and frequently deplored. A report published in 1961 by the Assembly Interim Committee on Ways and Means, reviewed a lengthy list of recommendations for reform, going back to a 1936 report to the Interim Committee of Twenty-five of the California Conference on Government and Taxation.[30] Nevertheless, the committee found that at least 37 new funds had been created in the decade 1950–59.[31] After careful study of the utility of various classes of funds, the committee recommended the elimination of upwards of 100 of the 155 funds then in existence, including those derived from highway user revenues.[32] Little progress was made in the 1961 legislative session, however, for while nine funds were abolished, six new ones were created.[33]

Special funds exist because interest groups wish to protect financial sources for particular purposes, because legislators do not understand that some of the purposes of special funds can be achieved through proper accounting systems, and, in some cases, because there are sound technical reasons for their creation. Many of the funds in existence involve no major political controversy, and there is some reason to hope that, as legislators become more sophisticated, many of the funds and dedications will be eliminated. On the other hand, it is doubtful that the strong opposition of automobile associations and other interest groups to the "diversion" of motor vehicle revenues can be overcome, or that sportsmen will accept the placing of license fee collections in the general fund.

Other Defects in Control

Although the system of control is generally quite effective, defects are brought to light from time to time. In 1959 the Legislative Analyst pointed out that the Social Welfare Board had authority to commit the state to substantial costs by changes in the basis of state aid for various categories of welfare recipients, noting that in one assistance program alone the board had augmented the cost by an amount in excess of $70 million.[34] The legislature subsequently placed in the budget act requirements for approval by the Director of Finance before any rule or regulation adopted by the board, adding to the cost of public assistance programs, could become effective. Recently, it was found that the state printing plant, whose operations are financed from a revolving fund, did not have an adequate cost accounting system for establishing appropriate charges to state agencies. In addition, the printing plant was accumulating surpluses by means of which it could augment its capital equipment without the legislative review entailed in a request for an appropriation. Beginning in 1961, the legislature placed restrictions in the budget act (1) to limit the working capital available to the Printing Division and (2) to require all equipment purchases to be provided through the budget act (except emergency replacements required to be reported to the Joint Legislative Budget Committee on a quarterly basis).[35]

The State Personnel Board has the authority to classify positions and set the salaries of civil service employees on the basis of general guidelines established by the legislature. Although the legislature does not control the salaries of individual classes, it exercises a general control over salaries; increases may be authorized by the Personnel Board only if funds are available for that purpose. On the basis of its regular surveys, the board recommends that the legislature appropriate lump sums for general salary increases or for selective salary adjustments.

In 1962, the legislature failed to include in the language of the budget act appropriation for special salary adjustments, the customary proviso that higher salary ranges should not result in a total annual increase in salary costs greater than the amount of the budget act appropriation. This proviso would have foreclosed the possibility that the Personnel Board, by making adjustments having effect during only a part of the budget year, could commit the state to increased salary costs in future years in excess of the amount appropriated by the legislature. The 1962 appropriation provided $2.6 million in special salary adjustments for civil service employees paid from the general fund. The Personnel Board granted increases creating an annual cost of $4.2 million, thus exceeding the 1962 appropriation by about $1.6 million.[36]

The budget act regularly prohibits filling any position vacant for longer than nine months without the approval of the Director of Finance, and requires a report to the Budget Committee regarding such approvals. The assumption behind this requirement is that positions vacant for a number of months may not be needed. The Legislative Analyst reported in 1961 that two devices were being employed to circumvent this control. Oldest vacant positions were filled first and positions were downgraded and filled at a lower classification in order to interrupt the period of vacancy. The Analyst recommended that agencies be required to fill the most recent vacancy first.[37]

Control of Spending by Extraordinary Majority Vote

A constitutional amendment adopted in 1933 attempted to limit the rate of growth of general fund expenditures by requiring a two-thirds vote in both houses to increase appropriations by more than five percent of the appropriations for the previous fiscal year (previous biennium, prior to 1946).[38] The limitation did not apply to appropriations for the public school system. If by a two-thirds vote the legislature exceeded the five percent limitation in any given year, the amount of the excess could not be included in determining the maximum for the following year. Whatever other effects the amendment may have had, it did not hold increases in general fund expenditures to five percent annually. Every subsequent budget act exceeded the limitation and therefore required a two-thirds vote. The gap between the authorized maximum and actual appropriations steadily widened, and it became clear that a two-thirds vote would always be required in the future. In 1962 the provision was amended to eliminate all reference to the five percent annual increase; the new language simply required that all appropriations from the general fund, except for the support of the public school system, be passed by a two-thirds vote of the total membership of each house. Presented as one of several measures to simplify the constitution and eliminate "obsolete" provisions, the amendment in fact presented a substantive issue of some importance.

The effects of requiring an extraordinary majority to pass appropriation bills are difficult to gauge, although the earlier provision certainly did not limit the annual increase to five percent. On at least three occasions, passage of the budget bill was prevented because of failure to muster a two-thirds vote. Twice during the 1958 struggle over appropriations for water development, and once in 1962, conference reports failed in one house, despite majority support in each case.[39] In 1962 the defeat of the conference report forced the calling of an extraordinary session to pass the budget bill. Although it is impossible to be sure that everyone would have voted the same way in the absence of the two-thirds requirement, these cases underline the potential importance of the provision.

There is some evidence that the extraordinary majority tends to encourage a higher level of spending rather than to restrict it. Senator Ben Hulse, member and subsequently chairman of the Finance Committee, stated in 1951 that the requirement "magnifies the power of the minority group in the legislature so that approval of the budget may be secured only after special expenditures sponsored by the minority groups have been accepted."[40] In 1955, eight senators were able to prevent passage of the budget bill until the chairman of the Finance Committee had agreed (1) to consider in conference their proposal to add an appropriation of $970,000 for capital outlay at the new site for the state fair, and (2) to permit a special appropriation bill for the same purpose to come from the Finance Committee to the floor. A majority of the elected membership of the senate had turned down attempts to amend the item into the budget bill, but because of absences and the two-thirds vote requirement, one-fifth of the house was able to exact these concessions. In conference, $200,000 for a master plan for the new site was added, although neither house had included this item in the budget bill.

The potential utility of the two-thirds requirement extends not only to "pork barrel" operations, but also to legislative controversies having no direct fiscal significance. Thus, in late 1960 two Republican assemblymen suggested that, if the Democrats enacted an unfair reapportionment and redistricting law, the Republicans should prevent passage of the budget bill; the Democrats, with 47 votes, needed seven Republican votes to pass the bill.[41] During the 1961 session it was reported in the press that assembly Republicans were considering such a move and that there were "strong hints that incumbents who fail to go along may find their GOP campaign funds cut off at the next election."[42] Although the reapportionment bill was bitterly criticised by many Republicans, in and out of the legislature, 11 Republican assemblymen joined all of the Democrats in voting for the budget bill. Thus, the constitutional requirement may have aided some Republicans in securing concessions in the reapportionment bill.[43]

To require a two-thirds majority vote for passage of the budget bill is to place in the hands of any minority of one-third plus one a powerful weapon for extracting concessions or for defeating the will of the majority, for the budget bill is not an ordinary bill. It must be passed if the government of the state is to function. Therefore, the extraordinary vote is not to be judged by the same criteria as those suitable for other legislation. It is impossible to demonstrate that the requirement of a two-thirds vote on general fund appropriations results in a lower level of expenditures than would result from following the majority principle. Plausible argument can be offered that the effect is likely to be in the opposite direction, and there is some supporting testimony for this argument from participants in the budget process. But the effect on the level of spending is unclear and unlikely to be established with any degree of precision. Like so many others, the issue ultimately turns on judgments about the degree of power and protection that should be afforded to minorities. The issue must be analyzed in terms of the entire structure of protections provided by written constitutions, separation of powers, the system of representation, the structure of interest groups, and so on. In any case, it is reasonable to assume that the extraordinary vote on general fund appropriations is a relatively insignificant defense against "excessive" spending. Far more decisive is the amount of revenue available, and a far more important bulwark is the political interest and opposition invariably aroused by proposals to increase taxes.[44]

[1] *Cal. Const.*, Art. IV., sec. 22.

[2] *Biennial Report of the Joint Legislative Audit Committee,* December 31, 1962, p. 13.

[3] *Cal. Govt. Code,* sec. 16304.6 (1963 ed.), p. 474.

[4] A notable case was the authorization of emergency funds in 1960–61 for air conditioning at Fresno State College shortly after the legislature failed to approve a member's request for appropriations for this purpose.

[5] *Analysis,* 1962–63, p. 279.

[6] *Cal. Const.*, Art. XVI, sec. 1 (Amend. 1962). Formerly, similar provisions were contained in constitutional amendments authorizing bond issues. These were repealed in 1962.

[7] *Budget,* 1962–63, p. 511.

[8] Senate Rule 12.5.

[9] See, for example, *Report of the Senate Fact Finding Committee on Agriculture* (1960), pp. 42–52.

[10] *Support and Local Assistance Budget,* 1966–67, p. A-17.

[11] *Budget,* 1962–63, p. A-21.

[12] *Budget,* 1963–64, p. A-40.

[13] U. S. Bureau of the Census, *Compendium of State Government Finances . . .,* 1955, 1965.

[14] *Support and Local Assistance Budget,* 1966–67, pp. A-72, A-73; *Capital Outlay Budget and Five-Year Construction Program,* 1966–67, p. xxi.

[15] *Cal. Water Code,* secs. 12935, 12938.

[16] *Analysis,* 1961–62, p. 740.

[17] For the veto message, see *Cal. Stats.* (1961), chap. 888.

[18] *Ibid.,* chap. 1955.

[19] *Recommendations for Obtaining Economy and Efficiency in State Government,* A report of the Assembly Interim Committee on Government Organization (Assembly Interim Committee Reports, 1957–59, vol. 12, no. 4, 1958), p. 63.

[20] See note 3, Chapter II, above.

[21] *Recommendations for Obtaining Economy and Efficiency . . .,* pp. 65–7.

[22] Cf. testimony of a spokesman for the Department of Finance, *ibid.,* p. 70.

[23] *Analysis,* 1963–64, p. 493. Beginning in 1964 the legislature included a provision in the budget bill which limited total welfare expenditures but permitted the limit to be exceeded under certain circumstances.

[24] *Report on Dedicated Funds,* Assembly Interim Committee on Ways and Means (Assembly Interim Committee Reports, vol. 21, no. 4, 1961), p. 21.

[25] *Progress Report on Dedicated Funds . . .,* Assembly Interim Committee on Ways and Means (Assembly Interim Committee Reports, 1961–63, vol. 21, no. 8, 1963), p. 21.

[26] *Ibid.,* p. 20.

[27] *Report on Dedicated Funds,* p. 10.

[28] *Support and Local Assistance Budget,* 1966–67, p. A-53; *Capital Outlay Budget and Five-Year Construction Program,* 1966–67, p. xvi.

[29] *Report on Dedicated Funds,* p. 24; "Accounting and Auditing for the State of California: Section One: Recommendations and Report," a survey for the Joint Legislative Budget Committee (1954), p. A-51 (process).

[30] *Ibid.,* p. 12.

[31] *Ibid.,* p. 10.

[32] *Ibid.,* pp. 33–7.

[33] *Progress Report on Dedicated Funds,* p. 15.

[34] *Analysis,* 1959–60, p. 30.

[35] *Analysis,* 1963–64, p. 810.

[36] *Ibid.,* p. 795.

[37] *Analysis,* 1962–63, p. XI.

[38] *Cal. Const.,* Art. IV, sec. 34a.

[39] The two 1958 cases occurred in the Second Extraordinary Session, one being senate rejection upon reconsideration of the first conference report, the other being assembly defeat of the second conference report. In each case, the other house adopted the conference report.

[40] Ben Hulse, "The Problems of Public Expenditures and Debt Control on the State Level of Government," *Proceedings of the Forty-third Annual Conference on Taxation of the National Tax Association, 1950* (Sacramento: National Tax Association, 1951), p. 156. Another former senator who served on the Finance Committee told the writer that, prior to floor consideration of the budget bill, it was necessary to satisfy senators in sufficient numbers to ensure a two-thirds vote.

[41] *San Francisco Examiner,* November 13, 1960, sec. I, p. 26.

[42] *Oakland Tribune,* May 23, 1961, p. 6E.

[43] Other weapons were at hand. The key figure in the reapportionment was Jesse Unruh, an aspirant for the office of speaker, which was expected to be vacant shortly. Reportedly, he saved the seats of some Republicans in exchange for support of his (successful) candidacy. William Buchanan, *Legislative Partisanship: The Deviant Case of California,* University of California Publications in Political Science, vol. 13 (Berkeley and Los Angeles: University of California Press, 1963), p. 132.

[44] The problem of the extraordinary majority would remain even if the 1962 amendment were repealed, since the Legislative Counsel has held that a two-thirds vote is required to give immediate effect to capital outlay appropriations. See note 5, Chapter II.

Chapter XI

RATIONAL DECISION-MAKING

As was to be expected, the process of making budget decisions in the California legislature bears little resemblance to the rational optimizing of the classic model. Rather, the process is strikingly similar to Lindblom's science of muddling through, referred to in Chapter I. The clarification and selection of goals in budget review are not separated from, nor chronologically prior to, the analysis of alternative means for their achievement. Both types of analysis proceed together. Often, intermediate goals are determined by the level and kinds of resources provided through the budget, rather than by a prior decision defining objectives.

Consideration of alternatives, consequences and affected values is severely limited. On most issues arising in connection with the budget bill appropriations, no more than three alternatives are considered—the governor's recommendation, the Legislative Analyst's alternative and perhaps a compromise lying somewhere between the two. If the Analyst concurs with the budgeted amount, it is unlikely that any alternatives will be considered. Although many special appropriation bills are offered as alternatives for consideration, only a small proportion receive serious attention from the committees. The analysis of consequences is limited by the character of the information presented to the committees in the budget document and the *Analysis,* by the perceptions and practices of the committees and houses, and by political considerations. There is little attempt to articulate the values underlying budget issues, much less to establish a clear ordering of preferences.

Lindblom's incremental method implies that (1) alternatives considered in decision-making involve "small"[1] changes from the status quo and (2) the decision-making process is one of successive limited comparison. In general, expenditure decisions do not involve radical departures from past policy, program, or practice. New programs are often proposed to be implemented on a small scale, as pilot programs. Experience with somewhat similar programs and the experience of other jurisdictions—national, state, or local—often aid in predicting outcomes of new programs.

Successive limited comparison means that the decision-making process is one of a chronological series of comparisons of the status quo with a small number of alternatives. In the context of the budget, such a process takes place through the annual budget review. The legislature does not decide once and for all that a program will be supported at a particular level or with particular instrumental elements, such as a specific staffing pattern. These are subject to adjustment every 12 months, except for continuing appropriations provided by the constitution. The legislature does not approach the budget as if it were deciding for the first time how to allocate resources among alternative programs and what instrumental elements are necessary to carry out those programs. Rather, it takes the status quo as its starting point and, in effect, asks: Who wants to change it and how, for what reasons, and with what expected outcomes? Thus, the legislative committees give special attention to proposed budget increases, comparing anticipated consequences with the consequences of maintaining the status quo; the outcomes of accepting a recommendation of the Legislative Analyst are compared with those expected to result from the governor's recommendation.

Agreement as a Test

According to the incremental method, the test of a "good" decision is agreement—on the decision, not necessarily on the objectives that it will serve. Decisions of the appropriations committees fit this pattern admirably. In the vast majority of cases, the committees assume that, if the Legislative Analyst, the department concerned, and interested groups make no objection to a provision of the governor's budget, the decision must be a good one, and they make no attempt to seek alternatives or to explore consequences. When the executive and legislative staffs are in disagreement, the committees sometimes ask them to resolve their differences and to return with an agreed decision. Full committees use the test of agreement in processing the recommendations of the subcommittees, normally accepting without further consideration decisions on which there is no appeal by the agency affected and no serious disagreement within the subcommittee. Similarly, the houses do not normally re-examine decisions on which there is wide agreement within the appropriations committee. The test of agreement also operates in the case of special appropriation bills: the unanimous opposition of the department concerned, the Department of Finance, and the Legislative Analyst are usually enough to kill a bill. Where the parties disagree, the committee or house must, of course, decide on the merits rather than on the assumption that lack of dispute indicates a good decision.

Lindblom presents the science of muddling through as a description of a method of decision-making that is widely used but whose elements have not been analyzed, a method that will often be superior to any other, including the rationality of the classic model, which makes impossible demands upon man's knowledge and capacities.[2] His analysis is especially useful, not because of the reminder that rationality is limited, but because it provides a realistic perspective for assessing the rationality of a decision-making process. It offers a broad bench mark for determining what can reasonably be expected of decision-makers operating in human institutions.

It remains, nonetheless, a general guide, for it does not specify which alternatives, consequences, and values the decision-maker may neglect, nor how widespread an agreement is necessary for a good decision, nor with what intensity particular alternatives and their consequences should be analyzed. The student of the budget process cannot be content to find that, because the process exhibits elements of the incremental method, it permits a relatively high degree of rationality in decision-making. Rather, he must ask whether it is possible to achieve a greater degree of rationality at a cost commensurate with the marginal improvement expected.

TOWARD MORE RATIONAL DECISION-MAKING

Review for Efficiency or for Best Total Result

The two basic goals of committee review of the budget are (1) to achieve administrative efficiency (the accomplishment of given objectives at minimum cost) and (2) to determine the goals and programs of the state government on a regular basis and in a more specific and flexible way than is generally possible by means of statutes. The latter requires that the benefits to be gained from alternative uses of resources be weighed in order to obtain what Smithies has termed "best total result."[3] Although these two goals are not in themselves incompatible, they represent competing demands on the time and attention of the committees, and they imply differing kinds of budget information and analysis. Best total result is concerned with the allocation of resources among programs, based upon an evaluation of the results expected from them. The goal of efficiency requires an analysis of the shortest path, the best method and the cheapest alternative for accomplishing objectives. Best total result requires consideration of "needs" in various fields of endeavor, as perceived by administrators, legislators, and interest groups. It requires projection of trends in school enrollments, welfare cases, car registrations, prison commitments, hospital population, and the like. It calls for analysis of approaches to meeting those needs, including program innovations, and of program costs, not only in the budget year, but also in the future. Efficiency requires the analysis of ratios of inputs to outputs, of the performance of a unit over time and compared with other units, and of the suitability of organization and procedure for accomplishing stated objectives. More than the analysis of best total result, it deals with instrumental and mechanical questions.

Approach of the Appropriations Committees

The appropriations committees do not have a clear policy regarding the relative emphasis to be given to review for efficiency and review for best total result. They move freely from one type of issue to the other, depending upon the alternatives that are presented to them by the Legislative Analyst or others. The mixing of issues does not facilitate determination of best total result, which requires a systematic review of programs, past and expected results, and relative values of those results in relation to cost.

A rational approach to their task requires that the committees determine how they will distribute their time and attention between the two types of questions, how they will perform each kind of review, and what information they require for each. These determinations will depend upon the perceptions of the committees and upon their evaluation of anticipated results. If the committees perceive that the administration is wasteful and inefficient, they will place more emphasis upon review for efficiency. If they place a high value on nicely calculating the social benefits to be expected from alternative uses of the marginal dollar, they will risk a certain loss of efficiency in the pursuit of best total result. Although the committees must determine for themselves the proper balance between the two types of review, the Analyst can suggest some of the factors that should be taken into account in making the determination and can offer guides concerning the kinds of information and procedures required for each type.

A number of considerations suggest that the committees should devote more of their time and effort to review for best total result. California is a dynamic state, steadily growing in population and urbanization, changing in economy and social problems. Its population is greater than that of most of the countries of the world. The allocation of its $4 billion of annual expenditures among a multitude of purposes and programs, and the determination of the allocation of resources in the light of constantly changing conditions, is a continuing and complex task. A fundamental function of the legislature, as a representative body, is to reflect the value preferences of the citizenry.

If the legislature concentrates too much on the problem of efficiency, it runs the risk of giving the executive undue influence in the determination of best total result. Instead of performing the function for which it is eminently suited, it becomes involved in administrative management, for which it is poorly equipped. The determination of the efficient course often requires intimate knowledge of operational details, as well as judgment about imponderables that puzzle the administrators most closely concerned. To acquire enough information to judge the efficiency of an organizational structure, a complex procedure, or a staffing pattern may be very costly in time and effort. In an effort to control efficiency, the legislative committees find themselves deciding many details regarding the personnel, equipment, and expenses of the departments. Some legislators believe that review of these details is important because it keeps the departments on their toes and deters them from putting questionable expenditures in the budget.

Although plausible, this is a proposition difficult to demonstrate. It implies that, if the legislative committees did not scrutinize expenditures in detail, the governor, the Department of Finance, the department heads, and departmental budget officers would be unable or unwilling to maintain reasonable control of efficiency. In certain times and places, such an implication would be justified, but the current character of administration in California gives reason for more optimistic assumptions. The state bureaucracy is highly professionalized, the merit system is well-established and protected by the constitution, methods and organization are progressive, corruption is negligible, and there is a well-developed system of control within the administration—too much control in the opinion of some line administrators. It is not credible that the existing degree of efficiency is due solely or even in large measure to legislative scrutiny of budget details. Efficient management depends fundamentally upon the motivation and capacity of administrators themselves. Compelling an agency to accept a particular solution to a specific problem may save a few dollars, but it does not ensure that the agency will be efficient and frugal in all of the other areas of its activity.

Whatever one's judgment about the deterrent effect of extensive scrutiny of budget details, the fact is that the committees go beyond the measures necessary to deter wasteful and unjustified expenditures. Of the committee's decisions on matters of efficiency, the vast majority turn on questions upon which men can reasonably disagree. This is evidenced by committee rejection of many of the Analyst's recommendations, by divided votes within committees, by disagreement between committees, and by repetition of budget requests that have been turned down by the committees in prior years. It is also evidenced by the infrequency of committee criticism of departments for submitting requests that the committees reject. The logic of the deterrent argument is that the committees must eliminate from the budget expenditures that have little or no justification, not that the committees should substitute their judgment for that of management on questions where opinions may reasonably differ.

Legislative and Executive Controls

Finally, in determining how much emphasis should be placed on efficiency, and how much on best total result, the committees should take into account all of the means of controlling efficiency that are available to the legislature and the executive. Legislative controls include: specifying organization and procedures by statute, postaudit by an agency responsible to the legislature and independent of the executive, investigations by legislative interim committees, informal influence, and management studies by the Legislative Analyst. Executive controls include internal auditing by the Department of Finance, central budget review and control of budget execution, and the work of administrative analysis units in larger departments, as well as that of the Organization and Cost Control Division serving all agencies. While these controls do not guarantee efficient administration—no system does—they make it unnecessary to place primary reliance on budget review.

INDEPENDENT POSTAUDIT AND
RETROSPECTIVE CONTROL

Independent postaudit of expenditures is a method of retrospective control that has not received the recognition it deserves. The postaudit performed by the Auditor General is aimed primarily at the legality and propriety of transactions and the protection of the assets of the state. It is not an audit of the efficiency of administrative operations. The activities of the Legislative Analyst and the appropriations committees are oriented toward the future; they do not include a systematic review of past performance to evaluate efficiency.

British experience suggests that retrospective methods can be effective in the control of administrative efficiency. Because, as a practical matter, the House of Commons may not change the expenditure plan proposed by the government, retrospective control is the principal method available. The Auditor General performs the postaudit and reports to the Public Accounts Committee of Parliament, which calls high administrative officials to justify, if they can, the transactions and methods to which the Auditor General has taken exception. On the basis of the reports and the testimony of the responsible officials, the committee publishes reports criticizing unsound practices and making suggestions for improvement. The Treasury takes corrective action; the Public Accounts Committee has no authority to require acceptance of its recommendations, although it has been highly influential.[4]

Retrospective control of efficiency has important advantages. It permits budget review to concentrate on best total result, and it encourages the appropriations committees to avoid making decisions better left to management. It directs legislative attention to questions of system and method rather than to the correction of particular decisions believed to be erroneous. Retrospective control is based on an examination of decisions and actions after the fact, which comes too late to prevent expenditures believed to be unjustified. The relevant question is how to prevent similar errors in the future, which in turn leads to a consideration of defects in system and methods that permitted the error to arise.

The basis for a strengthened system of retrospective control of efficiency already exists in California. The appropriate institution is not the Auditor General, which is a new agency and is staffed by specialists in auditing and accounting rather than by management analysts. Rather, the function should be performed by the Legislative Analyst, whose reports should be submitted to the Joint Legislative Budget Committee. In the interim between legislative sessions, the committee should hold hearings at which departments would respond to questions and criticisms raised by the Analyst. On the basis of the Analyst's findings and the testimony of responsible administrators, the committee should issue reports criticizing administrative deficiencies and recommending improvements. Although the prime responsibility for correcting deficiencies should rest with the departments themselves, the Department of Finance should take the lead within the administration to ensure that the committee recommendations are given serious consideration and that needed action is taken. It would be the responsibility of the Legislative Analyst to report on the implementation of recommendations and to bring to the attention of the Budget Committee any foot-dragging or unjustified resistance.

This proposal builds upon existing institutions and practices. It calls for a continuation of management improvement studies by the Analyst, but on a more systematic basis and with a different method of implementation of recommendations. Instead of relying on the appropriations committees to implement recommendations during the course of budget review, it makes the Budget Committee the prime instrument of legislative stimulus and places responsibility for action on the departments and the Department of Finance. In so doing, it reduces the need for review of efficiency questions by the appropriations committees during busy legislative sessions. Rather, the review would take place during the interim between sessions.

The discussion thus far has argued that the appropriations committees should give greater attention to best total result because (1) the changing character of public problems requires continuous adjustment of the allocation of governmental resources; (2) the representative role of the legislature implies major concern with the value questions implicit in the determination of best total result; (3) legislative committees are handicapped in making "correct" decisions about management efficiency; (4) the deterrent effect does not require that the committees substitute their judgment for that of management on debatable issues; (5) the character of the bureaucracy permits review for efficiency to be de-emphasized; and (6) budget review is only one of a number of actual and potential methods of control of administrative efficiency. It has been suggested that retrospective methods of control of efficiency should be developed more fully. Specifically, critical examination of efficiency should be the function of the Legislative Analyst and the Budget Committee.

Redesign of the Budget and the Analysis

If the appropriations committees are to give more thorough and effective consideration to best total result, the budget document and the *Analysis of the Budget Bill* must be redesigned to provide the kind of information and analysis required. The budget document contains massive detail on objects of expenditure, which is useful to the legislature for occasional reference, but its treatment of programs and performance is highly condensed. Although proposed increases are stated in program terms, the accomplishments anticipated from the additional expenditures are not fully and clearly explained. In many cases, total expenditures of a department or unit are not presented by programs; the legislator does not have before him a picture of all of the programs of the unit, but only proposed expansions or new programs. Overall indices of performance are offered—enrollments, degrees granted, net releases from mental hospitals, per capita costs—but there is insufficient information about the contributions of individual programs and activities. Many of the indices employed, although useful, do not permit conclusions as to the extent to which underlying objectives are being achieved. It is useful to know, for example, that a regulatory agency issued or suspended a certain number of licenses and investigated a certain number of complaints, but these workload factors do not indicate how well the regulatory job is being done, what kinds of problems the agency is encountering and how it is solving them, or how changes in the profession or industry will affect regulatory activities in the future.

The *Analysis of the Budget Bill* compensates in part for the deficiencies of the budget document, for it analyzes program and performance more fully. Nevertheless, the *Analysis* continues to place considerable emphasis upon the justification for objects of expenditure. The legislative committees tend to direct their attention to issues raised in connection with expenditure details, making less than full use of the program and performance information the *Analysis* offers. For their part, the operating departments tend to limit the information they supply to the amount and kind considered necessary to secure approval of the budget and to give the proceedings an aura of rationality. Neither the committees, nor the Department of Finance, nor the Legislative Analyst, nor the departments themselves place full responsibility upon the departments for providing information to the committees. Rather, the Department of Finance tries to make up for the failures of the departments, and the Analyst for the deficiencies of both.

As noted in Chapter VI, the Assembly Committee on Ways and Means recommended in 1963 that the publication of detailed expenditure information in the budget document be discontinued. Rather, it said, the document should be a statement of programs, expected accomplishments, work units, related resource requirements, and program costs.[5] The committee also suggested the possibility of using a computer to give rapid answers to questions about financial implications of alternatives involving program changes.

We can foresee the time when all the facts—the work units, the workload, cost factors and the like—are stored in the computer. . . . Specific information supporting any part of the program [of the governor] will be immediately available to legislative committees through a communication link between the committee room and the computer. As specific items are debated and committees weigh the possibility of adding to, subtracting from or altering programs, inquiry can be made to the machine concerning the fiscal consequences of each decision and an answer can be ready while the committee considers the question.[6]

These proposals require extensive change not only in budget presentation, but also in the budget-making process itself. It would require years of work to identify suitable programs, determine work units and work standards, and establish defensible formulas for overhead and supporting services, equipment and supplies. Moreover, as the committee recognized, there are many programs whose results are relatively intangible and difficult to gauge. A great deal of imaginative effort would be required, and the results would frequently be far from ideal. Nevertheless, there are many areas in which significant steps can be taken in the direction of the objectives set by the committee.

The proposed transformation in the budget document is highly desirable, although it would be preferable to continue publishing the expenditure details as an appendix to the budget rather than to eliminate them entirely. These details have value as a reference source; they must in any case be assembled for management purposes, and their publication would remove any suspicion that the program estimates were pulled out of thin air or that pertinent data were being withheld from the legislature. If the document were recast along the lines suggested by the committee, not only would the appropriations committees be encouraged to focus their attention on best total result, but also they would have at their disposal more and better information for this kind of review.

Although the committee is silent on this point, the recommendation also implies changes in the *Analysis*, which should examine critically the program and performance data provided in the budget document. It should analyze the adequacy of program statements, the relationship between programs and the basic objectives they are established to serve, the validity of estimates of future accomplishments, the value of programs in terms of cost, the consistency of programs and policies, the adequacy of measures of performance, the basis and justification for workload and staffing standards, and the extent to which actual accomplishments fulfill the expectations of previous budgets. As suggested in Chapter VI, the *Analysis* should not undertake a comprehensive review of all expenditures in the budget bill, but should direct particular attention to program changes and to selected operations whose improvement could be expected to bring about substantial economies or significant increases in efficiency. Unusual increases in objects of expenditures should be noted and questioned, and a check should be maintained on changes in the proportion of administrative and personnel costs. On a very limited sampling basis, details of objects of expenditures should be examined by the Legislative Analyst, but in order to minimize the substitution of legislative for management judgment, the *Analysis* should recommend cuts in such items only in relatively clear cases lacking justification.

It was suggested in Chapter IX that information about long-range plans and projections would provide a basis for more significant and responsible budget discussion on the floor of the houses, especially with respect to trends in aggregate income and outgo. Such information would also be useful to the appropriations committees in their consideration of best total result, for it would permit them to take into account not only the anticipated consequences of a program "mix" for the budget year, but also the outcomes in future years of present commitments. The plans and projections would not require that formal commitments be made for longer than one year. Because programs once adopted tend to continue and expand, it is important to consider the longer run at the stage of initiation.

LEGISLATIVE BUDGET STAFFING

What generalizations can be drawn from more than two decades of experience with the office of the Legislative Analyst? There is ample evidence that a professionally oriented and competent staff can contribute substantially to rational budget decisions and to legislative control of spending. The *Analysis of the Budget Bill* has provided useful information, offered specific and considered alternatives, assessed administrative performance and stimulated the formulation of performance standards, scrutinized the justification for expenditures, and reported upon administrative compliance with legislative mandates. Criticism of the *Analysis* should not be allowed to obscure the important values it has served, nor the marked improvement it has shown in recent years.

Under the conditions existing in California, at least, it has been demonstrated that without endangering its existence or its usefulness, a legislative budget staff can make specific recommendations to legislative committees regarding appropriations. Three important conditions have been noted: legislative acceptance of the legitimacy of such recommendations, the caliber of the staff, and the weakness of parties. The making of recommendations has both advantages and disadvantages. It tends to insure that specific, considered alternatives are presented to the appropriations committees, that staff review of the budget is critical and penetrating, and that advocacy is open rather than covert. At the same time, recommendations may be discounted by legislators, the capacity of the staff to maintain objectivity and balance is strained, and the staff is subject to pressure from legislators on behalf of particular propositions. One advantage of having a committee to supervise the staff is that the committee serves as a buffer against pressure.

One of the values of the office of the Legislative Analyst is that it contributes to harmonious relationships between the legislature and the bureaucracy. Because the Analyst scrutinizes information provided by the departments and keeps an eye on their operations, the legislators are less inclined to suspect that something is being put over on them. At the same time, the Analyst interprets administrative problems and viewpoints to the legislature.

California experience suggests that a legislative budget staff presents certain potential dangers. One is that the staff will be drawn into budget execution and administrative decision-making. Another is that it may become involved in political maneuvering and campaigning with respect to legislation. A third is that staff services may encourage the legislature to believe that it can correct erroneous administrative decisions on a comprehensive, detailed basis. As a result, the legislature substitutes its judgment for that of management on issues it is poorly equipped to decide, and it may fail to give attention to the system for making budget decisions.

Finally, we may note certain ground rules that have controlled and protected the budget staff. Strict rules of confidentiality surround requests for service from individual members. The staff does not issue press releases; public statements, except before committees, are discouraged, and reports are released by the Budget Committee (or other committee for which they are prepared). The staff does not campaign for or against legislation; it limits itself to providing information and making recommendations before committees when requested. If a recommendation is to be made against a bill, the author of the bill receives a copy of the recommendation and analysis in advance.

In deciding whether to provide itself with a budget analysis staff and how that staff is to be used, a legislature should ponder carefully its own purposes, which must be related to the problems that it expects a staff to help solve. In the context of a progressive, relatively efficient administrative system, the commitment of staff resources to the analysis of a myriad of detailed questions of efficiency is likely to result in benefits that are more symbolic than real. The legislature may experience an agreeable sense of being in control and of having trustworthy information, but the effect on the efficiency of the system is likely to be marginal, even trivial. The greatest challenge to the legislature stems from the need to decide what is to be done, what should be the level of effort, and what the pace. To make these decisions well—in the light of feasible alternatives, reasonable estimates of consequences, and relevant values—the legislature must employ all the resources at its command, including staff. Failure to accept this challenge not only impairs the quality of the decisions taken, but also diminishes the legislature's role in the political system.

[1] Examples of incremental policy alternatives cited by Lindblom make clear that changes can be substantial and at the same time "small" enough to be "incremental": lowering reserve requirements for banks, an increase of 50 percent in national military expenditure, repeal of the Taft-Hartley Act, or establishment of a Missouri Valley Authority. Charles E. Lindblom, "Policy Analysis," *American Economic Review*, 48 (June, 1958), 302–3.

[2] Lindblom, "The Science of 'Muddling Through,'" *Public Administration Review*, XIX (Spring, 1959), 88.

[3] Arthur Smithies, *The Budgetary Process in the United States* (New York: McGraw-Hill, 1955), p. 146.

[4] For the history and an evaluation of the Public Accounts Committee, see Basil Chubb, *The Control of Public Expenditure* (Oxford: The Clarendon Press, 1952).

[5] *Report on Long-Range Program and Budget Planning*, Assembly Interim Committee on Ways and Means (Assembly Interim Committee Reports, vol. 21, no. 5, 1963), pp. 30–4.

[6] *Ibid.*, p. 37.

Index

Administration, characteristics in California, 196

"Administrator." *See* Governor's Committee on Organization of State Government

Administrative agencies: as source of information, 77; as source of alternatives, 78; performance evaluation by, 79; clearing with Legislative Analyst, 101; requests for augmentations, 126; directives to, from appropriations subcommittees, 132; criticism of, by appropriations committees, 132–133; referral of Auditor General's recommendations to, 177

"Agency." *See* Governor's Committee on Organization of State Government

Agreement, as test of "good" decision, 8, 193–194

Alternatives: administrative agencies as source of, 78; proposed by Legislative Analyst, 77–78; parties as source of, 148–149; consideration of, in budget review, 192–194. *See also* Rationality

Alternatives, appropriations committees: search for, 125–126; budget reduction, 126; kinds, 126; sources of, 126; institutionalization of search, 126; reasons for limited search, 126–127; conditions for broader search, 127

Amendments, budget bill: in senate, 141; in assembly, 141; types 141–142

Analysis of the Budget Bill: use by legislators, 67; coverage, 67; guides for preparation, 67–68; size, 68; form and content, 68–69; as source of alternatives, information on consequences, 73, 77–78; compared with other information sources, 76–77; insistence on accurate information, 80; legislative action on recommended reductions, 81–82 (table); subcommittee action stimulated by, 132; proposed changes in, 201

Analysis of the Budget Bill, evaluation of, 202; utility in rational decision-making, 76–80; performance evaluation in, 78–79; scrutiny of justification for appropriations, 79–80; compliance with legislative intent, 80; improvements, 81; excessive detail in, 82–84; insufficient attention to budget method, 84–85; conception of legislative control, 85–87; prospective control of spending; 86–87; argument against creating consumer counsel, 88–89; inconsistent argument, 89–90; new services in budget session years, 90–91; utility in rational decision-making, 91; deficiencies, 200

Analysis of the Budget Bill, recommendations: types, 70; resource, 70; program, 70–71; unallocated cuts, 71; arbitrary reductions, 71; regarding financing, 71; for studies, 71; organization and procedure, 72

Annual budgeting: adoption, 17; reasons for, 18–19; in states, 19

Appropriation bills. *See* Budget bill; Special appropriation bills; Implied appropriation bills; Continuing appropriations

Appropriations committees: review of expenditure program, 15; work before legislative session, 18; importance, 114; workload, 115, 117; influential role of chairman, 118; voting in, 119; subcommittees' reports, 121; field inspection, 121–122; and policy, 123–124; role perceptions of members, 125; criticism of agencies, 132–133; conditional approval by, 133; arbitrary decision avoided, 133; role of chairman in house debate, 140–141; and aggregate expenditures, 154; review of revenue measures, 164; membership overlapping with revenue committees, 164; objectives of budget review, 194–197. *See also* Hearings, ap-